OUR BETTER NATURE

OUR BETTER NATURE
Environment and the Making of San Francisco

PHILIP J. DREYFUS

UNIVERSITY OF OKLAHOMA PRESS: NORMAN

Library of Congress Cataloging-in-Publication Data

Dreyfus, Philip J., 1954–
   Our better nature : environment and the making of San Francisco / Philip J.
Dreyfus.
      p.   cm.
   Includes bibliographical references and index.
   ISBN 978-0-8061-3958-6 (hardcover : alk. paper)   1. San Francisco
(Calif.)—Environmental conditions.   2. San Francisco (Calif.)—History.
3. San Francisco Bay Area (Calif.)—Environmental conditions.   4. San
Francisco Bay Area (Calif.)—History.   5. City and town life—California—
San Francisco—History.   6. City planning—California—San
Francisco—History.   7. Landscape—California—San Francisco—History.
8. Urban ecology—California—San Francisco.   10. Nature—Effect of
human beings on—California—San Francisco.   I. Title.
   GE155.C2D74   2008
   304.209173'2—dc22
                                                                    2008009295

1 2 3 4 5 6 7 8 9 10

To Julie, Madeleine, and Rebecca,
who fill my days with meaning and joy

CONTENTS

ILLUSTRATIONS

PREFACE

This book is inspired by love of urban vitality and by awe at the beauty of nature. It emerged as a product of my teaching environmental history at San Francisco State University, and of my interest in the relationships between cities, their human occupants, the landscapes that house them, and the natural world that sustains them.

Our Better Nature is a set of interrelated stories about the human beings who have occupied the physical space of San Francisco for centuries, and about their relationship with nature. My choice of San Francisco as a focal point is both circumstantial and intentional. The circumstance is that I happen to live and work here, and studying one's own backyard is convenient, as well as worthwhile if sufficiently interesting. As a loyal New Yorker, my decision to resettle in the San Francisco Bay Area over two decades ago was driven by impressions that reveal themselves herein, particularly the dramatic impact of the northern California landscape on the uninitiated. The city's remarkable natural setting, almost unimaginable from afar, piqued my curiosity about how San Francisco had assumed its modern form—a shape in which the presumed opposites of "urban" and "natural" seem to be entwined. Further, the Bay Area's quite pervasive popular environmental consciousness, and the strength of its environmental and urban planning movements, provided me with ample motivation to write this book as my curiosity about environments deepened over the years. I therefore chose San Francisco quite intentionally as my subject because it seemed an ideal place about which to raise interesting questions concerning the intersection of cities and nature.

Though the framework for *Our Better Nature* did not appear in my mind in full detail at the outset, I knew with certainty a few things I wanted to accomplish. First, I feel strongly that the history of a city as an environment should consider its pre-urban setting as nonurban space. There are environmental reasons that human beings settle where they do, and contemporary urban sites were populated long before they became cities. While people of different social and economic orders shape the external world differently, they share some understanding of nature's universal assets. Consequently, the first story in this book is about California Indians. As a first-generation American, I am struck by the arbitrary divide that often separates American Indian history and American history, as if conquest had somehow reset the historical timer to zero. I remember reading children's histories of France in elementary school, in which the story of Paris, for example, started in prehistoric times on the assumption—justified or not—that the ancient people who occupied the site were the tribal ancestors of its modern inhabitants. American cities deserve similar treatment, not to create a fiction of national continuity, but to recognize a significant constant concealed in a story of domination and usurpation—that of generations of human beings modifying and adapting to the same natural space in order to survive.

Second, I committed myself to narrative form. My instinctive tendency is to view stories as useful vehicles for stimulating analytic thought. Stories build a world in the mind through which we can grapple with and understand the self and the external universe. The field of urban environmental history is currently challenged by its youth and its unrealized potential. It is laden with possibilities that make it difficult to reach a consensus about what constitutes a definitive work. Because a great deal remains to be studied, synthesis is risky, and anthology has become the scholarly norm. Yet, in a field that has so much insight to offer the public and so much relevance to offer modern life, the assiduous collection of data should be supplemented by the broad interpretive sweep. We know enough to take the first steps toward telling instructive and thought-provoking stories about people and nature that illuminate the emergence of cities, urbanites, and urban environmental consciousness. *Our Better Nature* is an attempt at such a narrative tale, in which I make use of particular historical markers to create a story line—specific junctures on the path to urban development, followed by new land uses, resource extraction, the building of parks, the search for water, and the emergence all the while of new attitudes toward nature and human needs.

Finally, I wanted principally to produce a book that would interest an intelligent readership of nonhistorians and stimulate some thought among them regarding one of the most important and inescapable issues of our time—the relationship between urban civilization and our environmental well-being. I hope I will have succeeded.

My work was not produced in a vacuum. I have several predecessors to thank for having launched the study of cities in nature. William Cronon's work on Chicago remains a highly influential book-length study of the interaction between the great city of the northern plains and its expansive hinterland. Before

I began work on the manuscript for this book, Andrew Hurley had already edited a fine set of essays on St. Louis; and since my work began, the growing interest in urban environmental history has been gratified by the publication of invaluable anthologies edited by Char Miller on San Antonio, Craig Colten on New Orleans, Joel Tarr on Pittsburgh, William Deverell and Greg Hise on Los Angeles, and Martin Melosi and Joseph Pratt on Houston. Mike Davis's and Gray Brechin's critiques of Los Angeles and San Francisco, respectively, are also tremendously useful in heightening our awareness of the pitfalls of ill-considered urban growth. I have found much inspiration in the earlier, seminal work of the environmental history and politics scholar Samuel Hays, as well as in the magnificent and transporting narrative works of world history produced by the French historian Fernand Braudel.[1]

I am thankful to my colleagues at San Francisco State—Bill Issel, Robert Cherny, and Jules Tygiel—for their early faith in the merits of my project. I thank Bill additionally for his reading of early chapters and his unflagging enthusiasm for the mission of my book. I am also grateful to my editor at University of Oklahoma Press, Matthew Bokovoy, who found my goals sufficiently worthwhile to endorse publication, and whose steady support and insightful commentary helped me draw my manuscript to a timely conclusion. Thanks also go to Christina Moretta, photo archivist at the San Francisco Public Library, for her diligent help with identifying useful illustrations. My students deserve thanks as well for being brave enough to test the waters of a seemingly peculiar field. Their questions and our discussions have sharpened my understanding of commonly held attitudes toward nature in modern urban America and have helped me more clearly to perceive the degree to which these are embedded in the culture of city life. As for myself, I derived tremendous pleasure from producing this work. I struggled with its limits, rejoiced at its potential, and relished crafting every phrase. I am hopeful that the reader will take away something of use.

OUR BETTER NATURE

INTRODUCTION

NATURE AND THE CITY

Contemporary San Franciscans appear to share little in common with the area's first Native American inhabitants but for their humanity and their geographic locale. Yet these seemingly banal similarities are essential to the universal nature/human nexus: human beings in all places at all times transform their external world in order to survive—in order to further their own physical and social reproduction. This process of transformation is an interaction, both creative and destructive, that occurs not in a vacuum but within the larger web of life that we call "nature." Like the area's first people, modern San Franciscans exist within nature, although their urbanism may challenge their ability to see this. In the course of the last two centuries, dramatic changes in the scale of human economic activity—the work of providing sustenance—have altered perceptions of and relationships with the external, nourishing, nonhuman world. This change of scale, perception, and behavior is integral to a modern metropolitan way of life in which "urban" and "natural" appear to city dwellers as two extremes on a continuum that has both material and moral dimensions. San Franciscans, and modern industrial peoples in general, inhabit a paradox of urbanization. Modern urbanites have achieved an extraordinary mastery over the nonhuman world while they simultaneously experience an inordinate alienation from it.

On the one hand, cities have become so much second nature to us that we take their existence for granted much as we do the presence of our species. On the other hand, asked whether they believe that their environment is a natural one, a random collection of city people will likely give a negative response. Asked to describe a natural environment, they are likely to portray a rural setting, perhaps even a national park they visited last summer. One presumes to be able to establish a rank order of things natural by moving closer to or further away from the heart of the metropolis. Few people are conscious of the strange and contradictory dualism that leads them to distinguish between the course of nature and the hand of *Homo sapiens*. Few of us are troubled by the deeper question of how natural the process of urbanization is in the first place, but just as our presence in this universe is of physical and philosophical interest so too is our crafting of a metropolitan way of life as a means of harnessing the rest of nature to human ends.

Eighty years ago, it became fashionable in intellectual circles to draw analogies between urban growth and plant ecology. Much like the succession of plant species in a given environment results from a struggle for space and food and light, the evolution of urban space can be seen as a product of human competition over contested habitats.[1] The merit of the argument is that it quite appropriately places human activity in a natural context, but its drawback is its tendency to reinforce often cruel social Darwinist assumptions about the biological essence of human social relations and social conflict. Because of the danger of treating cities as purely biologically determined, later critics, including the Marxists, have preferred to treat urbanization as a product of the uneven economic development endemic to capitalism. In this scenario, metropolitanization is not natural, but driven by the economic interests and manipulations of elite classes. The strength of this view is that, to some extent, it can be verified and documented from the historical record. There is no doubt that whenever opportunities presented themselves, wealthy and powerful individuals used every means at their disposal to direct urban growth in ways that enhanced their own position. Consider, for example, the well-known story of the tremendous fortunes accrued from real estate speculation in twentieth-century Southern California.[2] However, one weakness of the lust-for-money argument is that, by linking the process of urbanization to self-serving, and sometimes corrupt, sponsors, it generates the distressing view that cities may be, at best, avoidable aberrations and, at worst, cancerous growths on the social organism. Most urbanites (this author included) find this image hard to accept.

The debates among scholars of urbanism are further complicated by a broader question that informs the work of environmental historians but to which most ordinary people have no immediate intuitive response—to what extent are human beings in nature and to what extent are they of nature? If we are in nature, then what we call nature is an environment separate from us upon which we act to positive or to ill effect. If we are of nature, then all of our activities are natural—like those of every other species with whom we share this Earth—even city building, though it seems to separate and alienate us most from what we think is real nature. This second view may have equal merit to the first, but it is very difficult to assimilate. Urbanites and nonurbanites alike typically experience the city as an artifice, and all of their judgments about what nature is or what it should be relate to this fundamental feeling.

The problem with all of this is that cities are, in fact, intimately entwined with what most of us consider nature. Whether cities are an inevitable outcome of human social evolution, technological progress, and economic efficiency, or are specific products of class societies, they occupy spaces that were once nonurban, and they occupy these spaces for some reason. Some landscapes lend themselves more readily to urban development than others, and all landscapes present physically or economically insurmountable barriers to unlimited growth. For example, there is a reason that New York City is at the confluence of the Hudson River and the Long Island Sound, that Chicago sits on Lake Michigan, that St. Louis rose from the gently sloping prairie on the west side of the Mississippi, and that San Francisco grew from a tiny settlement on an enormous and magnificent bay. There are also geographic and topographic reasons—hills, mountains, cliffs, bogs, and bodies of water—that explain why these and other great cities did not grow evenly and endlessly across the land.

In addition to the impact of landscape on the urban setting, developing cities affect environmental conditions far beyond their limits insofar as they need to be built, whether from wood, brick, or concrete and steel, and their people, incapable of independent subsistence, need to be fed, watered, and clothed. Further, the economic activity characteristic of urban life, the making of product and the mercantile activity that moves it around, is what defines cities as great concentrations of labor power and of the wealth it creates. And what is human labor if not the application of intelligence to nature? We are therefore compelled to consider what we mean by terms like "natural" and "social" when addressing the relationship between human beings and their environment. Urbanization is unquestionably a social phenomenon, as is all human enterprise, but it is also important to understand it as a natural process or, at the very least, as a process by which human beings engage nonhuman nature in a most dramatic, spectacular, and far-reaching way. This engagement is shaped as much by environment as by culture and produces in turn both environmental and cultural change.

Any city can lend itself to an investigation of the nature/human nexus, but San Francisco is of particular interest because of its powerful natural appeal. While San Francisco obviously evidences the work of human beings, the canvas on which it has been painted seems of equal importance in shaping the city's image. Can we really imagine a flat San Francisco, a city sweltering in the desert heat, or a San Francisco without a broad blue bay or the thunderous waves of the Pacific? The city's natural setting clearly adds much to its perceived beauty, and to what contemporary urbanites often call its "quality of life." Virtually constant ocean breezes keep the air surprisingly fresh and breathable for a major city. The retreating morning fog leaves the sky a remarkably brilliant blue that in turn enhances the beauty of the waters that surround the city on three sides. The many precipitous hills, once an impediment to cost-efficient urban growth, offer spectacular views of the surrounding land and seascape and, perhaps most importantly, create a sense of urban edges, or limits, beyond which we imagine finding another, truer nature in its unmitigated glory. Unaware that much of San Francisco's "natural" landscape was crafted in the same way as its buildings and streets, the observer sees an amalgam of intrinsic and man-made settings that together conspire to foster the feeling that nature is at hand. One presumes to be able to breathe. Looking at the happy and dazzled tourists lined up for the Hyde Street cable car, one can almost hear Tony Bennett's dulcet tones as he sings "I Left My Heart in San Francisco." Oddly enough, this simple, popular song is a testament both to our eternal attachment to nature and to the success of urbanization as a central feature of modern life. The lover pining for his beloved city remembers the beautiful qualities with which nature has endowed her—hills, morning fog, blue sea, golden sun—and holds these to his heart as if they represented her essence.

The visceral, often inexplicable feeling that San Francisco has compromised with nature has important intellectual implications. Even if this feeling is partly illusory and even if it rises from the soul of a typical modern urbanite who has not given any serious thought to what nature really is, there is value in examining its material source. What we imagine to be true in San Francisco, just because the evidence for it so forcefully confronts our senses, really should be regarded as a general rule of urban development. Even where our perceptions fail to reveal this truth, the effort to create, shape, and reshape our urban environments is a story of interaction, and ultimately compromise, between the human and nonhuman worlds. Unable to foresee with any consistency the consequences of our engagement with nature, we continually adapt ourselves, alter our environment, and then respond to the changes we have wrought with great ambivalence. San Francisco's place history exemplifies these things. This book is not written as a paean to San Francisco, but as an effort to reveal something of the way the city assumed its modern form. It is a history of place, with primary attention to the ways in which people used a geographic space to live and to thrive. And it is the story of a changing environment, altered by successive waves of human inhabitants whose cultural expectations—both economic and ideological—shaped their interaction with and uses of the nonhuman world.

San Francisco's story can be told in stages that exhibit the pairing of two phenomena. First, there has been continual growth of the region within which the current locale of the city functions economically—in other words, an expansion of interdependency between the northern tip of the San Francisco peninsula and the concentric rings beyond. Second, there is the constant human struggle to draw from, reshape, and define the nonhuman world to satisfy human physical and spiritual needs. The transitions of California history provide a framework for the city's evolution, from Native American settlement to Spanish colonial outpost to Mexican rule to U.S. conquest; from subsistence hunting to commercial pastoralism to industrial extraction and production; and from "wild" to rural to urban. It is in transition that the adaptive interaction of people and environment is most clearly revealed.

In the beginning, and for an immeasurable time, there was no city at all. Over the short space of a few thousand years, the land where the city now stands was used by its first human inhabitants as a direct source of sustenance. What we are now inclined to call "wilderness" was their universe. It brought them to life, nourished them, and swallowed them in death. They imagined it as eternal and immutable and eminently useful. They hunted and gathered in substantial isolation from the larger world and maintained tentative trading relationships with others barely more than a stone's throw away. Experientially, theirs was a small world indeed, broadened only by the certainty that no real barrier separated each material being from that much vaster universe of the spirit. They never could have conceived of the metropolis that now occupies their hunting and gathering grounds and envelops their graves. The life to which we others have become accustomed would certainly have been unfathomable to them. Their integration into nature was so thorough that if any point in time could challenge the conceptual folly of the nature/human dichotomy, this was it.

Then, as in other parts of the American continents, the Europeans came. While a centuries-old complex of events and historical fortunes brought the British to the East Coast of our present United States, these same instruments of fate brought the Spanish to the West. It was the Spanish who carried the world economy to the northern tip of the San Francisco peninsula and unwittingly established the preconditions for future urban growth. Armed with ambitions of empire, with techniques of Mediterranean agriculture and animal husbandry, with the tools of maritime trade, and with a religious creed that offered them "dominion . . . over every living thing,"[3] they set about making their new land serve their old and thereby initiated the Bay region's now-permanent relationship to the world marketplace. Nature began to serve ends beyond subsistence as it yielded to intensifying commerce. Yet even these first agents of Christian civilization could not have foreseen the ultimate results of their imperial adventures. The

Mission San Francisco de Asís and the presidio that defended it in 1776 could hardly be viewed as even proto-urban compared to the British Atlantic cities of Boston, Philadelphia, and New York. Nonetheless, the Spanish disrupted and altered the ancient lifeways of the Bay Area's natives and supplanted their subsistence and highly spiritualized relationship to the land with a commercial system that would have far-reaching consequences to the region's development.

However, it was not until 1835 that one could speak of even the rudiments of a town on the present urban site (using the term "town" reservedly at this point). The founder and sole inhabitant of the new town of Yerba Buena was William Antonio Richardson, a British mariner whose principal motive for being in California appears to have been escape from his whaling ship's captain. Richardson converted to Catholicism, married a daughter of the comandante of what had become the Mexican presidio, and secured the right to lay out a small village within which he was granted a number of lots. Within the next year, the American merchant Jacob Leese took up residency as the town's second inhabitant, drawn by the Mexican-sponsored hide and tallow trade and the Republic of Mexico's encouragement of mercantile activity. Leese's shipping business presaged at least a modest commercial future for the little settlement on San Francisco Bay.

A decade later, American conquest followed. The Mexican-American War of 1846–48 and the subsequent gold rush turned the village of Yerba Buena into the city of San Francisco. No historical convergence could have accomplished this more effectively than United States control coupled with the extraction of gold. The hemisphere's dominant and most ambitious commercial power now presided over a boomtown whose lifeblood was the most precious of commodities—the stuff of money itself. Value was created everywhere—seemingly from thin air and water—as hopeful fortune seekers vied for access to the goldfields and to the city of golden dreams. Even if one grants the cyclical unity of birth and death, creation and destruction, few great cities arose from as monumental an act of destruction as San Francisco. Few, if any, of the new San Franciscans considered nature's value as a source of nourishment or warmth, much less as an inherently beautiful thing. Commodity value reigned supreme, and gold was the ultimate commodity. Wherever nature dared to conceal it, the landscape was rent asunder. San Francisco, the rising metropolis at the Golden Gate, presided over the riot and eagerly laundered its spoils. In the city, as in the goldfields, Californians were busy crafting a new civilization by aggressively rearranging their received environment, and they were often caught off guard by the pangs of birth.

By the end of the nineteenth century, in the wake of the California gold and Nevada silver booms, San Francisco had settled down into the more genteel role of "grande dame" of the Pacific Coast. A genuine and economically diverse commercial and industrial metropolis by the 1890s, San Francisco presented its inhabitants with all of the typical opportunities and drawbacks of modern urban life. The rapidly urbanizing United States was just a few years away from becoming a nation of city people, and Americans in Chicago, St. Louis, and elsewhere worried about the potential ill effects of changes that had overtaken them so swiftly. Like the others, San Franciscans engaged in lively debates and heated contests over the quality of their urban environment and over their city's relationship to other far-flung lands that were quickly yielding to the march of progress. Environmental concerns were driven by sentiments noble and crass, idealistic and pragmatic, and they often produced ironic results. As the intense cadence, imposing grandeur, and wealth and misery of urban life took on an air of inevitability and permanence, San Franciscans worried about water, about urban parks, and about how to keep their lives wholesome. Gripped by a sense of loss, a generation of erstwhile urban boosters turned their attention to the defense of forests and wild lands. Their unease gave them a dualistic conception of corrupted versus pristine space that played an important role in the birth of the modern environmental movement. In 1892, a small group of upper-middle-class outdoorsmen joined with the legendary John Muir in the law offices of Warren Olney at 101 Sansome Street to found the Sierra Club. In the financial center of a city built from the forests of Northern California and the Pacific Northwest, the activists gathered to rescue and preserve the woods that had so graciously housed them. The club would soon be actively engaged as well in the conflict over San Francisco's famously controversial efforts to secure water rights in Yosemite Park's Hetch Hetchy Valley. The attendant debates over natural preservation, public health, municipalization, and urban growth represented one of the most famous events in American conservation history and one of the first efforts by San Franciscans to seriously consider the proper relationship of their city to its natural setting. When Hetch Hetchy was finally put in service to the city, its abundant water played a key role in the emergence of the modern metropolitan Bay Area. In the second half of the twentieth century, the new set of environmental conditions this produced led to the rise of the modern environmental movement—a fundamentally urban creation.

The two centuries that separate the pre-mission era from contemporary San Francisco present a remarkable tale of environmental relations. Native Americans, European colonists and their progeny, and several generations of American city folk have altered the same inherited space, ultimately producing today's mature urban edifice. Each step toward the creation of the modern city reduced the immediacy and intimacy of the relationship between people and the nonhuman world, while preserving their eternal interdependence. The ironic consequence is that the growing power of our species, as reflected in urban life, leaves us struggling to understand exactly what we have power over and how best to exercise it. Nature, like the socially powerless, is always present and is always speaking, but is most often heard when it is glaringly disruptive. San Franciscans who lived through the great earthquake of 1906 discovered, for example, that the city conceals but cannot break free from its natural moorings. But is it really sufficient for us to respond only to cataclysm? One would hope that a better understanding of cities as our most dramatic engagement of nature might help us repair a conceptual breach that urban life itself fosters. In the sage words of the environmental historian William Cronon, "We need to embrace the full continuum of a natural landscape that is also cultural, in which the city, the suburb, the pastoral, and the wild each has its proper place, which we permit ourselves to celebrate without needlessly denigrating the other."[4]

Rather than maintaining that cities are engines of efficient progress or, alternatively, consummate destroyers, it is time to reintegrate cities into our natural history. And as history shows, it is also time to give human beings credit at least for the capacity to imagine that reintegration, however flawed and halting our efforts thus far have been. The rise of urban civilization on San Francisco Bay destroyed older, well-established ways of being, but our inseparability from nature compelled the city's unwitting progenitors to develop new environmental perceptions and ultimately new environmental concerns. That inseparability, even when we are ill-equipped to grasp it, is in part the message of this book.

CHAPTER 1

COYOTE'S CHILDREN

On October 6, 1812, in Cádiz, Spain, Don Ciríaco González Carvajal, secretary of the Department of Overseas Colonies, penned an order to the viceroys of New Spain. The monarchy wished to gather, in regards to its distant possessions, "the knowledge and information [necessary] for [the] impartial guidance, rule and administration of [its] subjects."[1] Not coincidentally, Mexico had already set out on the decade-long course of rebellion that culminated in its independence, and officials of the mother country experienced some urgency in gauging the efficacy of their colonial enterprise. While Don Ciríaco addressed his message to both the civil and ecclesiastical authorities, in California it was the priests who shouldered the burden of response.

At Mission San Francisco de Asís on November 11, 1814, Fray Ramón Abella concluded and signed his *respuestas* and forwarded them to Fray José Señán at Mission San Buenaventura, where their trip home ended due to the disruptions of war. Fray Abella, like the other mission priests, had few Spanish subjects to describe but for the *Indios*. Although he dedicated his life to molding his "benighted" flock into proper and civilized Christians, and he knew his Indian "children" fairly well, he seemed neither to understand nor to respect them. Thirty-eight years had passed since the establishment of the mission, but the essential character of the native population appeared to him unchanged. Fray Abella reproached, "Everything that requires labor they naturally shun."[2] The priest's premise was remarkable—had the Indians really managed to survive for centuries in this place by avoiding work? This is inconceivable. Yet to Fray Abella, their activities in a natural state were too insignificant to qualify as labor. Abella evinced a perspective on the environmental role of human beings that was embedded in the culture of modern Europeans but that was not shared by the native peoples of California, who had always worked, but differently. The distinctions between the two peoples' ways of being in nature were at the crux of the transformative role of Spanish colonization. The needs of empire were straightforward—control and production—but to accomplish these goals it was necessary to reorder nature, both human and nonhuman, by reorganizing work.

This reorganization involved a dramatic complex of interrelated social, techno-logical, biotic, demographic, and ideological changes. One can only grasp the enormity of these changes by appreciating, as Fray Abella did not, what the natives had made of their world in the first place. This requires us to step back to the mid-eighteenth century, to the moment of Spanish contact with the natives.

Imagine standing on a clear day at the nine-hundred-foot summit of one of the Twin Peaks, near the geographic center of today's city of San Francisco. If, from that lofty perch, one could look two and a half centuries into the past, the city would melt away, yielding to grasslands, sand dunes, rolling hills, marshes, precipitous cliffs where the Pacific crashes against headlands, and the occasional stream wending its way to the vast blue expanse of bay. Acuity of vision, or a good pair of binoculars, would then afford a sight of a different sort. Due east in the valley of Mission Creek, today flowing through a culvert and buried out of sight, were human habitations—Sitlintac and Chutchui. Two miles to the south-east in Visitacion Valley lay the villages of Amuctac and Tubsinte, and off to the northwest stood Petlenuc, not far from the Golden Gate.[3] The Yelamu made their homes in these settlements and, from them, linked their lives by marriage and trade to other proximate Ohlone, or Costanoan, people on the east side of the bay and on the peninsula to the south. The inhabitants of those villages were people like ourselves, busy with love and hate and wonder, and with the workaday rou-tines designed to keep themselves fed and comfortable, but they approached all of these things differently.

The Yelamu were a subset of a human population that for thousands of years had fanned out across the landscape of west-central California. The Yelamu ended up in what is now San Francisco. Who were they? While it is tempting, for simplicity's sake, to speak of a Native American way of life, the reality of human experience in the Americas prior to European contact is more complex. This is especially evident in California, where eighty different native languages and dialects were spoken in an area comprising only 5 percent of the modern United States. For convenience of study, tribe has come to be identified with lan-guage, and the Yelamu were one of many bands of Costanoan speakers. How-ever, the inference that one might then draw regarding group identity is false. Five languages were spoken in the San Francisco Bay region alone—Coast Miwok, north of the Golden Gate; Pomo, for a dozen miles north and south of the Russian River; Wappo, in the areas surrounding the Napa River valley; Patwin and Bay Miwok, respectively north and south of Suisun Bay and the Sacramento River Delta; and, finally, the most widely spoken, Ohlone, or Costanoan, on the San Francisco peninsula and for five to fifty miles outward on radial lines reaching from the bay shore. Each language group comprised numerous independent, often competitive, and sometimes hostile groups. The existence of these significant linguistic variations within a distance now easily traveled in two to three hours by car therefore falls short of accurately portraying the area's diversity of native experiences, identities, and loyalties.

California's greatly varied climatic and topographical characteristics, so appealing to travelers today, yielded a variety of cultural adaptations by its earliest human inhabitants. Specific and narrow ecological niches shaped native economies, and highly localized familial bonds shaped native political and social structures. Environmental setting did not correlate precisely to language, but was probably a significant determinant of distinctions between human groups. The San Francisco Bay region's tidal wetlands, estuaries, hills, grasslands, riparian woods, forests, coastal ridges, escarpments, and rocky oceanic shoals offered a broad range of sustenance around which human social life could revolve. Where people lived and what they made of it played a large role in defining whom they were and how they in turn defined who constituted "others." Certainly, resource-based micro-regionalism was reflected in the tendency of tribes and tribelets to refer to themselves as "the people," and to others as "those from north of here," or some other such self-referential term. The relative isolation and independence of small kinship groups and villages of a few dozen to a few hundred persons is largely unimaginable to most of us in today's small world. The Yelamu, for example, probably numbered no more than two hundred persons at the time of Spanish contact. Three bands of Yelamu families shared the northern peninsula. One band moved seasonally between the Visitacion Valley settlements of Amuctac and Subsinte; another did the same in the Mission Creek villages of Sitlintac and Chutchui; and the third occupied the Golden Gate beachheads at Petlenuc.[4] Yet their isolation, independence, and localism were not absolute. Kinship ties linked the Yelamu bands to one another as well as to the Huchiuns across the bay where Berkeley is now and to the families at Pruristac, near today's fog capital of Pacifica. All of these groups were Costanoan speakers whose spatial separation was a necessary adaptation to the limits of territorial resources. Separation ensured sustainability, and intercommunal marriage promoted trade, while access to a broader range of ecological niches, when politically possible, facilitated the food quest.

Native Americans could count on perhaps five hundred different plant and animal foods within the current borders of California. Of course, since these were not distributed evenly, but varied with geography and climate, natives created distinct alimentary cultures suited to their group's habitual territory and

13

migratory range. The people of the San Francisco Bay area, including the Yelamu, were principally coastal tideland collectors and foothill hunters and gatherers. The bay shoreline and rocky coastal shoals yielded an abundance of shellfish. Blue mussels, California oysters, and bent-nosed clams were good sources of protein, as were the deer, elk, bear, and rabbit that inhabited local grasslands and chaparral.[5]

The significance of shellfish to the Ohlone diet is evident in the size and number of shell mounds surrounding the San Francisco Bay, of which one notable example lies just south of Islais Creek within the modern boundaries of the city of San Francisco, not far from the Yelamu sites in Mission Valley. Almost a century ago, before much of today's familiar waterfront landfill and development occurred, archeologists had identified no fewer than 425 such sites.[6] Their original number might even have exceeded that figure, as nineteenth-century agriculture and ranching, as well as the natural effects of tidal action, probably took their toll. There is today some controversy regarding the function of these vestiges of ancient human activity. Generally, the mounds have been viewed as remnant villages or seasonal habitations, kitchen middens, or garbage dumps—functional reminders that filling the belly is a primary human activity. More recently, native descendants, self-identified or reconstituted tribal entities, and their legal advocates and supporters have stressed the ceremonial and sacred purpose of the mounds as formal cemeteries and cremation sites for elite and distinguished members of Ohlone society.[7] Regardless, it is evident that huge quantities of shellfish were consumed or prepared for consumption at these locations. A substantial accumulation of clam and mussel shells rests at Ellis Landing near Richmond on the east shore of the bay. A settlement the size of which probably never exceeded a hundred souls produced this one-and-a-quarter-million-cubic-foot mound over a period of two thousand to four thousand years by consuming an unfathomable eight billion mussels and half a billion clams.[8] Considering the size and apparent age of the shell mounds, evidence of the scale of human habitation, and assumptions regarding dietary needs, archaeologists guess that natives of the bay shore regions ate about fifty mussels per person per day, along with a couple of the more labor-intensive clams, which had to be dug up rather than merely gathered. Although mollusks were less protein-rich than terrestrial and sea mammals, Native Californians ate a wide variety of foods, including plant products, which, taken together, yielded an adequate diet.

Despite the high degree of organizational and territorial independence maintained by native communities, food provided a principal motive for contact and interaction between groups. On that score, perhaps a quarter of the shell mound deposits represent export trade to the interior. Costanoans carried dried mollusk meats especially in trading expeditions to the territory of the Yokuts people of the San Joaquin Valley, who exchanged these for local pine nuts.[9] The Yelamu may also have acted as middlemen for the easterly trade of coastal shells and north coast obsidian. Because we modern folk have conceived of the great bay of San Francisco as the hub of a national and global trade network since at least the mid-nineteenth century, it would be proper to recognize that some of our "improvements" have been in scope rather than in kind. Trade has always played a significant role in the lives of the region's inhabitants, but in earlier times the concentric rings formed by the spokes of export trails were of necessity far smaller on account of the technical limits of production and transportation.

A fundamental difference from our time, however, was the absence of commoditization. The most prevalent type of trade was a direct barter of items considered of roughly equal value, and most such goods were judged on their subsistence merits. Natives also on occasion sold or leased usufruct rights from one another on a communal basis, establishing reciprocity in, literally, the "use of the fruit" of the land in a mutually beneficial fashion. These forms of exchange were, of course, only useful in situations of resource dissimilarity and therefore occurred across environmental settings. It is worth noting here as well that while topographic barriers limited trade, thereby promoting exchange between proximate neighbors, long distance trade was also restricted because tribes were generally loath to launch expeditions across one another's territories. Food could be as much a source of friction and warfare as a source of cooperation and trade. Only the fearsome Mohave of the South and Modoc of the North passed with impunity through the territories of others in a world where the loss of one man in battle would, among most tribes, be sufficient to bring a general retreat. And while presumed shamanistic malevolence—the casting of spells resulting in misfortune or disease—frequently caused warfare, territorial encroachments arising from food collection were a more material root of conflict.[10]

While food sources might vary widely from environment to environment, as between the Pacific coast and the Sierras, others were fairly universal. Much has been made, for example, of the California Indians' great affection for the acorn. Even the shellfish eaters of San Francisco Bay depended on this bitter fruit of the oak tree, but here the Yelamu may have been at a disadvantage. Eons of drifting sand produced an unusually sparse landscape between the bay and the sea. The virtually constant Pacific breezes that provide natural air-conditioning to the city today have been blowing immeasurable quantities of sand eastward from the beaches since long before the arrival of human beings. The entire northern peninsula is consequently one huge sand drift of varying depths, punctuated by the occasional rocky outcroppings we now refer to as Mt. Davidson, Mt. Sutro, Twin Peaks, the smaller Nob and Russian Hills, and so on. One should imagine a primeval landscape of far more precipitous heights and far deeper valleys, all filled in, smoothed out, and softened by sweeping sand. The power of the wind and the passage of time left very few places untouched, from the gently rising slope of our Sunset and Richmond districts to the low-lying downtown areas occupied by the Civic Center and Market Street. Today's city hall, over five miles from the ocean and thankfully sheltered from the full force of the wind, sits on eighty feet of sand.[11] While in modern urban usage these sandscapes pose engineering challenges, in pre-urban times they presented problems of sustenance. Contemporary University of California soil studies confirm this in identifying essentially two soil types within the city limits. The western two-thirds of the city consists of acidic, sandy, wind-modified soil that normally sustains some clump grasses and scrub, while the eastern third contains more clay and is more amenable to grassland and chaparral.[12] There was therefore a natural logic to the small number of Yelamu and to their preference for settling on the eastern, or bay side, of the peninsula. The few relatively small creeks were there, supporting a greater variety of flora and fauna than the western sections but, unfortunately, only small oak groves.

Perhaps transbay marriages like that of the mission-era Yelamu headman Guimas to two Huchiun women helped provide access to the oaks of what is now Oakland.[13] *Quercus kelloggii* and *Quercus lobata*, the California black oak and the valley oak, were both hardy natives of Costanoan territory. Their acorns were good sources of fat, fiber, and carbohydrates, with small amounts of vegetable protein. Oaks generated fruit so prolifically that balanophagy—the consumption of acorns—must be considered one of the most logical and effective human uses of California's native landscape. During the bearing season, average acorn production per tree averages from two hundred to five hundred pounds for the black and valley oaks, making one grove of trees sufficient to nourish an entire village. The only significant variable that human beings had to take into account was the bearing cycle of the trees. Black oaks, for example, bear well every other year, while valley oaks are especially fruitful one year in three. Native Californians, whose lives were directly tied to subsistence from a minimally reordered natural world, learned by keen observation to collect enough acorns in one year to last a family for two. This wise practice did not place too onerous a burden on annual labor but did require rather consistent effort over a couple of weeks, during which dawn-to-dusk collection was the rule. Dutiful application of a family's energy might well yield ten to twenty tons of acorns over the short harvest season, explaining the presence of granaries as prominent structures in Indian villages.[14]

However, one should not imagine the native acorn harvest in the context of a contemporary jaunt in the woods. Human beings had to compete for their acorns not only with little squirrels and woodpeckers but also with powerful and fearsome bears. These omnivorous creatures loved all the same foods as humans and did not hesitate to assert their dominance. Grizzly bears, now extinct in California, presented a major threat to acorn-gathering expeditions. We know these bears today by the scientific designation *Ursus arctos horribilis*, and they must have seemed quite horrible indeed when they threatened to apply their eight-hundred-pound weight to a hapless human being. Sentries were a sensible adaptation to these formidable competitors.

Acorn collection, measured on the basis of volume per hour of work, was less labor intensive than preparation for consumption. This was not due to the acorns' texture, since they are no harder to chew than walnuts, but to the unpalatable tannins they contain. The San Francisco Bay Ohlones shared the same technique of tannin leaching as employed by all the other balanophagous Californians. Leaching was a two-step process that involved grinding and immersion, the latter being the more ancient method. Prolonged immersion of the acorns in water or mud, often for months, and then boiling or sometimes roasting effectively removed most of the tannins from the meat. The discovery that acorns were edible when soaked but inedible in their natural state may well have been an accident. But the habit of grinding the nuts into meal prior to leaching was no doubt a consequence of human ingenuity. The great variety of pulverizing devices used by different California Indians suggests that locals adapted tools already at their disposal to speed the transformation of acorns into comestibles. Because grinding accelerated consumption, the most common method of preparation was for a woman to remove the acorn hull and grind the meat into flour on a stone slab. She then placed the resulting meal on a bed of conifer needles in a shallow pit in the ground, while a tightly woven basket containing water heated with hot stones sat by her side. As she repeatedly poured warm water over the meal, its bitter taste abated. For the last step of the process, she used her basket as a container for combining the leached meal with hot water, producing an edible mush. Ohlones, and other tideland natives, ate their gruel with spoons of clam or mussel shells. All in all, the combination of proteins from shellfish and fats and fiber and carbohydrates from acorns contributed to an adequate, if incomplete, diet.

Judging from the vertebrate bones found in the upper strata of San Francisco Bay shell mounds, Ohlones supplemented their diet of shellfish and acorns with a wide variety of hunted or trapped game—deer, elk, squirrel, rabbit, gopher, raccoon, badger, skunk, and wildcat, in addition to numerous species of aquatic birds.[15] All but the latter were abundant in the grasslands, chaparral, and woodland areas that surrounded the bay. Topographic features were more favorable to these creatures to the south and east of the present site of the city, but the Yelamu could certainly count on a steady supply of birds from wetlands like the lagoon at Mission Valley. Captain Auguste Bernard Duhaut-Cilly of the French merchant marine came to the area in the 1820s and commented on the still ample hunt "of hares, rabbits, those tufted partridge, and particularly an astonishing variety of ducks and seabirds . . . all this for our table."[16]

Yelamu could hunt ducks and harvest shellfish by doing little more than gracefully accepting the munificence of nature, but they, and especially their East and South Bay relatives, were often eager to acquire many of the land-based supplemental foods. In the process, Ohlones, like most California Indians, engaged in their greatest act of environmental modification, the intentional setting of fire. It stands to reason that a human population of limited size and technology would instinctively gather from its lands that which nature had been good enough to provide in abundance. But human beings have apparently long considered how to help nature along in serving their ends. Mastery of fire was once as important a tool of production as it is today perceived as a tool of destruction.

Native Californians in general hunted and gathered across two or more vegetational belts. Consequently, they effectively exploited the resource base within transitional zones, or edges, between ecosystems. The edges, technically known as "ecotones," between forest and chaparral, chaparral and woodland, woodland and grass, house the greatest variety and density of life. Naturally occurring fires promote this density by forcing periodic rebirth. As fire affects chaparral succession, for example, grasses, forbs, and sprouting varieties of brush yield highly nutritious new growth for animals to consume. Native Californians repeated what they witnessed in nature; by burning small areas, they pushed back dense brush and trees, or mature landscapes, and effectively promoted in their stead a mixed cover of trees, grass, and shrubs that was more conducive to supporting the herbivorous mammalian population whose bones now rest among heaps of bivalve shells. In other words, humans created their own ecological edge zones and, in so doing, displayed our species' characteristic survival mechanism of applying technique and technology to environment.[17]

Given the use of fire to manipulate the nonhuman world, one naturally questions the lack of such interventions as agriculture and animal husbandry among the natives of north-central California. This is especially significant in light of the developmental schema we usually impose on human social evolution, which often equates agriculture with civilization, and thereby places the horticulturist on a higher plane than the hunter and gatherer. The absence of these means is subject to much debate and may be unanswerable with certainty, but a few facts are worth considering. First, California's typical annual cycle of winter rain and summer drought likely does not immediately bring agriculture to mind, especially if one has not imagined irrigation. In this case, the cultivation of corn, squash, and beans, as accomplished by the southwestern natives of the Colorado River valley, would have had no place further north and east. Yet it is conceivable that, if pressed by natural shortages, California's natives might have adopted some of the techniques of their southerly neighbors. Difficulty and ignorance therefore may not sufficiently explain agriculture's geographic limits. Alternatively, one could imagine a naturally occurring cornucopia in California, whose relative ease of exploitation militated against methods of production seemingly inappropriate for the environmental setting. California's aboriginal population density was the highest anywhere within the current boundaries of the United States, and without the benefits of agriculture. In terms of productivity and sustainability, here was a very effective collection of human societies. The acorn economy, coupled with coastal Indians' specialization to a prolific marine environment, may, in fact, have ensured a standard of living for California's natives that surpassed that of neighboring agricultural peoples. Although the American trans-Sierra migrants of later times could not have understood California's natural wealth in Indian terms, there was an element of truth to their images of the land of milk and honey that awaited them.

Understanding the uses to which Native Californians put nature is essential to grasping the impact of their ultimate contact with the Spanish in the mid-eighteenth century. But a mere analysis of material culture would provide an insufficient appreciation of the enormity of the changes that awaited the natives. The physical relationship of the Yelamu to their environment was reflected in and influenced by their spiritual beliefs. There is little ethnographic evidence of a specifically Yelamu faith, and, while Costanoan-speaking peoples covered an extensive area, they did not see themselves as a unified people any more than they identified with Pomo or Miwok speakers. Nonetheless, California's first people shared broad cultural attributes that linked their ways of seeing the world to their ways of being in the world. Consider, for example, one version of the Costanoan creation story, the Coyote myth:

> One day Coyote saw a feather floating on the water. As it reached the island, it turned into an Eagle, which then spread its wings. Eagle flew over to Coyote, where Hummingbird met them. Eagle told Coyote that he should find a wife and have children so they could populate the world, but Coyote did not know the facts of life. "How do you make children?" asked Coyote. Eagle did not answer. Coyote tried making children in the knee. Eagle laughed. Coyote tried to make children in the elbow, the eyebrow, and the back of the neck. Eagle laughed so hard, Coyote became angry. Hummingbird was watching and laughing too. Finally, he [Eagle] told Coyote, "This place will be good. Try the belly." Then Coyote went off with the woman and said, "Louse me." The girl found a wood tick on him and was afraid. She threw it away. Coyote made her look for the Louse. "Look for it, then eat it." The girl put it into her mouth, swallowed the louse, and became pregnant. Coyote did not like his first wife, so later he found another. He had five children by her and told them to go out and populate the world.[18]

On the one hand, this tale is three stories in one—Coyote's comical efforts to discover the means of reproduction, Coyote's successful act of procreation by compelling a girl to swallow a louse picked from his body, and Coyote's ultimate peopling of the earth with his progeny by his second wife. The apparent disjuncture of these stories suggests that the narrative, as handed down to the present, is a composite of several related ways of reflecting on the same question—how did we get here? Of course, as a preliterate people, the Ohlone could not have left us a theological canon, but more significant is that their creation of multiple variations of central myths exposes a sort of religious democracy linked to the independent nature of even linguistically related bands of people living only dozens of miles apart.

On the other hand, the Coyote myth in all of its manifestations, along with native sacred and folk tales generally, engenders a particular relationship to nature that transcended kinship, village, and tribe. Imagine a world of human beings for whom species was not the determinant of consciousness, a world of persons in human form descended from the ancient "persons" Bear, Rabbit, Deer, Eagle, Hummingbird, Coyote, and others whose sentience was unquestionably real. One does not do justice to the sentiments of Californian Indians by describing this as the anthropomorphization of their gods or demigods, because this term is itself anthropocentric. Rather, the native world should be understood as one of multiple communities of sentient beings in a variety of corporeal forms. One could argue therefore that the early people of California did not trust empirical reality, and to some extent this was true, but it would be better to ask what their experience taught them about reality and how they adapted their lives and beliefs to these lessons.

Everywhere in pre-Spanish California, the human quest was to survive by effectively harvesting the wealth of nature. Climate, terrain, water access, and regional flora and fauna all had a direct impact on human population density, technology, and style of habitation. It is not surprising that the direct intimacy between human beings and other more numerous life-forms on which people were utterly dependent would have produced a sense of interspecies equivalency. The idea that humans were actors in a play of equals rather than dominators has given rise to the currently popular notion of the eco-Indian, a contemporary variant of the noble savage theme. Romantics may propose with some justification that these were people who lived in harmony with nature. But one need not accept a romantic view of Indians' connection to their earth to understand that their vulnerability in the face of natural cycles made them acutely aware of nature's power and thereby instilled in them a proper sense of awe and respect for their surroundings. Materialists may harden the edges of this proposition by noting that these were people who, in the typical fashion of our species, by cleverness and necessity made the most that they reasonably could of their resources. This is valid as well but fails to arouse our hearts to the sense of joy, fear, and wonder attendant to living in a world of mystery.

Regardless of the image one prefers, the fact remains that for thousands of years, early Californians both accepted and required the presence of all other native species on a shared landscape. Consequently, Native Californians never devised techniques of survival and technologies of production that challenged the continued existence of their nonhuman neighbors. They could not behave as a narcissistic species because their self-interest necessitated recognition of others. Consequently, Native Americans in California drew from and even manipulated their environment while impressing upon the land a very small and shallow ecological footprint. Furthermore, their limited impact and their experience of species interdependency justified and supported their cosmology. The power of nature was so apparent that humans felt compelled to analyze its essential functioning and to carefully negotiate with it. The power embedded in nature was sentient and behaved as the motive force of the universe. Because all natural objects and beings—both inanimate and animate in our modern view—were potential and possibly perilous power sources, humans had to prepare for their capricious tendency to either serve or foil their interests. In their own minds, humans played a central role in the universal equilibrium of power, but this role could only properly be fulfilled by following the rules of reciprocity handed down to Coyote's children in early cosmic times.[19] From these understandings emerged the sorts of taboos and rituals that were later ridiculed by the Spanish missionaries as "pagan superstitions, vain observances, and foolish practices."[20] But, far from being foolish, time-honored rituals provided the ideological and moral support for a balanced relationship between human beings and nature, the likes of which is very difficult to imagine today. This was superstitious perhaps, but functionally important in establishing standards of interspecies behavior. It was analogous to the role that Mosaic Law has played in intraspecies relations for many of us in the last few thousand years. Although there were important variations that distinguished the religious stories and ceremonial details invented by tribal groups in different California regions, all native societies, the Ohlone included, held to a code that they hoped would ensure their collective persistence in a dangerous world. And so it did. On the northern San Francisco peninsula, this millennia-old set of behaviors and beliefs defined the lives of the Yelamu until the summer of 1776.

On June 27, 1776, the first "San Franciscans," priests Francisco Palóu and Pedro Cambón, led a party of seventy-five people—soldiers, settlers, and Rumsen Indians who had been assembled in Monterey—a mule train, and 286 cattle to the vicinity of Chutchui. The expedition made camp in Mission Valley, where the cattle especially produced quite a sensation among the locals. The initial encounter between the Yelamu and the newcomers was friendly, and the settlers began work on a presidio and a church within the next two months. The Yelamu neither were aware of the role they were about to play in the Spanish scheme nor could have imagined how much their lives would change. Since the sixteenth century, the Spanish had been effectively harnessing the labor power of sedentary Indians in Mexico and Central and South America for the needs of the empire. Church and state collaborated in a process that was mutually beneficial. The Church spread the Catholic faith while simultaneously acculturating the converts to European ways of life. The civil authorities thereby hoped to benefit from the natives' adoption of production techniques that were supposed to generate surpluses of benefit to the state. In 1776, it was the Yelamu's turn to be made over.

In the last few decades it has become increasingly common, if not mandatory, to recognize the tragic fate dealt out to the original natives of this continent by colonial powers, American governments, and immigrant settlers. That American Indians were at one time or another, and from place to place, brutalized and subjugated by violence or the threat of violence is incontrovertible. However, because conscious acts of cruelty make a gripping story, we tend to pay less attention to the arguably even more devastating impact on Indian lives of the unconscious ecological revolution that the newcomers unleashed. For example, the Yelamu and other first people of the San Francisco Bay region not only were confronted with the occasional use of Spanish military power but also faced an ongoing transformation of their traditional ecological relationships. The Spanish presence in California ultimately redefined the parameters within which natives could perform the essential activities of survival—production and reproduction—and did this so thoroughly that the old ways were gone within fifty years. In fact, by 1830 not a single Indian village existed within traditional tribal lands for dozens of miles to the north and east of San Francisco. All their inhabitants had either perished or moved to the mission. Why?

Indians initially reacted to the Spanish newcomers with a mixture of curiosity, apprehension, and awe. Natives seemed especially fascinated with domesticated animals, metal implements, woven clothes and priestly vestments, armor, and certainly firearms. Given the Indians' concepts of power and their spiritualized views of nature, it must have seemed that the Spanish exercised unique influences over the nonhuman world in order to produce their intriguing form of wealth. Even relatively minor displays of military force served to confirm this impression. When Spanish soldiers responded to a series of petty thefts at San Francisco with a flogging, a conflict ensued in which the soldiers fired their muskets into a small band of bow-and-arrow-wielding natives. One Indian death led to the quick surrender of the rest. Although there are many recorded instances of Indian resistance throughout California from this point forward, their frequency and the number of participants involved is not as significant as the number of individual, familial, and communal acts of cooperation or resignation that fed the mission system. Cooperation, or resignation, stemmed from the gradual constriction of traditional means of survival. For example, the 286 cattle that Palóu and Cambón drove up to Chutchui from Monterey represented only the advance guard of a much larger herbivorous invasion. By 1830, Mission San Francisco had accumulated a herd of 4,200, while Mission Santa Clara, established in the South Bay region in 1777, could boast 9,000 cattle. In addition to these were approximately 2,000 and 8,000 sheep, respectively, and about a quarter as many horses.[21] Although these numbers resulted from a steady accretion over years, they steadily eroded elements of the Indians' habitual food resources.

Cattle, mules, horses, and sheep grazed on lands that supplied native tribes with wheat grass, wild onion, wild oats, mustard, clover, dandelion, and many other plants that produced greens and harvestable seeds.

The mission fathers were aware of this problem although their concern was colored by their proselytizing ambitions. In San Francisco, the priests became increasingly worried about the despoiling of Christian Indians' planted fields by presidio cattle, and in Santa Clara, they argued with civil authorities over the impact of livestock from Pueblo San Jose on the wild fields of local "pagans," whom they hoped to convert. Their passions were not equally aroused by the threat of mission herds although the effect on Indian subsistence must have been similar. Indian villagers responded to this threat in predictable fashion, by killing some of the livestock that grazed on their lands and eating them to fill the void created in depleted fields. The logic of this is incontestable, but Spanish authorities did not appreciate it. Indians who butchered livestock were considered thieves and were hunted down by soldiers, arrested, flogged, and sometimes pressed into forced labor in the missions. If they or their fellows put up resistance, they faced the inevitable volleys of musket fire, with the survivors giving themselves up under even more unfavorable terms. Here was a good demonstration of how the Spanish civil and military authorities employed police power in a way that punctuated, or was adjunct to, the profound and continuous processes of environmental change brought about by colonization.

The whole livestock matter was emblematic of the relationship between the natives and the newcomers. A seemingly narrow question of land use had implications beyond the obvious. When Spaniards experienced a field of wild grasses, greens, and tubers as a pasture, they were failing to see it as another people's sustenance. While they could easily grasp the legitimacy of their own property rights in cattle, they could not always grasp the equivalency of natives' rights in wild fields. One person's food became another's fodder; one person's need to eat became another's theft. The problem was aggravated by the clearing of fields for planting—both at pueblos and at missions—and especially by the colonial authorities' ban on Indian burning practices, which the Spaniards considered threatening to the domesticated herds. It bears repeating here that Native Californians used fire to enhance ecotones, or transition zones, between ecosystems. The general effect had been to promote the regeneration of certain seed-bearing food plants and trees, as well as to create an environment favorable to the wild herbivores they preferred to hunt. The ban on burning further reduced production of humanly comestible wild vegetation and constricted accessible hunting grounds. And while domesticated beasts grazed away at grasslands that were increasingly unregulated by Indian action, what they consumed was really destroyed since it was not easily or quickly replaced. Presidio commanders and *pobladores,* or settlers, were forced to repeatedly move their herds to untapped lands to guarantee enough feed, thereby setting in motion a vicious cycle of depletion. This is one, but not the only, reason for the "voluntary" relocation of Indians to the missions. Mission food was neither intrinsically superior to the traditional diet nor necessarily abundant. Some studies suggest that mission Indians' diets were inferior in calories, if not in nutritional value, to those of European peasants at the time. But because conventional food supplies were under attack, mission food may have seemed at least to offer some promise of regularity.

While animal husbandry was an important source of ecological competition between the natives and the newcomers, mission agriculture was another. Crop production was the principal goal and economic mainstay of the mission economies. Its success depended on ready access to arable land and fresh water. Consequently, missions occupied prime real estate. Consider, for example, the settlement site chosen by Fray Palóu and Fray Cambón for San Francisco. They did not choose to build on the windblown and sand-swept western peninsula, but in the valley of Mission Creek. It was no coincidence that the Yelamu had placed four of their five settlements in the same warmer, wetter, and relatively greener zone. Soon after their arrival, the San Francisco missionaries benefited from an unexplained, but for them fortuitous, attack on the Yelamu by their Ssalson enemies from what is now San Mateo.[22] When the surviving Yelamu fled in fear, the Christian settlement party set their former village lands to the spade. This gave the Spaniards and previously converted Indians an imposing physical presence on the creek, its surrounding lands, and its marshes and on the lagoon and beachfront on the bay. The Yelamu who had fled found a village of sorts upon their return, but it was not theirs, and Spanish power precluded the rebuilding of what had been lost. Yelamu continued to hunt the Mission Bay wetlands for ducks and other water fowl, but the new inevitability of dealing in some way with the mission often changed these birds into articles of trade. Missionaries took advantage of this situation to proselytize. A people devoid of their old homes confronted an active reconstruction process by strangers who were not only frightening, but amazing. What could the Yelamu have thought of a people who commanded ploughs, axes, metal cooking utensils, pigs, chickens, and cows? Within a few years, many of the locals had joined the mission—first offering their children for baptism and then themselves.

Despite Mission San Francisco's early success in recruiting the Yelamu, the priests soon understood that their mission's location was a disadvantage in two ways. First, as the landscape was bounded on two sides by bay, on one side by ocean, and on one side by tall hills, the mission's accessibility to other Indian bands was poor. This limited the pool of potential proselytes and laborers. Second, the lands the mission cultivated in Mission Valley were insufficient to feed the large and growing presidio, making the settlement substantially dependent on grain imports from Mission Santa Clara—the location of which was far superior to Mission San Francisco's from both an agricultural and a human resources perspective. To rectify these limitations, in 1786 the San Franciscans constructed the farming station of San Pedro and San Pablo south on the Pacific coast at present-day Pacifica. This annex promoted peninsular migration while its labor force of three hundred converts planted and harvested much-needed supplemental crops. The cumulative effect of the San Francisco and Santa Clara missions, the outstation of *San Pedro y San Pablo*, along with Pueblo San Jose and the even more populous San Francisco presidio, was to create a semi-encirclement of the San Francisco Bay region by the agents of a new social and economic system that was alternately attractive and infuriating, but always magnetic. Ironically, Mission San Francisco's relative isolation from native villagers other than the Yelamu caused it to play a substantial role in rearranging the geographic distribution of native populations. Indians from the peninsula south of San Bruno Mountain and those from across San Francisco Bay to the east or across the Golden Gate to the north could not gain access to mission amenities by taking a daytrip. In the Santa Clara Valley, the level and unbroken landscape and the slightly higher population densities made it possible for natives to maintain their village lives and still visit the mission and pueblo. San Francisco's offerings, on the other hand, could only be obtained by relocation. This fact was ultimately manifested in the sheer variety of Indian peoples represented in the San Francisco mission population over time and in the continuing depopulation of surrounding lands for miles.

Although the missions held many attractions for the natives, Indians migrated to them in uneven waves. Motives for resettlement varied from person to person, family to family, village to village, and time to time. Indian communities faced substantial internal dissension on how to deal with the Spanish newcomers as well. Natural phenomena, however, could conspire to strengthen the missionaries' hand. Disruptions of native food supplies by Spanish agriculture and animal husbandry were aggravated in 1794 by drought. Although the mission fathers launched an aggressive campaign of conversion that year by sending Christianized Indian emissaries to "pagan" villages, this does not adequately explain the doubling of Mission San Francisco's population in a few months. The Christian

Indians received no military support and had no forcible means of compelling whole communities to uproot themselves, yet this is what occurred. Environmental crisis may have boosted the converts' powers of persuasion. Entire Huchiun villages moved to Mission San Francisco from the East Bay, as did their southeasterly neighbors, the Saclans, as well as dozens of Huimens from across the Golden Gate, and a few Carquins and Tatcans. A similar mass migration was under way at Santa Clara. The effect at San Francisco was a significant population transfer from as far away as present-day Benicia, Lafayette, and southern Marin County into the locale of today's city. Even the priests attributed this miracle to drought conditions that had left "the pagans . . . without food, having lost their harvest."[23] By the spring of 1795, the San Francisco mission housed over a thousand people. The settlement was then perhaps five times larger than even the largest traditional native village in the area, while the Yelamu were vastly outnumbered by outsiders. Because the oak-poor Yelamu had economically useful kinship ties across the bay, one incidental consequence of Huchiun relocation may have been the Yelamu's loss of acorn resources, which would have further deepened their dependence on mission wheat.

As usual, interaction between the native order and the Spanish order unleashed a spiral of events that strengthened the latter to the detriment of the former. Spanish/native interaction spawned a complete reorientation of the San Francisco Bay economy within a few decades. The relocation and concentration of human beings and their labor power into new centers of production—the missions—and the application of their labor to nature in new ways—agriculture and animal husbandry—created a new regionalism anchored by Spanish institutions. Spanish techniques, ideas, and expectations increasingly shaped the landscape, while the ability of Indians to impact that shape waned.

The missions not only affected the environment on which the area's people had traditionally depended but also profoundly altered the region's human ecology. Mission Indians experienced extraordinary rates of disease and death that brought terrible suffering and further weakened the social and economic integrity of the native way of life. Mission neophytes and native villagers suffered from ongoing bouts of gastrointestinal disease, measles, influenza, syphilis, tuberculosis, typhus, and diphtheria, all punctuated by epidemic outbreaks. In the spring of 1777, an unknown epidemic in Santa Clara appears to have killed half of the Indian children and an even higher proportion of infants. Even non-epidemic death rates at San Francisco and Santa Clara were twice those of the average native village between 1780 and 1784 and triple the average in 1785. In 1795, an outbreak of typhus decimated the natives at Mission San

Francisco, who already faced food shortages due to a sudden influx of refugees from the regional drought. Disease took an unimaginable toll on reproduction. Of the thirty-eight native children born at Mission San Francisco from 1796 to 1797, only two survived to the age of ten. In 1802, another epidemic struck the missions, making its way up the coast from Santa Barbara, and taking with it a disproportionate number of young women. A few frightened fugitives carried what may have been tuberculosis or diphtheria into surrounding villages, spreading havoc far and wide. As natives continued to migrate into San Francisco from the Marin peninsula and the East Bay over the next few years, they brought fewer and fewer children with them—a sign of a disease-driven reproduction crisis. This crisis deepened with a measles outbreak at San Francisco in spring 1806 that killed half of all women of reproductive age, three-quarters of all baby boys, and every little girl under five. Within thirty years of Mission San Francisco's founding, all of the native peoples for miles around had suffered devastating demographic collapse.[24]

While imported diseases taxed natives' immune systems, missionaries' efforts to remake the natives' physical environment contributed to high death rates. Indians gave up disposable clothing for woolen cloth that was not always easy to keep clean and could harbor dangerous parasites. Whereas natives had lived in lightweight and airy tule-grass structures that they burned periodically when infested with vermin, their mission accommodations were of adobe brick. Dark, damp, overcrowded, and unsanitary, these adobe dormitories were breeding grounds for disease. The priests' practice of protecting female virtue by locking girls and women into these often windowless dungeons at night with a single blanket apiece could not have been conducive to good health. Furthermore, mission population densities that were artificially large compared to those of native villages aggravated problems of sanitation and water pollution and promoted epidemic conditions.[25] The general effect (as already noted) was an extraordinarily high death rate, especially among women and children. This human tragedy delivered the crowning blow to traditional patterns of life and assured victory to the ecological revolution the Spaniards had unleashed.

Missions and pueblos reshaped the methods and goals of human productive activity in ways that altered the nonhuman environment. The missions in particular also distorted human reproductive activity in ways that made a return to pre-Spanish systems of production impossible. It is worth noting that human reproduction is both a physical and a social process. Spanish contact and concentration of natives in the missions so compromised the physical reproduction of California Indians that they could no longer muster sufficient productive capacity to sustain their communities. In other words, labor power was neither being maintained on an intra-generational basis nor being replicated on an inter-generational basis—the bodies just weren't there. Social reproduction was equally compromised. How does one transmit a culture, a way of life, when the children who are normally instructed in community norms are not surviving into adulthood? A community's loss of its women and children is a loss of communal existence itself. By 1810, Mission San Francisco had swallowed virtually the entire population of Indians proximate to the bay's north, east, and west shores and had absorbed them into a nonviable community. A sad progression of migration, infertility, morbidity, and death denuded the land of the human beings who had once used it, ensuring a Spanish institutional success that not only transformed what had come before but totally supplanted it.

The drama of ecological transformation portrayed thus far is not intended to ignore the use of military force by the Spanish against the Indians. In fact, natural conditions, environmental alterations, and Spanish force were all woven together into a compelling engine of change. While some Indians became loyal to the mission system, others became disaffected because of stringent labor demands, inadequate food, or excessive discipline. Still others avoided engagement with Spanish institutions as much as possible. The Spanish responded most harshly to the disaffected. Of course, Indian labor was necessary to the success of the missions as economic enterprises, but this material aspect alone does not explain the anger with which missionaries responded to recalcitrant workers, liars, thieves, and especially fugitives. A more significant cause of priestly outrage was the ingratitude of those who rejected civilization and the "light of truth."

As early as 1775, Father-President Junipero Serra had initiated a policy of engaging civil authorities in the use of military force to capture converts who fled Mission San Carlos Borromeo near Monterey. Indians of the San Francisco Bay became more and more accustomed to this sort of action from the late 1780s onward. Consequently, the story of native/settler relations was punctuated by periodic acts of native resistance and humiliating Spanish reprisals. Numerous small-scale military engagements between Spanish forces and natives occurred around the San Francisco Bay area in the decade following the typhus epidemic of 1795. These conflicts resulted from Spanish efforts to capture neophyte fugitives, from threats or acts of violence by non-Christian Indians against Christian Indians, or from native theft of harvests or livestock. All of these engagements ended very badly for native villagers, who lacked horses and firearms. But these battles can neither individually nor collectively explain the totality of destruction that befell the losers. Indians died in battle; their communities did not. Individual lives were lost; a way of life was not. Warfare may have ultimately weakened native resistance by demonstrating Spanish military supremacy, but it was the Spanish way of being that wrought the greatest destruction to native life. In many ways, Spanish civilization in California replaced one nature with another—a shift that not only had immediate consequences but that planted the seeds of future urban development.

By the mid 1820s, the cumulative effect of fifty years of Spanish/Indian interaction in the San Francisco Bay region was dramatic. The newcomers had completely rearranged regional land uses, ecological balances, consumption and trade patterns, population distribution, human reproduction, and even dominant ideology. That a relatively small number of Spanish and Hispanicized colonists could change so many things so quickly may be surprising, but at least one aspect of native life magnified their impact. Californian Indians lived in very small communities and functioned economically within very small territories. Planting an agricultural enterprise like a mission or a pueblo in the midst of such a territory produced an immediate sort of ecological competition from which there was no escape. The micro-region that housed the initial contact community became an incubator for a whole series of changes that ultimately fanned out across the land.

On the one hand, natives were fascinated and sometimes awed by the newcomers' tools, techniques, animals, and weaponry. On the other, new land-use patterns often constricted traditional food-gathering opportunities and drew natives into the colonists' economy. Once drawn in—once in the missions, for example—their transformation gathered momentum. The mission/pueblo/presidio complex could rarely be sustained within the same geographic limits as one or even a few native settlements. This was especially true as missions took on the task of feeding presidio soldiers as well as Mission Indian populations that grew quickly to exceed those of traditional Indian villages. Mission food production then required an expanding consumption of arable and grazing land both within and across the traditional geographic boundaries that defined one native group's land from another's. Coupled with the rising demand for labor, this brought the missionaries' reach, often through the use of native proselytes, into areas beyond those of the initial contact community. And hostility and violence toward the proselytes was always met with military reprisal. The missions' competitive push into relatively far-flung resource and labor pools created a new regionalism on a scale unparalleled in pre-Spanish northern California.

A significant feature of this regionalism was that it was completely unlike a native trading network, which had entailed the movement and exchange of occasional surplus product across the territories of fixed peoples. Rather, the missions became centers of regional power that drew both resources and human beings inward with magnetic force. It was especially tragic for the natives that these power centers were gaping maws that swallowed and destroyed entire peoples. Native communities whose members gradually entered the missions never recovered from devastating diseases and extraordinary death rates. But the human toll contributed substantially to the overall strength of the transformative forces that the newcomers had unleashed. The mixing and conglomeration of native peoples in the missions over time and their subsequent demographic collapse, especially evident in the death of women and children, destroyed a whole way of being. The instruments of Spanish civilization clearly rearranged the nonhuman environment in substantial ways, but they also rid the landscape of the human agents of an alternative, prior way of life. In effect, the elimination of people wiped the slate clean in both a physical and an ideological way. In physical terms, a relatively centralized, hierarchical, macro-regional, agricultural, and commodity-based way of being in the world replaced a way of life that was very much decentralized, kinship-based, localized, and rooted in hunter-gatherer subsistence. In ideological terms, and very much of equal importance, a way of seeing the world in which human dominance was a given—in which we were to "have dominion over the fish of the sea, and over the fowl of the air, and over every living thing that creepeth on the earth"—supplanted a way of seeing in which human beings could be "coyote's children." [26] When Yerba Buena, the city of San Francisco's innocent Mexican precursor, rose quietly on the shore of the bay in the 1830s, it occupied a very recently altered world. The small young bastion of commercialism sprouted quite literally from the dust and ashes of Native California.

Chapter 2

Urban Genesis

By the 1820s, the environs of San Francisco embodied all of the contradictions endemic to the Spanish colonial venture in California. Mission Dolores, which had been purportedly designed to save the Indians through Spanish acculturation, had destroyed many of them instead. The presidio, established in part to defend the mission, became its adjunct and its economic dependent. The priests, whose primary devotion was to the elevation of souls, remade themselves by force of circumstance into masters of labor and engineers of production. Like the other missions of California, Mission Dolores became an agricultural enterprise of some substance, with a resident labor force that at times exceeded a thousand. Social and economic life contained elements that were at once archaic and modern, semifeudal and capitalist. Native peoples who had once hunted and gathered to subsist were harnessed to yield surpluses through sedentary agriculture, but, like slaves in other corners of the Americas, their masters considered the benefits of civilization to be a sufficient wage. Entire communities were uprooted, leaving previously inhabited land at least temporarily barren of human activity, while mission complexes grew into new towns that bustled with life, death, and work. If these mission communities—often five or ten times larger than native villages and even larger than the widely scattered pueblos—were not recognized as veritable towns, it was for failure to adapt the vision of their initial purpose to the reality of their ongoing function. In many cases, the missions produced surpluses that were sufficient to allow them to sell grains, dairy products, wine, and clothing to settlers, thereby planting the seeds of a market economy on Californian soil.

However, in addition to the virtual enslavement of labor, two factors militated against a fully modern approach to development. First, there was the problem of geographic isolation. Like ancient Roman camps, mission/presidio or mission/pueblo/presidio complexes were garrisons planted in the midst of hostile expanses and were poorly linked across these "empty" spaces by very slow means of communication. This hampered their ability to link up with external—hemispheric or global—markets. Second, because Spain's imperial aims with

regards to California had a great deal to do with titular control and less with capital formation, the primary goal assigned to the regional economy was the support of its military personnel. Governors periodically issued an official price list,
or *arancel*, which established, in the typical premodern European fashion, the
prices at which the necessities of life were to be sold by the missions to the pre-
sidios. This restricted the emergence of a more extensive internal market. In
essence, Spain's exertion of power on the Native Californians successfully
destroyed their subsistence economy and replaced it with the forms of a commercial one, although the latter was politically constrained. It was left to the
Mexicans to unleash the new system from those political constraints.[1]

When Mexico achieved its independence from Spain in 1821, the new government at Mexico City inherited the distant province of California. By 1824,
with the birth of the Federal Republic of Mexico, an ambitious young constitutional regime took on the task of transforming *la frontera del norte*, the northern frontier, into a more integral part of the nation. By the 1830s, liberal
democrats like Vice President Valentín Gómez Farías and California governor
José Figueroa sought to advance economic development and social modernity
by secularizing the missions and integrating the Indians into Mexican society.
They were driven both by noble republican notions of equality and by fears that
the scant population of citizenry on the northern frontier left these Mexican
lands vulnerable to foreign conquest. By divorcing the missions from their lands
and the priests from seigneurial authority, they hoped as well to produce incen-
tives for private, entrepreneurial settlement. They also planned to open trade
with foreign merchants in order to convert the land's wealth into liquid capital.
The missions provided them with an invaluable pool of resources—ten million
acres of land, four hundred thousand head of cattle, roughly as many sheep, and
tens of thousands of horses. In the turmoil of the revolutionary decade that began
in 1810, the California missions and pueblos, cut off from the rest of New Spain,
had already initiated an export trade in hides and tallow. This was to become the
core economic activity of Mexican California, and an essential step toward the
founding of Yerba Buena, the town later known as San Francisco.

Yerba Buena exemplified the central role of foreign adventurers and merchant capitalists in the economic development of Mexican California. Although
the Mexican government pursued a logical course in encouraging foreign trade,
the predominance of Americans and Britons in the emerging commercialism of
formerly administrative towns like Monterey and San Diego reveals the subsidiary nature and inferiority of Mexican California to economies whose emissaries were the Hudson Bay Company and the Boston hide traders. Like

sixteenth-century Genoese merchants in Madrid and Italian merchants in Paris or seventeenth-century Dutch merchants in Leipzig, Americans and Englishmen quickly dominated the principal spheres of economic activity in nineteenth-century California on account of their experience, their access to liquid capital, and their links to substantial external markets. Since regional, national, and global markets are impossible without towns and cities, if anything distinguished the California case from the earlier European examples, it was that the California urban canvas was so barely sketched by the 1830s that the imprint of outsiders upon it can be seen in much bolder relief. The Genoese did not invent Madrid, but Britons and especially Americans were the principal architects—or perhaps conjurers—of what became the city of San Francisco.[2]

In 1835, the Englishman William Richardson secured the right to a building lot of 100 varas square (roughly 100 by 100 yards) set back from the beach of Yerba Buena cove, San Francisco's original anchorage. Richardson, a former first mate on the British whaler *Orion*, had jumped ship in 1822 and proceeded to marry the San Francisco presidio comandante's daughter, Maria Antonio Martinez. Around that time, early efforts by the Mexican government to spawn a civil pueblo from presidial seed failed on account of the military outpost's severe decline over the course of the revolutionary years. Later, with the secularization of Mission Dolores in 1833, the old settlement in proximity to the mission was placed under the nominal charge of *Alcalde*, or mayor, Francisco de Haro, but there was little for him to govern, as the population was too small for self-government under Mexican law. Richardson was luckier. Governor Figueroa at Monterey, whom he had convinced of the benefits of a town site on the beach by the bay, instructed de Haro to lay out the boundaries of a village with Richardson's assistance, and to grant him the first lot, subject to a two-hundred-vara-deep government land reservation extending inland from the waterfront. The fortuity of the site, as opposed to existing population centers at the presidio and in Mission Valley, became increasingly apparent over the years as seaborne commerce grew in economic importance.[3]

Commerce, in fact, was Richardson's driving ambition. From his hastily erected sailcloth tent near the intersection of today's Clay and Grant streets, Richardson acted both as harbormaster and as the operator of two schooners that carried produce from farms and ranches around the bay for transfer to oceangoing vessels anchored at Yerba Buena. As such, he became one of the pioneering merchants of the San Francisco hide and tallow trade. Richardson's ships carried hides at twelve cents freight apiece, tallow for one dollar per five-hundred-pound bag, and grain for twenty-five cents a *fanega* (roughly two and a half bushels). His business arose logically from the transformation of the local and regional landscape that was initiated by Spanish colonization and Indian concentration and depopulation and that was ultimately sealed by the Mexican land-grant system. Mexico made substantial land allocations to private individuals both to foster political allegiance and to promote economic growth. While grantees continued to employ Indian labor to cultivate crops on irrigable land, most took advantage of the unlimited supply of free grass provided by nature to raise cattle as their principal source of income. Several ranchos existed at only a stone's throw from Yerba Buena, within the modern city limits of San Francisco—José Antonio Galindo's Rancho la Laguna de la Merced to the southwest, José Cornelio Bernal's Rancho Rincon de las Salinas y Potrero Viejo to the southeast, Francisco and Ramon de Haro's Rancho Potrero de San Francisco, and José de Jesus Noé's Rancho San Miguel, which alone fed two thousand cattle on over four thousand acres near the geographic center of today's city. But it was the numerous other and more distant ranchos bordering the bay along the Contra Costa shore and south toward San José, along with the grain-producing farms of Santa Clara, that provided ample cargo for Richardson's shipping business.[4]

Richardson's first neighbor in Yerba Buena, Jacob Leese, was also the first American to receive a major land grant on the outskirts of the fledgling village. Rancho Cañada de Guadalupe Rodeo Viejo y Visitacion comprised almost nine thousand acres spanning the mid-southern section of modern San Francisco as well as northern San Mateo County. In May 1836, Leese came to Yerba Buena to establish a mercantile business with some partners based in Monterey. The authorities at first offered him a choice of land either at the mouth of Mission Creek or near the Golden Gate and the presidio, but neither plot held the commercial possibilities of Yerba Buena cove. After negotiating with Governor Mariano Chico and Alcalde Francisco de Haro, Leese secured a one-hundred-vara lot adjoining the south side of Richardson's and facing the beach, where he built a substantial home and store. Leese's potential contributions to the prosperity of the region were apparently evident to the political leaders, who subsequently awarded him eight more lots, one of which was on the beach within the original government reserve, in addition to the large grant at Rancho Cañada in 1841. In 1837, Leese married the sister of General Mariano Vallejo—the comandante of the San Francisco presidio—and within a few years, both families would seek out new fortunes in Sonoma. Before his departure for the North, Leese traded his San Francisco rancho to Robert Ridley for Rancho Calloyami in Sonoma, and he sold his beachfront home and business in Yerba Buena to the Hudson Bay

Company, which dominated the commercial life of the village from that point until its own departure in 1846.[5]

If it were possible to suspend time somewhere in the early 1840s, Yerba Buena would forever be carved in history as a small port whose existence both depended on and made possible the commercialization of a thinly populated agricultural hinterland. The economic reciprocity between Yerba Buena and its countryside was typical of nascent towns in other parts of the world and in earlier times. The village demonstrated the presence of markets for the yield of the land and promised the emergence of the division of labor and diversification of consumption that characterizes urbanizing societies. Yet Richardson and Leese's Yerba Buena, the Hudson Bay Company's Yerba Buena, was really no more than a trading post. As late as 1844, the village had merely fifty inhabitants, almost all employed by the company. Although the cumulative product of the ranchos that encircled San Francisco Bay was not insubstantial, its transit could not realistically support a large number of great mercantile establishments. A few wealthy individuals and firms would have quickly exceeded the competitive limits of the regional economy, buffeted as well by the vagaries of natural cycles of deluge and drought with their unfortunate consequences for crops and cattle. The fact that Jacob Leese could foresee greener pastures only five years after his arrival clearly indicates that the future preeminence of San Francisco could in no way have been foreseen before the gold rush. Soon after the outbreak of war between the United States and Mexico in 1846, the almost uncontested seizure of California by the United States led to a significant increase in American immigration, but, even then, the village's population was barely five hundred by the summer of 1847. Nonetheless, Yerba Buena—officially renamed San Francisco in January 1847—played a key role in regional development.

San Francisco's principal asset, well-understood by those first merchants who so determinedly set up shop on Yerba Buena cove, was the bay itself, although the relative advantages and disadvantages of the site evolved over time along with changes in transportation technology and the sources of commodities traded. The existing centers of population and authority at the San Francisco mission and presidio laid the basis for the establishment of Yerba Buena insofar as these provided the miniscule mercantile colony with physical security and legal legitimacy. The ranches and farms encircling the bay were the economic raison d'être for Yerba Buena, to which the most logical shipping routes were by water due to the primitive state of land transportation. The bay's proximity to the Golden Gate offered ready access to the oceangoing trade, as long as an adequate harbor could be provided for the ships. The harbor opposite the pre-

This sketch of Yerba Buena cove as it would have appeared in 1847 shows the sheltered harbor that gave the town its initial commercial value. Courtesy of the San Francisco History Center, San Francisco Public Library.

sidio might have sufficed, but it sat at the foot of a cliff and was open to the Pacific winds and proximate to an often tumultuous sea. Yerba Buena cove was at least sheltered, a benefit already well-established in the 1820s by whaling captains who made this their preferred anchorage. Furthermore, San Francisco Bay was one of only three convenient harbors on the California coast, the others being at Monterey and San Diego. In most other places, goods had to be ferried back and forth in small boats from ships anchored three miles out at sea. Yet, in the days of the hide and tallow trade, San Diego enjoyed certain incomparable advantages to Yerba Buena, which San Francisco ultimately overcame only by accidents of history.

Because Southern California had the largest ranchos, a southern harbor appealed to the trading companies that, in turn, maintained large warehouses there. The substantial numbers of hides procured from the area's ranchos were cured in the San Diego sun. Raw hides were softened by soaking in the ocean, after which they were pickled in brine, scraped clean of fat and grease, and spread out in the sun to dry. The entire process could be undone, and the hides thereby spoiled, if they should happen to get wet again when loaded onto a ship.

Aside from its proximity to the raw material itself, San Diego Bay offered calm waters with ease of loading and unloading on a broad, flat landing. Had ranching remained at the core of California's economy, San Diego may well have eclipsed San Francisco as the principal port in the state, but conditions changed rapidly soon after conquest. The catalyst was gold.

When James Wilson Marshall made his famed discovery of placer gold in January 1848 on the south fork of the American River, he gave no thought to its origins. Over many millennia, the dramatic geologic upheavals that created the Sierra Nevada mountain range had incubated, fragmented, and scattered tons of ore-bearing rock. Some of this rock found its way into the silt and gravel of the rivers and streams that formed to drain the western slope of the Sierras. This was the placer gold that set off the 1849 boom on account of its extraordinary accessibility. A geologic phenomenon with an accidentally democratic bent allowed anyone with a shovel and a pan to dream of fortune. Forty-million-year-old river channels, carved out by climatic conditions that shaped eons of precipitation cycles, brought most of this placer gold into the northern and central Sierra Mother Lode Country. At the onset of the historic period, the Yuba, Bear, and American rivers were prime beneficiaries of this process. Consequently, the almost immediate result of Marshall's find was a human flood into the Sierra foothills and the creation of a narrow, one-hundred-mile-long band of mining camps and towns along auriferous streambeds from Downieville to Rough and Ready and from Hangtown to Groveland. The same snowmelt and rain that fed the gold-bearing streams also drew their flow downslope to the Sacramento and San Joaquin rivers, both navigable and both winding through a shared delta into Suisun Bay, through the Carquinez Strait, and out to San Pablo Bay and its partner, the San Francisco Bay. In the blink of an eye, the glimmer of gold reoriented San Francisco's inland commerce. No longer would the magnificent bay serve principally to ferry agricultural product from its perimeter to the Golden Gate. The most lucrative trade was now to be had upriver and downriver, well inland, linking the Sierra gold country to the nation and the world through the tiny commercial settlement on Yerba Buena cove.

San Francisco Bay's primacy as the transit hub of the gold trade was geographically determined, but San Francisco's ascendancy was not. Technology, history, and politics contributed mightily to the city's rise. In the interest of time and carrying capacity, small schooners that could navigate both ocean and river were replaced early on by seafaring clipper ships and steam-powered riverboats, each confined to its own nautical niche. This specialization eliminated the likelihood that the river ports of Sacramento and Stockton could ever become more than adjuncts to some bay port at which cargo could be reloaded to continue its journey inland or out to sea. The bay port required a deep and sheltered harbor, and a number of sites could have been exploited to this end, not the least of which was Benicia on the Carquinez Strait. But San Francisco was already established and by 1850 had an enormous advantage both in population and in invested capital over any potential rival. Not only did late starters find it difficult to overcome San Francisco's early lead, but the burgeoning city's interests were defended in Congress by Senator William Gwin, who secured San Francisco's monopoly as port of entry and as the site of the U.S. customhouse and mint. Further risks of being outflanked by Oakland, across the bay to the east, were fended off with the construction of a rail line from San Francisco to San Jose that offered any future transcontinental railroad an opportunity to bypass Oakland and link up with existing port facilities at San Francisco. In sum, growth begot growth, and those who stood to benefit did all in their means to defend their advantage. This also required drastic modifications to the landscape on which San Francisco was situated, as the spatial needs of the city were of a distinctly different order than those of its predecessor, Yerba Buena.[6]

Writing of Constantinople, Bahia, Cologne, and Canton, historian Fernand Braudel once noted that "every town grows up in a given place, becomes wedded to it and, with few exceptions, never leaves it. The original site may or may not be a wise choice: its initial advantages and disadvantages stay with it forever."[7] San Francisco was no different. From a functional perspective, the city's environmental disadvantages were numerous. Although Yerba Buena cove offered a sheltered harbor, the anchorage was at some distance from the beach. A broad mud flat extended out a quarter mile into the bay, covered to eight feet at high water but laid bare at low tide. When the tide was low, the narrow projection of Clark's Point at the foot of Broadway, beside which Telegraph Hill rises, was the only place that even small boats could land. Under the circumstances, the timely shipment of cargoes was as much at the mercy of daily natural rhythms as it was dependent on the cadence of the market.

Without human manipulation, the waterfront was ill-adapted to the needs of a booming commercial port. At a short distance from the port, the land was broken in all directions by a series of hills and ridges from one hundred to three hundred feet high—Telegraph, Russian, Nob, and Rincon hills among them—leaving limited level ground on which the city could easily expand to the west and north. Beyond the ridges were the inhospitable windblown sand dunes that progressed eastward for miles from the ocean beaches. The low-lying land to the south along the shore of the bay was equally ill-suited to building, as it comprised the marshy estuaries of Mission and Islais creeks, which extended far inland and prevented the city from pushing at any great distance below Market Street. While the eastward-flowing freshwater creeks had some short-term utility as sources of drinking water for cattle and humans alike, the more extensive tidal estuaries into which they drained were not potable and were only marginally navigable. Small craft could negotiate the ebb and flow of these broad and shallow tidal basins, but to what end? There was not much serious business worth having but for that at Yerba Buena. Consequently, places such as these, which had been the hunting grounds of the area's first human inhabitants and the homes of the birds, shell-fish, and small mammals they ate, were seen increasingly as obstacles to "ratio-nal" urban development. City building would require substantial environmental transformations.

Mature cities project such an effective illusion of imperviousness to natural forces that we rarely consider the intensity of the contest that brings them to life. Like other pioneer urbanites, Gold Rush–era San Franciscans cobbled together a city fitfully and haphazardly through a trial-and-error struggle with its setting. As they crafted a new environment, they found themselves inescapably bound to water and earth. The constraints these elements imposed, as well as the human effort required to manipulate them, shaped the growth of the city and the exploitation of its hinterland. San Franciscans seemed quite consumed by the concern that their city had been graced with too much water and too little earth. The urban site had too little developable land while the harbor was separated from shore at too great a distance by tidal flats and marshes. San Franciscans' principal early goal was to create commercially viable real estate despite these spatial shortcomings and to provide a means for cargoes to land directly in port instead of being lightered ashore. Both of these goals were accomplished by the relentless extension of the city on pilings across the mudflats of Yerba Buena cove—by gradually filling with rubble the interstices of these new streets that stood aloft the tide and by throwing long piers out from the made-land business district into the deep water of the bay. Within two decades, San Francisco's mim-icry of Venice had transformed Yerba Buena cove into the city's commercial dis-trict and had created a new waterfront with approximately its modern configuration.

The process of reclamation reveals a great deal about the culture of urban-ization. The use of the word "reclamation" has become second nature to us, especially in regard to our understanding of economic development in the Amer-ican West. In fact, for most of the twentieth century, the word's connotations were largely positive, as it was associated with modernization and progress. Its

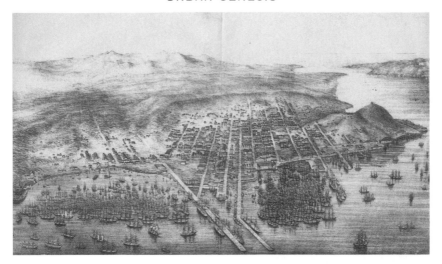

A bird's-eye view of San Francisco in 1852 shows the city's encroachment into Yerba Buena cove, with wharves becoming streets. The Market Street wharf is farthest left, and Telegraph Hill rises on the far right, past the Broadway wharf. Courtesy of the San Francisco History Center, San Francisco Public Library.

conventional meaning is "the bringing of wild, waste, desert, marshy, or sub-merged land into a condition for cultivation or other use."[8] While there is nothing inherently unjust or morally destructive about this kind of human activity, the language we have chosen to describe it with reflects a particular frame of mind. Is not "to reclaim" the act of taking back a thing to which one has a prior right? As San Franciscans, like other city builders, stood in opposition to nature in its pre-urban state on the basis of their prior right, they were applying a new concept of value to their environment and justifying its alteration. If we look further at the Latin root of "reclamation"—*reclamare*, "to cry out against"—we develop of very good sense of the emotional content of the process. The reclaimer experiences the received environment as inadequate, cries out against it on account of its withholding nature, and then proceeds to transform it into more congenial space. Reclaiming San Francisco from the bay went hand in hand with dramatic shifts in the value assigned to various elements of the landscape as well as to various economic uses of it.

Even before the gold rush, Jasper O'Farrell's survey of San Francisco confirmed the high value that subsequent occupants would place on waterfront and submerged properties. O'Farrell delineated water lots in Yerba Buena cove by extending the existing street grid into the bay. While ensuring that Yerba Buena preserved a block pattern in which actual and planned streets crossed at right angles, O'Farrell also sketched out the diagonal path of today's Market Street. Although the logic of this may evade the viewer of a contemporary map of San Francisco, there was some justification for planning a street grid in this section of the imaginary city that ran parallel and perpendicular to existing overland traffic patterns connecting the commercial bay front to the Mission, and that avoided bringing every street to a dead end on the banks of Mission Creek. O'Farrell's geometric sleight of hand unwittingly laid the basis for future cultural and economic distinctions between the commercial and financial heart of the city and what came to be known as "south of Market," or "South of the Slot." Here, both the blocks and the lots were substantially larger and cheaper, reflecting the premium that buyers were willing to pay for port access on the northern side of the imaginary line. Conversely, the design and pricing of south of Market lots were due to the obstacles that stood, quite literally, in the path of immediate development. When the straight line of Market Street was transferred from the map to the actual landscape, its outbound southwesterly course was interrupted by a series of impassable sand hills from eighty to hundred feet high. O'Farrell clearly anticipated substantial grading work from the very beginning, which provides yet another reason for the large size of the proposed blocks— fewer streets to grade and a greater quantity of developable private property. In 1858, more than a decade after its initial mapping, Market Street began to take physical shape at the hands of David Hewes, the "Maker of San Francisco."[9]

David Hewes was a Yale graduate and early San Franciscan who devised an earth-moving invention that was referred to as the "Steam Paddy." The label's not-so-veiled image of an Irish automaton was derived from the similarity between Hewes's street grading techniques and those of railroad construction, in which Irish laborers figured prominently. Irish laborers also filled the ranks of the work crews that moved Hewes's steam shovel and railroad car combination around the unimproved urban outback. By laying temporary tracks linking the alternating marshes and sand hills that characterized the south of Market landscape, Hewes's crews could use the steam shovel to daily move up to 2,500 tons of sand out of the way of prospective streets and into railcars that carried it away to fill marshes, tidelands, and ponds.

Hewes graded and filled in a southwesterly direction, starting with the most valuable property. He filled the water lots closest to downtown in the early 1850s, during and right after the peak period of placer gold production in the Sierras. He then moved his operation gradually outward along the mapped line of Market Street, opening streets sequentially toward Mission Creek. By 1868, the building of Long Bridge opened a horsecar line across Mission Bay to the

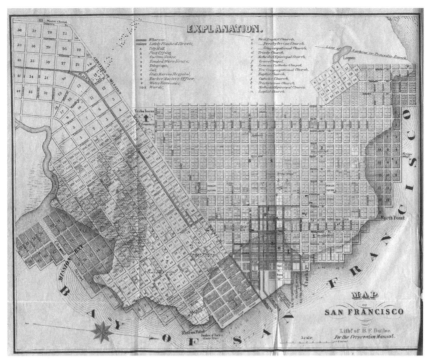

This map of San Francisco in 1852 reveals the original shoreline, with shaded areas showing city blocks built or soon to be built on landfill. The disappearing Yerba Buena cove appears at the bottom of the map, and Mission Bay is to the left. The mouth of Mission Creek is on the far left center, and the shaded fingers running inland from Mission Bay indicate the location of the marshes that once extended toward Market Street. Courtesy of the San Francisco History Center, San Francisco Public Library.

Potrero district and went on from there to span the Islais Creek estuary to Hunters Point. An aerial view would reveal the original shoreline as two peninsular promontories interrupted by two extensive reaches of bay water. Long Bridge transected these perpendicularly and became a potential future frontage road.[10] By 1873, Hewes had begun filling Mission Bay, which had been enclosed by the bridge and severed from the main body of San Francisco Bay. This work was completed a quarter century later by the Southern Pacific and Atchison, Topeka & Santa Fe railroads, which had used their political influence to acquire the submerged water lots thus created in the shallow lagoon. Hewes, his machine, and his work crews were responsible for both the flat topography of far eastern San Francisco and the linear aspect of the bay shoreline of today's city, both of which are far removed from their pre-urban state. In 1870, Reverend

John Todd of Massachusetts reflected the urban boosterism of the age in his appraisal of Hewes's impact: "On the end of [the] peninsula is San Francisco—a city built on and among the most dreary sand-hills. Originally no spot could be more uninviting. But in twenty years the high hills have been cut down and carted into the water, rocks blasted, sloughs filled up, till now you find a wondrous city . . . with nothing that looks young . . . or unfinished."[11]

The process of urbanizing the space that the city grew to occupy was uneven, however, and involved false starts and wasted resources on the one hand, and compromises and sensible adaptations on the other. Early efforts to create suburban arteries were a good case in point. In 1851, just as Hewes was beginning his work, the Mission Dolores Plank Road Company spent ninety-six thousand dollars to construct a two-mile-long toll road linking the business district to the mission and followed this within a year with the parallel Folsom Road, which ran to its south. The private company received a seven-year franchise for toll collection, after which the roads were to revert to the city. Profit concerns thereby assured that these thoroughfares would be built as quickly and cheaply as possible. Avoiding the precipitous sand hills that no horse-drawn vehicles could ever hope to scale, the roads ran alternately over dry land and marsh, of which the latter presented obvious engineering problems. Pilings were often swallowed up by seemingly bottomless mud, so sand fill became a preferred foundation. Unfortunately, the sand often did nothing more than displace the existing water and peat, producing a morass of shallow, muddy pools with contorted earthen banks that negatively affected the uses of surrounding land. Impassable still, the spongy roadbeds were then planked to accommodate wagon traffic. Oregon fir planks, four inches thick, were one of the emerging city's first significant extractions from its wooded Pacific hinterland. Although the impact of San Francisco's roads and streets on the region's forests was as yet small, the plank roads presaged the city's more substantial future dependency on the woods of California and the Pacific Northwest. And, as remained the case for a very long time, builders showed no concern for waste. The fir planks had little or no resistance to the rot they suffered in their watery setting, but frequent replacement was still cheaper than stone pavement would have been. The road companies' focus on short-term gain also blinded them to the effects of tidal action, seasonal streams, and subsurface water flow, all of which led to washouts, land subsidence, the broadening of flood plains, and other unanticipated consequences of altering the balance of water and land with no attention to the causes of their natural shape.[12]

On a more sensible note, land uses along the new roads were typically appropriate to the well-watered environment that had once nurtured the seasonal set-

Mission Plank Road in 1856, looking southwest from Ninth Street. Courtesy of the David Rumsey Map Collection, www.davidrumsey.com.

tlements of the Yelamu and then the fields and pastures of the mission. Until the rampant real estate speculation and development of the 1860s pushed the city far beyond its initial limits, agriculture was still the predominant economic activity in Mission Valley. While most cities emerged as a consequence of agricultural surpluses generated in the countryside, San Francisco's development was not so linear. Yerba Buena had arisen, of course, as an agricultural entrepôt but was hardly a city. The city of San Francisco emerged as a gold port but then grew too quickly for its agricultural hinterland. In any case, few ardent gold seekers had any interest in farming. For many years, San Francisco was fed from a great distance—flour from Virginia and Chile, apples from Massachusetts, farm products of all sorts from New York and Pennsylvania, rice from China, coffee from Java, sugar from Hawaii, and oranges from Tahiti. The breadth and quantity of San Francisco's imports reflected what geographer Gray Brechin has identified as the burgeoning city's "imperial" qualities. Positioned at the center of an extraordinarily far-reaching global trading network, in 1853 alone San Francisco imported essentials valued at almost $12 million—100 million pounds of flour, 20 million pounds of butter, 25 million pounds of barley, 400 thousand bags of rice, 115 thousand bags of coffee, and 1 million pounds of tea. Its noncomestible imports included 80 million feet of lumber and 80 thousand tons of coal. The latter, initially extracted from places as far-flung as Chile and the British Isles, was ultimately derived at lower transport cost from Bellingham Bay in Washington Territory. The coal fueled a growing fleet of steamers on the bay and its tributaries, providing the arterial network that turned San Francisco into a "mother of cities," spawning urban growth in the almost undeveloped regions of the interior.[13]

Despite the enormity of its demand for external resources, San Francisco still enjoyed a favorable balance of trade, thanks to its export in the same year of $65 million in gold. Nonetheless, three factors mitigated the benefits that San Franciscans derived from so much long-distance trade. First, there was the expense related to shipping costs and external dependency; second, the irregularity of shipping led to periodic gluts and shortages; and, finally, in those days long before refrigeration and high-speed transport, fresh meat and fresh produce could not be shipped. As a consequence, a few enterprising souls planted market gardens and established sheep ranches and hog farms along the plank roads and creek banks south of the built-up city. Fairly large commercial gardens occupied former mission lands, while smaller-scale production became an increasingly characteristic transitional use of newly created one-hundred-vara lots south of Market Street. Hewes's reclamation project, therefore, did not often lead to immediate urbanization, but instead created the conditions for economic activities to take root that were ancillary to the process of city building. The fact that Hewes's made land was flat and readily accessible to the downtown made it ideal for short-term agricultural use. The fact that it sat on, in, and around water made it easy to irrigate by means of windmills and wells.

Over a few decades, as industrial and residential development swept progressively south and west from the heart of the city, agriculture on the urban periphery was displaced, but it did not completely disappear until the twentieth century. One consequence of the completion of Long Bridge as the urban core expanded was that it facilitated the relocation of San Francisco's market gardens southward to cheaper land around Islais Creek and Hunters Point. Eventually, the market for regionally grown produce would push agriculture outward along the banks of San Francisco Bay's tributaries, giving rise to the extensive system of valley farms that supported the state's economy in the aftermath of the gold and silver booms. But even with the growth of commercial agriculture in the city's fertile Central Valley hinterland, as late as the 1890s urban and suburban market gardening continued to occupy the time of field laborers drawn from the ranks of recent, non–English-speaking immigrant groups, like the Italians, as it had the Chinese at midcentury.[14]

The suburban Mission District in 1865. Courtesy of the San Francisco History Center, San Francisco Public Library.

If market gardening partially reduced San Francisco's initial dependency on the "civilized" farming regions of the East, animal husbandry reduced its reliance on the California wilderness. A meat diet that included venison, bear, and all sorts of wild game reflected the early city's status as a genuine frontier outpost. However, from the early 1850s onward, evident from the local gardens themselves, the city increasingly shaped its own hinterland, rather than the reverse. As urbanism demanded urbanity—not to mention regularity of supply—hunter's fare was replaced by a farmer and rancher's menu of pork, lamb, and even beef. The first two of these, and even some of the latter, were procured from within the city limits and processed in the Butchertown that grew on the banks of Mission Creek.

The Mission Creek site had a number of natural advantages that suited the needs of the meat-processing business and its allied industries of tanning and soap making. All of these advantages derived from water. Hogs were easy to raise on the well-watered creek banks, as were sheep in its neighboring pastures. Cattle from around the bay could be shipped in shallow draft schooners to the slaughterhouses on Mission Creek wharves. Water was easily drawn up to scour the packing plants, and the tides allowed the butchers to use the bay as a sink to carry away the carcasses, blood, and undesirable organs that would have been either expensive or even more noisome to dispose of in any other way. The tanneries that converted animal hides into a marketable raw material for the city's leatherworks were equally water-dependent. The soaking, cleaning, brining, and tanning stages of the process each required great quantities of water, which also needed to be flushed away as waste. In fact, in a city whose economy was so driven by shipping, Butchertown was an early example of industrial, rather than commercial, use of waterfront property. Although most of Butchertown's wastes were organic, their sheer volume drastically affected the ecology of the bay as well as the quality of the human environment that surrounded it, presaging the foul and polluted urban bays and waterways of our own time.[15]

Butchertown's resource impact also illuminates San Francisco's unplanned creation of a web of environmental relationships that were completely novel and unforeseen and which at first aroused no serious concern. For example, the tannins required for turning hide to leather came from tree bark. The chestnut oaks of Santa Cruz performed this function so well that their numbers were seriously depleted by the 1880s. Their depletion is emblematic as well of the speed of cultural change that in just a few generations transformed a tree that was once a living food source for Native Americans into an abstraction whose bark alone was an industrial raw material.

Furthermore, as Santa Cruz provided wood for tanning, it also provided much larger quantities for building. In their haste, early gold rush San Franciscans either imported prefabricated houses from New England or threw up rudely constructed house-tents whose canvas walls and roofs were tacked to wooden framing members. When they were ready to build a more permanent city, sailcloth would not do, and large-scale importation of homes was impractical and expensive, so the pioneer urbanites turned to the enormous stands of virgin timber in the Santa Cruz Mountains. Three Americans and a French-Canadian had already started lumbering operations there in 1840. During the Mexican period, Isaac Graham, Henry Neale, Joseph Majors, and Francisco Lajeunesse secured the right to Rancho Zayante, thanks to Majors's marriage into the family of Comandante General José Castro. The partners set up a mill on Mount Hermon and were joined by dozens of other producers by the early 1860s. In 1847, the lumbermen built a 20-mile-long flume from the headwaters of the San Lorenzo River to the Pacific Ocean, and in 1851, a wharf was built at Santa Cruz Harbor to facilitate the shipping of lumber and other raw materials. Santa Cruz became one of the principal sources of building materials for the growing city of San Francisco.[16]

The abundant Santa Cruz forests, coupled with one of the legacies of the Spanish colonial economy, also triggered the imagination of two Massachusetts engineers. A. P. Jordan and Isaac E. Davis sought to adapt mission-era lime production to modern commercial purposes. Lime was widely used in the construction industry of the 1850s for making mortar, plaster, and whitewash. The Santa Cruz region was naturally rich in limestone, which was converted to building lime by burning it in large kilns, stoked by local wood. So, while gold mining in the Sierras fueled the growth of early San Francisco, the city's cyclical construction booms fostered another, less highly renowned, but nonetheless significant, type of mining in the mountains to its south in the limestone quarries. Besides the physical impact of the quarrying itself, firing the limestone into lime had a substantial effect on the forests because of the huge amount of wood consumed in the kilns and in the production of barrels to store and ship the finished product. Davis and Jordan's business thrived, allowing them to build their own wharf and operate their own schooner, the *Queen of the West*, to ship their lime to San Francisco. As in the lumber industry, their success promoted competition as new companies entered the field over the subsequent decades. In the 1860s, Santa Cruz County yielded eight thousand barrels of lime per month. By the 1880s, three Santa Cruz companies—Davis and Cowell, Holms, and IXL Lime—produced half of the state's supply. By the 1890s, thoughtless resource exploitation brought industrial decline, as years of intense logging had virtually denuded the Santa Cruz Mountains of the virgin forests that were the source of their initial attraction.[17]

While harnessing and even destroying the Santa Cruz forests to build a city of wood was by no means unusual by nineteenth-century standards, San Francisco's recurring problems with both arson and accidental fire triggered a curious loop of environmental and social effects. Less than a century before the gold rush, the region's Native Americans had used fire to create use value. They protected their health by setting their homes ablaze when these became hopelessly infested with fleas, and they burned the chaparral to encourage the proliferation of favored comestibles. The Spanish and Mexicans who followed saw fire only in destructive terms as it threatened their capital in livestock. The Americans felt quite the same, although by 1849 the capital they sought to protect was not livestock but the physical infrastructure of the city of San Francisco. Wooden buildings jammed together and joined by plank streets and wharves made a perfect tinderbox. In the early days, the city burned, at least in part, seven times—in December 1849, May, June, and September 1850, May and June 1851, and November 1852. The lost investments were appalling; however, fire had a uniquely positive effect on the real estate values of water lots and waterfront properties, where bay water and artesian wells could most readily be tapped to combat future flames. This fact made David Hewes's reclamation work all the more compelling.

Yet if fire generated value on American wetlands as it had on the Natives' chaparral, the analogy is a limited one. Real estate profits are an inedible abstraction, and most San Franciscans ate by using urban land to engage in some sort of commercial enterprise or productive activity. Preventing fire was therefore an urgent matter for almost all of them, especially in light of the frequency of conflagration. Between 1851 and 1856, the *Alta* reported 253 fires in the city, almost a third of which were attributed to arson. On the one hand, the criminal nature of so many of these flames provided a justification for the famous, or notorious, San Francisco Vigilance Committees of 1851 and 1856, which provided an extralegal outlet for the frustrations of the city's "better class" of citizens. On the other hand, San Franciscans organized volunteer fire brigades, the city built cisterns and restricted the locations of canvas shanties and even of wooden houses, many builders switched to masonry at the behest of their customers, and George Hossefross made his name forging some semblance of centralized fire service for the city by 1853.[18]

San Francisco's evolving system of fire suppression benefited as well from the sturdy leather hoses produced by the Butchertown tanneries, adding a certain irony to the story. While woodsmen provided builders in the growing city with Santa Cruz redwood only to see this turn to kindling, they likewise provided tanners with the Santa Cruz oaks whose bark cured the leather that made the fire hoses. As the creative use of technology seems to know no bounds, the same hoses would one day prove themselves valuable tools of hydraulic gold mining. And here we have come full circle to what is well-known as San Francisco's most dramatic engagement of nature and its very reason for being. The goldfields and the city were symbiotic, but neither was static. In gold country in 1849, simple men with simple tools initiated a complete reordering of San Francisco's auriferous hinterland that had profound environmental consequences. Within a decade, neither the city nor the Sierra foothills would have been recognizable to mission-era Californians, and even the human beings who brought these changes about could barely recognize themselves.

The gold-era migrants who transformed the northern California landscape were a varied lot who held various motives. It is easy enough to understand the commercial ambitions of the city folk in San Francisco, since cities by their physical nature require their inhabitants to participate in the cash marketplace.

In the city, commercial ambitions cut across lines of wealth and produced a broad range of hopeful businessmen, from the fabulously wealthy merchant and real estate mogul Sam Brannan to the more numerous middling tavern keepers, blacksmiths, shoemakers, butchers, and tailors to the market gardeners and peddlers who represented the economic fringe of the self-employed. San Francisco's wageworkers, although they were not necessarily aspiring entrepreneurs, were obviously a part of the larger cash economy as well. But in the countryside, the gold rush created overnight a cash economy as well. In San Francisco's hinterland, there was no gradual evolution leading isolated subsistence farmers into the marketplace over several generations. Nineteenth-century San Francisco was not eighteenth-century Boston. The subsistence economy of the California frontier belonged not to settlers but to those Native Americans who had escaped the reach of Spanish and Mexican institutions. Both this economy and its members were suddenly and rapidly supplanted by the explosive arrival of the market and the argonauts. But what did these newcomers want and how did their dreams shape the land?

From our modern perspective, it is easy enough to understand the allure of gold, but to grasp its significance in 1849 we need to imagine its potential applications at that time. Gold is and was liquid capital. It has little intrinsic use value other than ornamentation but can be exchanged for almost anything one might desire. In the mid-nineteenth century, the object of greatest desire was land, which many a gold seeker hoped to acquire after a few successful months in the goldfields. Immigrants aside, ordinary American men came from far and wide and set to work in the cold, clear water of California's mountain streams with shovels and pans to build themselves farms in Illinois, Ohio, or Tennessee. In so doing, they were driven by the very same patrimonial ambitions as their contemporaries who had not taken the California risk. While most of these men have faded into historical oblivion, a few of their letters and diaries, like those of Lucius Fairchild, have survived. In 1855, Mr. Fairchild wrote from California to his sister in Wisconsin: "I could not think I would be doing justice to my friends at home, or myself, in leaving here, when I knew that I could in a few years make an independence, which I might labor and toil for a life time at home."[19] The patrimony, or grubstake, was an essential component of the nineteenth-century American dream. Freeborn American men strove to create and maintain some form of fixed capital that would ensure the comfort and economic independence of their families. Before 1865 and the emancipation of African American slaves, a farm, a store, or a ranch was also a substantial component of the distinction between a free or independent person and an unfree or dependent slave. The economic changes that accompanied the march of urbanization and industrialization over the course of the nineteenth century threw recurring and increasingly severe obstacles in the path of those yearning to be free. Gold was certainly a potential quick fix on the road to personal fulfillment.[20]

The hopes of ordinary men who sought to build their family patrimony elsewhere explain much about their behavior in California. In brief, they did not plan to stay. California was simply a means to an end. Their lack of attachment produced among them an alienation from California's nature that was just as profound as if they had been physically removed from it through urban concentration. This is especially notable because so many of the argonauts were of rural origin and knew nature at the very least in the way a farmer would. Farmers find themselves compelled to husband the land, however imperfectly, or the latter fails to live and thrive and to support farmers in their own lives. Miners extract inanimate rock from the earth. The land's living qualities are of no value in this context. What is extracted is commoditized, and life must be purchased with it. Insofar as the gold seekers began to know nature in their new environment, it was largely as an unyielding and poorly arranged landscape in need of serious adjustment: "The hills resemble the color of the Windham soil and are high and steep . . . [with] some very steep ravines. . . . The rivers appear to a person standing on the bank almost sunk out of sight and in places very difficult to descend and ascend on foot. . . . And most of the country . . . never can be made productive and consequently never will be worth anything for agricultural purposes."[21] Not unlike the people of San Francisco, the miners began to think about the inadequacy of their received setting of water and earth. And while San Franciscans' efforts to impose a uniform and geometrically predictable pattern on their urban site can easily be interpreted as the imposition of order, the city's parallel life in the goldfields shows us how disorderly this human order can be.

Both Native American hunter-gatherers and Hispanic pastoralists, for example, had known nature in their own ways. They certainly had been well aware of the impact of the seasonal cycle on their livelihoods. Dry summers and wet winters, punctuated by occasional years of deluge or drought, at first determined nature's yield of edible forbs, wild herbivores, and fish, and later that of cattle and wheat. By 1849, the same cycles shaped the extraction and marketing of gold and of the miners' necessities of life. Just as Yerba Buena was fueled by hide and tallow, San Francisco's economic engine was stoked by gold. For the first few years of the city's existence, it had little else of value to exchange. But gold, though inert and inanimate, was as water-dependent a crop as wheat. Miners could only efficiently harvest placer gold from Sierra riverbeds in late spring and early fall. In summer, the dry months severely reduced the flow of the streams and thereby curtailed the process of panning, cradling, and sluicing silt from ore. And from late fall through early spring, heavy fall rains, winter snow, and spring snowmelt turned even seasonal dry creeks into mighty torrents that could hardly be approached.

Gold production's seasonal cycle was occasionally replicated in longer-term patterns as well. The Bay Area's rancheros remembered the relentless downpours of the winter of 1824–25, which destroyed the crops of the missions and flooded the valleys of the Sacramento and its tributaries to a depth of fourteen feet. Natural history repeated itself with great irony in the first year of the gold rush. The first ambitious and starry-eyed argonauts, who in the spring of 1849 found barely enough water to flush their diggings, were flooded out by the end of the year. The same cycles determined the flow of essentials from the city up to the goldfields, on account of the primitive conditions of overland travel. While wet weather usually did not hamper waterborne deliveries to Sacramento and Stockton, the roads from there on became virtually impassable mud wallows in winter, and freight charges soared when transport was conceivable. Consequently, San Francisco wholesalers did their best business in late spring, when the roads had dried out, and in early fall, when interior merchants placed orders to tide them over the rainy season. In the early days of the rush, winter and summer were as quiet in the city as in the goldfields.[22]

Natural limits and their economic consequences compelled miners to extract as much gold as possible when their product was in season. Self-imposed seasonal speedups, coupled with competition among the growing numbers of prospectors, quickly depleted the easy gold, and the miners moved on. The population mobility that gave mining camps their rough-and-tumble social qualities thereby led to the progressive exhaustion of the resource that justified their existence. In 1851, Daniel Woods, a prospector who had recently returned home to Philadelphia, offered an ominous warning: "Who should go to the mines? It is very sure that a man with a family depending upon his daily efforts should not go. He should not exhaust his slender means, and run himself in debt, with the hope of making himself independent in one or two years. Let such a one, who is inclined to do this, picture to himself his wife struggling alone with poverty or sickness, his children left without a father's presence and love to guide and protect, and himself a homeless wanderer."[23] Woods's words went unheeded, and by 1852 there were one hundred thousand miners in California, but the placer gold was gone.

In the short span of the gold rush's first three years, state politics reflected American migrants' high expectations, their collective sentiment that California gold was the patrimony of white Americans, and the ultimate depths of their frustration at diminishing returns on their labor. The first California State Constitution, which was drafted at Colton Hall in Monterey in 1850, had made California a free state. But California's ban on slavery was not based on the moral abolitionism of New England, but rather on western free soil notions that gave primacy to the economic interests of ordinary white men. The gold was for them, and not for the privileged few who held others in bondage. Besides, slaves in the goldfields would have insulted the dignity of the free worker. It was no coincidence that the first Foreign Miners Tax was passed in the same year, in hopes of driving the Sonorans back to Mexico. After all, had not Americans wrested this piece of earth from Mexico just a few years earlier? By what right did Mexican immigrants now compete with the new owners of California? In fact, many Sonorans either found the tax too onerous and left the state or were expelled for nonpayment. As the placers shrank, another Foreign Miners Tax targeted the Chinese in 1852. The so-called Celestials were not only seen as peculiarly inassimilable but were legally handicapped by federal immigration laws that limited naturalized citizenship to Caucasians. In California, a special charge on the earnings of "aliens ineligible for citizenship" sought to protect the privileges of the native-born. Yet none of the political efforts to defend one group of hopeful miners against another could do anything to regenerate the supply of gold, which was, after all, a finite resource. Instead, from 1852 on, labor yielded to capital as more complicated and environmentally destructive means of extraction prevailed. Formerly independent prospectors sank into proletarian conditions, becoming employed miners on company crews. The bitterness of personal failure could only have been compounded by the steady decline of wages from $10 a day in 1850 to $3 in 1856. Exploitation of people and of nature marched hand in hand.[24]

San Francisco and Sacramento investors provided the capital for mining companies to harness gangs of labor to large-scale extractive operations. These could get at the gold that was inaccessible to a single miner or small crew armed only with shovels, pans, and picks. Since the prospectors had already exhausted the riverbanks, primary targets of the big companies were the gravels and soils of the deep riverbeds where a man in boots could neither stand nor brave the current. Mining companies cut the Sierra forests to provide lumber for the construction of huge wooden flumes into which they lifted and diverted entire rivers to expose the beds beneath. By 1853, for example, twenty-five miles of the Yuba River ran through an artificial channel. Hundreds of workers picked away at the exposed riverbeds, hurrying as in times past to complete their work before the winter rains. Invariably, the seasonal floods would come, now bringing other costs besides idleness, as tons of debris, along with the flumes built at the forest's expense, washed downstream.[25]

Besides the gold in the beds of flowing rivers, mining companies sought out the even greater supply that had hardened in the dry beds of volcanically rerouted river channels eons ago. Because these ancient, dry riverbeds were buried up to hundreds of feet in the Sierra foothills, extractors needed to adapt their technology to mine them cost-effectively. In 1853, Edward Matteson of Connecticut used an improvised canvas hose with a wooden nozzle to wash soil away from ore-bearing rock and became the progenitor of hydraulic mining. As the new technique gained popularity, canvas hoses gave way to the leather ones that originated in San Francisco's tanneries, then to iron conduits from San Francisco's foundries, and finally to water cannons. The more that mining companies increased both the volume and the pressure of water directed at Sierra hillsides, the more debris they created. In thirty years, hydraulic mining flushed almost one and a half billion cubic yards of gravel debris downstream from the vicinity of the Feather, Yuba, American, and Bear rivers—more soil erosion than natural processes had accomplished over the preceding six hundred million years. One witness commented, "Nothing can be more dreary than a territory where the soil has been washed out as low as the water will run off. Ten thousand rocks of all shapes, and forms, and sizes are left; acres and acres, and even miles, of the skeletons of beauty, with the flesh all gone, and nothing but hideousness remaining."[26]

The demand for water also drove mining companies higher and higher into the mountains to build waterworks that could provide enough pressure at the point of extraction. San Franciscans' rearrangement of water and earth within the city limits paled by comparison to parallel events in their symbiotic Sierran economy. Companies built almost six thousand miles of ditches, flumes, and canals across the Sierras to move water down to the mines. They destroyed forests, despoiled salmon spawning grounds, denuded hillsides of their vegetation, and raised riverbeds by yards, broadening their flood plains and aggravating the effects of the natural flood cycles that had preceded the days of gold mining. In particularly wet years, the silted tributaries of the Sacramento River turned the river into a muddy lake as wide as fifty miles across in places, while the famous Yuba rose sixty feet over its natural level, threatening settlement, agriculture, and all earthbound life.

Finally, after particularly devastating floods in 1875, usually remembered as the submergence of Marysville, farmers began to mobilize against the miners in defense of their own property rights. As was not unusual in the nineteenth century, the voiceless nonhuman world had few defenders, but competition between

Hydraulic mining. Courtesy of the Society of California Pioneers, San Francisco, Gift of Florence V. Flinn, LH795/SCP585.

different users of nature could produce substantially different results. Mining companies defended their uses of water, however destructive, as if they were no more than simple extensions of early miners' appropriationist principles—"first in time, first in right." Because the miners came first, they had prior right, and farmers should have known better than to settle downstream of them. In 1884, that argument didn't hold water anymore. Sacramento and San Joaquin Valley farmers won a major court victory when U.S. Ninth Circuit Court Judge Lorenzo Sawyer issued the first of many injunctions that would ultimately drive hydraulic mining operations out of the state. Unfortunately, the effect was similar to many of today's national environmental regulations—the problem was exported elsewhere, to the Klamath Mountains, Colorado, and overseas. And though important, the shift in California's legal climate was hardly altruistic, as it reflected the decline of the gold industry and the rise of agriculture in their relative contributions to the state's economy and future. The enormous dollar value of flood-damaged property, the cost against future development and economic activity, and the support the farmers received from the Southern Pacific, anxious to protect its rights-of-way from the ravages of bloated rivers, all contributed to the legal victory.[27]

The city of San Francisco itself played multiple roles in the gold economy. It was the port of entry for that portion of its inhabitants who did not arrive by the overland route. San Francisco was the transit point for outbound gold and for inbound products that served the gold seekers as well as the city's own burgeoning population of workers and businessmen. As such, its port and warehouses, its wholesale and retail trading houses, and even its real estate were inextricably linked to events in gold country. San Francisco produced industries that provided some of the tools of mineral extraction, such as iron conduits, water cannons, dredges, and explosive powder. The city also housed the merchants, manufacturers, shopkeepers, craftsmen, wageworkers, and financiers who acted within the web of economic relations that bound the people and businesses of the city to one another and to those of the golden hinterland. For a decade or two at least, San Franciscans' collective dependency on and contribution to the mining economy was so thorough as to raise questions about the nature of motive and responsibility in their interactions with their acquired environment.

It is easy enough to say that wealthy capitalists were the driving force in both the spatial development of San Francisco and the extractive economy of its hinterland, but this simply states a given—that the United States was a class society consisting of a hierarchy of social groupings, each exercising more or less economic power. This is an important fact, but it is equally useful to consider the systemic relationship between all Americans, and in this case all of the "new Californians," and their environment. As surprising as it may seem, California's native tribes had traditionally functioned as class societies as well, with distinctions of wealth; ownership rights; social, political, and religious privilege; and even condition of servitude. Nonetheless, our tendency is to understand their collective relationship to the external world in systemic terms—hunting and gathering, minimal reordering of the landscape, cautious use of the environment, and spiritualization of other species. Similarly, Spanish California is generally understood as a culturally cohesive entity whose principal characteristics were the creation of pastoral and agricultural surpluses along with the propagation of a Christian monotheism that at least in part justified Spanish uses of nature. We know very well, of course, that this too was a class society, and partly capitalist albeit with some premodern forms. Its ruling class, at least locally, was of a theocratic bent, and its working class—the Indians—was ethnically distinct and essentially unfree. What equivalent characteristics defined mid-nineteenth American society?

The United States was an industrializing nation. An ongoing transportation revolution was building an ever-expanding national market system. Subsistence farming was losing ground everywhere to commercial agriculture. The products of the land, whether grown by farmers or extracted by miners and lumbermen, were processed, transformed, and reshipped by a growing network of cities that sprang up as the people pushed relentlessly westward. Americans were a mobile population of producers, and after the end of slavery in 1865, all Americans were at least theoretically free to join in the great migration. Capital's mobility was even freer and more rapid than that of the ordinary people themselves, as every new landscape to be settled opened opportunities for investment. In American society, nature was a flexible resource, full of potential as untapped capital. The extraordinary natural wealth of the continent was the nation's blessing, and, for all social classes, getting a piece of it was the key to the future.

What made California appear marvelous to so many people was the fact that its principal crop was money. With a little luck, one hoped to buy a piece of America with a piece of California. As one would imagine, those fortune seek-ers who started with the most capital at their disposal had some advantage over the others, especially if they had timing on their side. Sam Brannan, who arrived in San Francisco in 1846 with a party of Mormons, was a good example of a clever fellow who happened to be in the right place at the right time. After set-ting up a general store at Sutter's Fort near Sacramento in 1847, he responded quickly when he discovered that some of his customers were paying for their purchases in gold. Brannan immediately began to hoard goods in his warehouse and then broke the news of Sierra gold in the streets of San Francisco in May 1848. As his mercantile business boomed to the tune of five thousand dollars a day, he reinvested his profits in real estate, railroads and shipping, and waterfront development. By the mid-1850s, he was one of the two largest landowners in downtown San Francisco, proving the adage that those who served the miners often were more financially successful than the miners themselves. But Bran-nan's wealth was made possible by thousands of ordinary men with ambitions of their own—ambitions that may have differed in scale but not necessarily in kind. California was a means to an end, with gold as the intermediary.[28]

The presence of the common folk was evident in the social geography of San Francisco. Even before the gold rush, residents understood the commercial potential inherent in the city's site, but no one could effectively plan for the future distribution of a random population of migrants attracted by a boomtown economy. By 1850, the gold rush had packed thirty-five thousand people into a roughly forty-acre district around Portsmouth Square. Very quickly, the city took on the combined social characteristics of commercial metropolis, frontier town, and mining camp all at once. Business luminaries like Sam Brannan and Joseph Folsom were joined by hundreds of lesser merchants, hotel and saloon keepers, butchers, bakers, grocers, brewers, blacksmiths, coopers, and shoemakers. Thousands of teamsters, stevedores, sailors, carpenters and masons, and common laborers made up the ranks of the city's wage-earning class. And when gold was out of season, San Francisco's hotels and rooming houses filled with miners waiting for their next chance at the diggings. The city grew so quickly and was so busy with activity that its inhabitants must have felt that it had a life of its own. This is a common illusion among city dwellers, and one that most of us harbor today. We urbanites find ourselves so completely preoccupied with and engulfed by the specific activities of urban life that we hardly give a thought to our total dependency on the external. Yet, dependent we are—as the root of all that we have and all that we do is planted in our specific uses of nature, in the way that nature's capital is transformed through labor into human wealth.

For all of the people of early San Francisco and for the organism they called "the city," that life-giving root was the extraction of gold. Gold determined the manufacturer's profits, the middleman's commission, the worker's wages, and the miner's fate. It determined the labor supply and the rate of immigration. It affected the cost of rent and the price of real estate. It led to business success or business failure, and it underscored something very essential about modern city life—the city is a distillation of the system of commodity exchange, which has created it and which it in turn promotes. As a city built on a figurative foundation of gold, San Francisco, however small by Eastern standards, was the quintessential modern metropolis. Consequently, San Franciscans enjoyed the benefits and suffered the consequences of metropolitanism.

With a whole city crammed into those initial forty downtown acres, one can readily grasp the problems that occurred. Aside from the crowding, inadequate waste removal, muddy morass of winter streets, and prevalence of summer and fall conflagrations, the undifferentiated class character of the place made San Francisco a sort of social tinderbox. While social violence was a common fact of life in mid-nineteenth-century cities, it is hard to deny that the gold economy had something to do with the manifestations of such violence in San Francisco. An entire regional economy fueled by gold left no or few spaces outside of the marketplace to which the poor might retreat in hard times. The first year of the gold rush was a good one for all social classes, but a downturn came in 1850 and

1851. Good times returned for the next two years, but wages declined steadily from 1853 through 1856. Employment opportunities were also conditioned by the relentless influx of newcomers, most of whom failed in the diggings and fell back on an increasingly competitive job market in the city. Poverty must have been accompanied by desperation and anger as well, as hopes dashed in a golden land imposed a special burden on the psyche. In any case, San Francisco was rife with robbery, murder, and mayhem.[29]

The social disorder so characteristic at the onset of bust periods in mining camps was superimposed on a young city with world-class pretensions, to the horror and dismay of its higher-class citizens. Individual acts of violence were compounded by the depredations of gangs. Transplants from Australian penal colonies formed the Sidney Ducks, while a disbanded regiment of New York Volunteers comprised the Hounds. In addition to murder, robbery, and rape, the former were renowned for extracting protection money from merchants, while the latter developed some notoriety for their assaults on foreigners, particularly Latin Americans. Individual and gang violence led to vigilantism, especially the famous San Francisco Vigilance Committees of 1851 and 1856, which consisted in part or in whole of the mercantile classes of the city. But vigilantism, although temporarily satisfying the fearful, scored no permanent victories over crime.[30]

Fears of violence, as well as fears of congestion, rudeness, filth, and fire, were partially quelled over time by another consequence of the overall long-term growth created by the gold economy. As San Francisco planked its streets, graded its hills, filled its wetlands, and promoted private omnibus service, the original amalgam of commercial, industrial, and residential land users who were clustered around Portsmouth Square began to sift themselves out into a more distinct pattern of product-, service-, and class-specific districts. In this way, environmental transformations of the city's site intersected with both the economic needs of expanding and emerging San Francisco businesses and the social needs of those classes able to escape the villainy of the port. While this process of expansion and spatial separation was a boon to wealthy real estate speculators, it was driven by the hopes, fears, and ambitions of a whole mosaic of San Franciscans, from merchants and manufacturers to wage earners, without whom a demand for the creation of new urban space would not have existed.

Consequently, economic and social pressures helped push urban infrastructure development forward. Through the 1850s and 1860s, middle- and upper-class San Franciscans increasingly abandoned the port and downtown for higher ground—Rincon Heights, Russian Hill, and Nob Hill—or followed the planked or otherwise improved roads westward to new neighborhoods like the Western

Addition. South of Market Street, the steam paddy created new commercial and industrial space proximate to the bay, enabling the expansion and ultimately the relocation of Butchertown, the construction of the sugar refineries of Adolph Spreckels and George Gordon, various foundries including the Union Iron Works, factories like the Kimball Carriage Works, and shipping and warehousing facilities such as those of the Pacific Mail Steamship Line. The relocation, expansion, and creation of commercial and industrial enterprises also generated a demand for working-class housing as many wage earners began to settle in the south of Market area. The building of Long Bridge in the late 1860s, and the opening of a horsecar line there, brought further working-class migration southward along Fourth Street to the Potrero and later to Hunters Point. The overall effect of business expansion, as well as the emergence of new residential neighborhoods, was the rapid diminution of spaces available to nonurban activities and the resultant expulsion of pasture and field in favor of the factory, warehouse, office, townhome, and tenement. None of this process was peculiar to San Francisco, but the speed at which it occurred had few parallels. Certainly by comparison to the old cities of the Atlantic Coast, San Francisco's growth was astounding. A combination of gold, nineteenth-century technology, and the existence of an effective national and international market system helped San Francisco accomplish in a few years what used to take centuries. As such, the city by the bay serves as an exemplary laboratory of urbanization and its relationship to environmental change.

There are two linked phenomena that characterize the emergent phase of a city's growth, such as occurred in San Francisco from the 1840s through the 1860s. First, the people whose settlement decisions make the city happen are all collaborators in a conscious effort to eliminate environmental diversity at their urban site. We can say "conscious" because that is precisely true of an active decision, for example, to level inconvenient hills that might interfere with a planned street grid. Yet people make these decisions not because they are conscious enemies of the hills, bogs, creeks, flora, and fauna that preceded them but because they have something else in mind. Entrepreneurs wish to homogenize space to maximize its ability to generate such capital as they imagine the space will produce for them. Workers accede to and contribute to this homogenization to the extent they imagine it will create work, and thereby life. Life is therefore redefined as urbanization redefines space. San Francisco's growth displaced nonhuman life on the sand hills, in the creeks, in the marshes, and in the bay, and also exiled in short order those means of production that sustained human life directly—the raising of crops and livestock. As the city's site de-ruralized, its

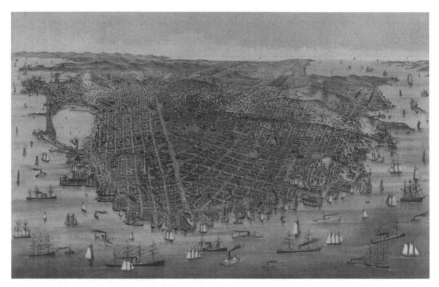

This bird's-eye view of San Francisco in 1878 shows Long Bridge on the left,
completely severing Mission Bay from San Francisco Bay, and continuing through the
Potrero district and onward across the Islais Creek estuary to Hunters Point. The wide
swath of Market Street, its path cleared of sand hills, cuts through the center of the
image. The Golden Gate is at the top left. A very young Golden Gate Park cuts
westward across the dunes at the top center. Drawn by C. R. Parsons for Currier and
Ives, courtesy of the David Rumsey Map Collection, www.davidrumsey.com.

people became more and more genuinely urban, meaning that their lives became
more and more dependent on external sources of sustenance, while they experienced their lives as being more and more bound up with distinctly urban economic activities. This truly urban separation of those human activities that
directly support human life from those activities that city people call "their lives"
is at the crux of the alienation from nature that begins to take root early in the
city-building process. As urban space begins to appear as life itself, more of it is
needed, and few people will stand in the way of progress as streams are cul-
verted, wetlands are filled, hills are leveled, and their mute prior occupants are
banished from the life of the city.

The second phenomenon relates to the costs of sustaining an expanding urban
infrastructure. The grading of streets, their planking or paving, the earthmoving
and bay filling, and the construction of water mains, sewer lines, factories, warehouses, and homes all represent a tremendous capital investment that cannot just
lie fallow. Furthermore, there are too many livelihoods at stake for a city simply
to rest or to accept decline. A city requires continual infusions of nature's capi-

tal to support the investments that human beings have made in urban residential, production, and distribution systems. In San Francisco's early days, gold provided the necessary infusion, but as the gold rush days waned, the city was rescued and its life sustained by silver. And had it not been silver, no doubt it would have been something else, but the city's hinterlands must always be tapped and harnessed in some way to secure the city's continued existence.

San Francisco's silver era further strengthened the links between the fortunes of the city's general populace and those of the often-manipulative wealthy few. And, as in the dramatic case of gold, it brought significant environmental change both to the cityscape and to distant lands beyond. Prospectors discovered Virginia City, Nevada's Comstock Lode while searching for gold in 1859. Unlike the early California placer gold, Nevada silver could not be extracted without substantial labor power and technology. In addition, buried as it was across the Sierra ridge, silver could not be moved directly by water to the port of San Francisco. Consequently, silver required and attracted the attention of substantial capitalists from the outset.

In 1860, it was Nevada silver that turned Theodore Judah's dream of a trans-Sierran railway into Collis Huntington, Mark Hopkins, Leland Stanford, and Charles Crocker's determined mission. It was Nevada silver that led to the founding of the San Francisco Stock Exchange in 1862 and to William Chapman Ralston's Bank of California in 1864. It was Nevada silver that transformed Nob Hill into the literal and figurative commanding heights of California, and the intersection of San Francisco's California and Montgomery streets into the heart of finance in the American Far West. Ralston and his allies in the "Bank Crowd"—Darius Ogden Mills and William Sharon—swallowed up mines, mills, and timberlands and redirected their profits into insurance, coastal transportation, telegraph lines, gasworks, railroads, and hydraulic mining. On the one hand, their business operations had an even more devastating environmental impact on the eastern face of the Sierras than gold mining had exerted on the western slopes. The Bank Crowd laid bare Lake Tahoe's pine and fir forests in less than two decades to provide hundreds of millions of feet of lumber for the Nevada mines and tons of cordwood for the mills. On the other hand, Comstock's mines turned San Francisco's south of Market and Potrero areas into a major metallurgical center, teeming with foundries and machine shops full of molders and machinists dedicated to producing the pumps, hoists, drills, boilers, and increasingly inventive tools of hard rock mining. Comstock industrialized the commercial city, promoted the Central and Southern Pacific rail links that tied it to the nation, and was largely responsible for San Francisco's stature as a genuine metropolis by the last quarter of the nineteenth century. Although industrial San Francisco was never comparable in output or character to Pittsburgh, Detroit, or even Philadelphia, the city nonetheless emerged from the depression years of the 1870s as an economically diversified, cosmopolitan, gritty, and urbane metropolis, blessed and saddled with the entire benefits and burdens attendant to "real city" status. The speed of change and second nature aspect of urban development caused few San Franciscans to pause and consider how they had gotten there.[31]

Barely thirty-five years separated the last days of Yerba Buena in January 1847 from the quarter-million-inhabitant city of 1880. In 1828, insofar as statehood was concerned, the American nation extended no farther west than Missouri. An American born there in the fall of that year, after Andrew Jackson's election to the presidency, might have come to California as a gold seeker at the age of twenty. Had he stayed, by his early fifties he would have seen San Francisco transformed from sleepy port to boomtown, and from rambling tent colony to preeminent city. In the bat of an eye, over the course of one person's short adulthood, Mexico's second-tier hide and tallow port grew into the ninth largest city in the United States—a city whose urbanity could be measured in a proportion of lawyers unmatched even by New York and Boston, and whose global reach was reflected by a population 70 percent of which consisted of immigrants and their children.[32]

San Francisco's birth involved a monumental human effort to reorganize nature in ways that would produce the most desirable results—human comfort, wealth, and advancement. The environmental revolution that the city characterized was no less radical in its impact than the unexpected arrival of Fathers Palóu and Cambón with their faith and their cattle in 1776. And just as in 1776, no one could have fathomed the extent of this revolution at the time. Perhaps one way of grasping San Francisco's environmental importance is to imagine the city's site as a way station on an extraordinarily long road. Our imaginary Missourian would have been among three hundred thousand very real people who set out west on the Oregon-California road between 1841 and 1859, bringing with them 1.5 million cattle, sheep, horses, and oxen. Eighty thousand of the human migrants set out in 1849 alone. Without a second thought, travelers timbered the watersheds while their livestock trampled and foraged the grasses of the plains, leaving indelible ecological marks across a wide swath of territory that extended for miles on either side of the westward trail. Once in California, the road formed a junction on the western face of the Sierra Nevada from which a number of branches ran through the gold deposits of the Mother Lode. The migrants paused here, while their product continued westward by stage and down the tributaries of the Sacramento and San Joaquin rivers to the wharves of Commercial and Market streets in San Francisco. In effect, the long wharves that stretched out over the city's disappearing mud flats into the deep water of the bay were the terminals of a long transcontinental road and the transit points at which the people and products of the world met those of the United States.

San Francisco's position as the principal juncture and the largest conglomeration of capital and labor power along this international artery was shaped by a nature that the city altered in turn. The interaction between the city's growth and the transformation of its hinterland occurred within a hierarchy of more or less powerful actors, all of whom nonetheless played a role in giving the city and its partnered environments their ultimate design. Among the human actors, those who commanded greater wealth exercised more power than those who had the least. Merchants, industrialists, and financiers like Sam Brannan, Leland Stanford, George Hearst, James Phelan, and others exercised much more economic and political influence over events than their lower-class counterparts. Without these wealthy and influential men, the city's site would not have developed as it did and the resources of its hinterland could not have been extracted, processed, and shipped to the extent that they were. The gold era would have ended in 1850 with the depletion of the placers; there would have been no hydraulic operations, no Comstock Lode, and no mining industry, and Lake Tahoe's old-growth forests would have lived on for a few more generations. On the other hand, it was ordinary folks whose dreams fueled the early gold rush, and whose hopes and ambitions brought them to San Francisco to live and to work when their golden dreams failed them. It was ordinary folks whose willing labor ran the foundries, factories, and streetcars of the burgeoning city and whose earnings and desires made the working-class homes of the Potrero district marketable. We likewise should not forget that it was ordinary men driven by anger and greed who hunted and murdered thousands of California Indians during the 1850s and 1860s to clear the goldfields or to avenge the lives of white men's cattle and pigs out of an extraordinarily perverse sense of equivalency.[33]

And then there is the voiceless nonhuman world. How does nature itself become an actor in what appears to be very much a story of human choices and human agency? One of the best examples of nature's power was its response to William Ralston. In 1866, Ralston consolidated a number of smaller hydraulic mining operations into the North Bloomfield Mining Company. Ralston's Ring spent over a million dollars to build a reservoir, dozens of miles of ditches, and a mile-and-a-half-long tunnel to channel debris into the Yuba River. Ralston's company was largely responsible for the already noted submersion of Marysville during the deluge of 1874, to which farmers and townsfolk ultimately responded with litigation. The Yuba River, like the American, Feather, and Sacramento, may appear voiceless, but when sediment generated by human action raised their beds by dozens of yards, they spoke quite loudly. Their voices were heard in the havoc wrought to valley floors, the destruction of orchards and farmlands, the despoliation of riparian woods and salmon runs, and even the loss of human life.

In the city proper, nature's agency may not have been felt so clearly and powerfully most of the time, but this was more often due to urbanites' false illusions of imperviousness to nature than to any objective appreciation of reality. Besides, it took a cataclysm to awaken rural folks to the depredations of hydraulic mining, and, even in the positive resolution of that case, a practical economic conflict of interest trumped any larger appreciation for environmental balance. In San Francisco, human beings were crafting an environment of their own. Over time, they shaped the urban site in such a way that every trace of the nonhuman world was seemingly harnessed to human ends, very effectively concealed, or completely obliterated. An ironic consequence of this was that by the late nineteenth century, many San Franciscans came to dislike some of the more noxious aspects of their acts of creation. Like the citizens of other American cities of the time, they started to worry about crowded quarters, industrial wastes, and the cadences of mechanized routines. They began to miss nature and to long to restore some aspects of its presence in their daily lives. But oddly, they had also forgotten what it was.

CHAPTER 3

GREENING THE CITY

A curious aspect of nineteenth-century American urbanization was how the drive to convert every square inch of land into marketable and productive cityscape quickly gave rise to the notion that every great city required a great public park. It was as if, in their building frenzy, urbanites had suddenly found an error of omission on their blueprints. Where was nature? Had it no place within the city? Of course, the question itself revealed the conceptual distance between city dwellers and their pre-urban ancestors. It crystallized the experience of nature as an externality and its division into categories of use. It reflected a disintegrated universe of component parts—human beings, production, and nature. Insofar as cities were the apotheosis of concentrated human labor power, they were the ultimate means by which people transformed the objects of nature—trees, minerals, crops, and animals—into human wealth. But the very success of cities as engines of production divorced their inhabitants both physically and emotionally from the same nature that fed, clothed, and housed them. Unable to experience work and nature as integral, urbanites increasingly came to understand nature as something far away, something other than them and other than their cities, and something that was not used, where work was not performed and where the nonhuman world escaped the grasp of the market.

When nineteenth-century city leaders imagined urban park space, they drew from the intellectual reservoir of a newly industrialized America. They felt the separateness of humankind and nature and wished for a managed reunion of the two. The application of an industrial society's managerial impulse to the creation of natural-feeling environments is certainly fraught with irony, but it had at least the positive legacy of leaving open spaces for future generations to enjoy. This legacy is taken so much for granted today that few citizens consider that their playgrounds and refuges once had to be made. And if the mechanics of park creation elude the contemporary user, then the context within which they were built is all the more removed from everyday consciousness. Yet like all that is historic, timing is everything. It is not a coincidence that the drive for public parks came alongside the mid- to late-nineteenth-century industrial and transportation revolution. This upheaval magnified urban growth rates, intensified production and distribution, mechanized work, extended industrial discipline to all walks of life, attracted millions of immigrants to America's cities, vastly increased the proportion of working-class Americans, transformed gender roles and the dynamics of middle-class family life, created the conditions for unprecedented accumulation of wealth, and propelled Americans into a world they could not have imagined a generation or two earlier.

The generational context of the park movement explains the emergence within a narrow time frame of Central Park in New York, Delaware Park in Buffalo, Forest Park in St. Louis, Brooklyn's Prospect Park, the Niagara Falls Reservation, and the first national park—Yellowstone. San Francisco's contribution to the trend was the city's substantial and beautiful Golden Gate Park as well as Yosemite State Park in the city's hinterland. Although the two parks had different native landscapes, means of acquisition, and levers of political control, their concurrent birth in the immediate aftermath of the Civil War was no accident. In part, both parks were products of an urbanizing people's yearnings for a lost and often mythologized past. Both also revealed the complex of material ambitions and social and environmental attitudes that shaped urban Americans' efforts to re-create nature—ambitions and attitudes that, at least initially, had a distinct class basis.

Between the 1850s and the early 1900s, upper-middle-class park advocates around the United States variously argued that grand public green spaces conferred stature on the cities that contained them, that parks increased real estate values and thereby benefited both private landowners and the public coffers, or that the aesthetic of parks was a morally transformative force that could soothe the ills of an urban industrial society. San Francisco followed in the larger national mold, as boosterism, real estate profiteering, urban environmental concerns, and middle-class utopianism all contributed to the creation and evolution of Golden Gate Park. However, these factors were of uneven weight, and their relative influence was conditioned by San Francisco's distinct economic development, regional role, social composition, and environmental setting. As fate would have it, certain peculiarities of time and place relegated the perceived negative effects of industrialization, urban concentration, and social transformation to the smallest role in shaping the city's park movement. In fact, because Golden Gate Park's inception preceded San Francisco's most industrial phase, one cannot fairly see the park as a corrective response to existing industrial blight, working-class misery, or residential crowding. What then was its motivating force, and how was it affected by San Francisco's specific pattern of growth?[1]

The principal factors driving San Francisco's park movement were neither mass demand nor reformist altruism, but the forethought and ambition of city leaders who were determined to make their home the unrivaled metropolis of the Pacific Coast. This goal fostered inevitable comparisons to New York City, with its unquestioned dominion over the East Coast, and which in 1857 had embarked on its own ambitious mission to create Central Park.[2] However, San Franciscans' wish to imagine their city as a sort of New York of the West should not be considered a reflection of genuine similarities between the two metropolises in all aspects of social condition and economic function. Any direct comparison between the two cities was particularly weak insofar as municipal parks in the East—New York especially—could realistically be portrayed to the public as essential refuges from desperate levels of physically and mentally jarring urban congestion. But in 1870, when San Francisco embarked on its preliminary land surveys for Golden Gate Park, the city was home to just over 149,000 persons, while New York held in excess of 942,000. On the one hand, it is true that San Francisco had become the tenth largest city in the United States in the mere two decades of its existence, and the impression that this made on its people was significant. On the other hand, a substantial gap separated it from the largest American city when measured in terms of population density. San Francisco's populated area, almost all of which fell within the city's 1851 charter line, covered approximately nine square miles extending from the Bay to Divisadero Street to the west and Twenty-fourth Street to the south. Ninety-five percent of New Yorkers lived below Eighty-sixth Street on Manhattan Island in an area of about eleven square miles. There were consequently about sixteen thousand San Franciscans and seventy-nine thousand New Yorkers per square mile. This disparity was even more apparent in the area of New York below Fourteenth Street—the Lower East and Lower West Sides—which was roughly analogous in function to San Francisco's downtown and south of Market districts. There were almost 126,000 New Yorkers per square mile in those densest quarters. Even in 1860, shortly after Central Park began to take shape, New York was four and a half times as dense as San Francisco would be ten years later.[3]

San Francisco's low-rise buildings and its solitude as an urban pocket in a nonurban region made it a different environment than that of the East Coast metropolises. One could take less than an hour's walk from the deepest recess of San Francisco and abandon all trace of the city. Similar in effect, the constant winds that blew across the peninsula from the Pacific kept the air fresh enough to remind the urbanite that the city's edge was not far away. In addition, the city's immediate hinterland on the peninsula and north and east across the Bay was still too thinly populated to present an image of regional urban concentration, even with Oakland's emergence as a port in its own right. Consequently, it is improbable that a San Franciscan of the 1860s or early 1870s would have yet penned the words of Bostonian Robert Woods: "Isolated and congested working class quarters, with all the dangers to moral and material well-being that they present, grow along with the growth of all our great cities."[4] At least in 1870, San Francisco was not plagued with an equivalent physical and social "malady."

San Francisco's pattern of growth through the early 1870s was not characteristic of major American industrial cities. Golden Gate Park was imagined at a time when its city was still overwhelmingly commercial, home to the mercantile establishments that handled around 90 percent of the Pacific Coast's trade.[5] The port was the city's principal economic feature and its most clearly defined social space. San Francisco's shipping firms, banks, and insurance companies overwhelmed the physical and economic visibility of the city's industrial sector. As was more typical of a frontier railhead than of an industrial metropolis, before the 1860s two of the three leading San Francisco industries were related to food processing. George Gordon opened the San Francisco Sugar Refinery in 1856, which was supplanted by Claus Spreckels's large refinery at Eighth and Brannan streets in 1863. Able to refine tens of millions of pounds of raw sugar a year, the industry generated $4 million in value in 1870 and employed hundreds of workers. Slaughtering and meatpacking, especially of locally raised hogs, were second in economic importance to sugar production. San Francisco had an advantage in this over other California locations since its cool climate allowed packers to produce a better-tasting product with less salt. Yet, despite their importance, the sugar and meat industries left a relatively small footprint on San Francisco's physical and occupational landscape. Their firms employed hundreds, not thousands, of workers, and their need for substantial daily supplies of water forced them to concentrate their facilities in geographically confined spaces at the bay front, in particular on the estuary of Mission Creek.[6]

San Francisco's metallurgical firms—its foundries and machine shops—were infinitely more evocative of our general image of industry. Collectively, they were more spatially imposing and more occupationally significant with their thousands of employees. Peter Donahue's Union Iron Works was the first of these, established in 1849. As the date suggests, the entire industry developed in response to the mining industry's need for drills, pumps, and amalgamating pans, and it grew over time to produce steam engines, rails, and beams as well.

If anything gave San Francisco's south of Market area an industrial atmosphere, it was the clamor and din of these hundred or so small metalworking shops. Additionally, in 1853, under contract to light the city's streets, Donahue and his brothers built a coal-burning gasworks at First and Howard streets. The San Francisco Gas Company allowed the thick, coal tar by-product to run off onto an adjacent lot until discovering its usefulness as roofing and paving material. The gas company's waste products earned the neighborhood the less-than-appealing name of Tar Flat.

Yet in 1870, San Francisco's industrialization had not produced the pockets of seemingly intractable poverty or slum-like, working-class residential concentration that were chronicled there by Jack London in the early twentieth century. The 1860s were years of general prosperity for the people of San Francisco. The continuing silver boom, the economic benefits of the Civil War, and speculative investment in anticipation of the completion of the transcontinental railroad all fueled economic growth and job creation. Workers were not yet confronted with the flooded markets and labor competition that followed the completed railroad after 1870 or with the terrible predicaments of the 1873 depression. Work was abundant, trade unions were on the rise, and the physical conditions of working-class life were in some ways better than average for the time period. Worker housing in the south of Market area was characterized by two- or three-story wooden buildings, many of them small individual houses, as well as a fair number of small hotels and rooming houses that served a transient population of single men. While the latter accommodations were rudimentary at best, and while property owners did experiment with tenement housing in some areas as early as the 1860s, many working-class families lived in small, single-family homes.[7] The steam paddy's southward enlargement of the city, along with the proliferation of streetcar lines and the completion of Long Bridge across Mission Bay, also all contributed to working-class residential mobility.

Only two neighborhoods really possessed all the characteristics associated with nineteenth-century urban blight—the Barbary Coast and Chinatown. The former, a collection of brothels and gambling dens along Pacific Street near the waterfront, had plagued genteel San Franciscans since gold rush days. But hemmed in as it was by an ever-imposing downtown commercial district and a crescent of middle-class neighborhoods to the west, this old sailors' haunt had nowhere to go. Chinatown, on the other hand, was a genuine ghetto shaped by the cultural integrity of its inhabitants as well as both informal and legal discrimination and exclusion by the larger society. However, the Chinese ghetto's virtual autonomy, coupled with the anti-Chinese racism so typical of the West, ensured that city leaders and white residents of all social classes would always view the Chinese as a special case rather than as representative of evolving urban conditions.

All in all, the social, aesthetic, and environmental problems of San Francisco's industrial districts and working-class neighborhoods in 1870 did not dominate to the point that they much alarmed guardians of the city's character, fame, or respectability. Perhaps because the physical aspects of life in the city were not abominable, or perhaps because whatever poor conditions existed were well-contained, prominent citizens gave little attention to urban concentration until the late 1860s. One San Francisco editorialist who did express concern that future densities would become intolerable did so only within the context of the park debate in 1868: "As the few vacant lots fill up and wood buildings are replaced with lofty bricks, the streets will appear to become narrower and the want of clear sky spaces will become more than ever felt."[8] Unlike reformers of later decades, the writer offered a straightforward aesthetic critique of the city rather than an indictment of environmental conditions that might have threatened its social fabric. In defense of a future park, he simply argued in favor of the coexistence of open sky with the "lofty bricks" of progress.

If leading San Franciscans did not yet link crowding to social breakdown, some—like urbanites elsewhere at the time—were increasingly upset by the impact of noxious industries on their quality of life. Because comparisons to a city of New York's magnitude would be a bit unfair, analogies with another western city, St. Louis, might be instructive here. In 1870, St. Louis was the nation's fourth largest city, with a population twice that of San Francisco. Unquestionably commercial by virtue of its position as a Mississippi River port, St. Louis was also far more heavily industrialized than its Pacific cousin. As one of the nation's largest manufacturing cities, St. Louis housed numerous flour mills, slaughterhouses, breweries, and machine shops, all of which had direct counterparts in San Francisco. But, unlike San Francisco, St. Louis was also a city of steel mills, brick kilns, and belching smokestacks, with a well-deserved reputation for filthy air.[9] This characteristic, which was probably the most powerful indicator of industrial progress and one of its most glaringly noxious by-products, did not figure significantly in the image of San Francisco.

Despite the smoky emissions of companies like the gasworks and Thomas Selby's pig lead smelter in North Beach, San Francisco's manufacturing base was smaller, and its rarely abating ocean winds thankfully scoured the atmosphere and blew particulate residues eastward across the bay. Consequently, San Franciscans' concerns regarding the ill-effects of industry were fairly limited in scope. During the 1870s and 1880s, they included successful efforts to force the relocation of malodorous slaughterhouses and tanneries, as well to exile the powder works that served the Nevada mines. By 1871, mounting public pressure had resulted in ordinances banishing all of the city's slaughterhouses to the Bay View district at Islais Creek. Tanneries, fertilizer plants, and tallow works soon followed them to the new Butcher's Reservation, which was far from any of the well-inhabited sections of the city. While the removal affected the animal-processing plants of working-class south of Market, much of the political will behind the effort came from affluent businessmen whose Rincon Hill and Nob Hill homes were aerated by the stinking breezes that wafted up from the flatlands.[10] As for another industrial nemesis of the era, in 1870 the Giant Powder Company was forced to leave its home in the Mission District's Rock House Canyon—now Glen Park Playground—after a series of major explosions. For the next nine years, the company occupied some sand dunes south of Golden Gate Park, but long-range plans for the latter forced the company across the bay to West Berkeley in 1880.

The struggle against awful odors and explosive substances showed that San Francisco faced a typical urban dilemma of the time—in the words of historian Samuel Hays, "a conflict between the city as a source of production and work on the one hand and the city as a place to live on the other."[11] Prominent San Franciscans in pursuit of environmental wholesomeness did not explicitly connect the restraining of industry to the goal of park development, but the concurrence of these efforts was not entirely coincidental. In fact, the connections were very apparent to the man first engaged to design Golden Gate Park, Frederick Law Olmsted. In his view, the *rus in urbe*, or country in the city, was the wise planner's ultimate remedy to the ills of industrialization. But were leading San Franciscans really so concerned about problems that accrued disproportionately to the working-class districts? And again, how industrial was San Francisco really? In terms of noise, pollution, congestion, and working-class poverty, there were many cities that were immeasurably worse. If parks were a remedy to such ills, why did San Francisco need what would turn out to be one of the grandest urban parks in the nation—bigger, in fact, than New York's? The answer lies not in what past or present failings San Francisco's leaders wished to correct but in what they wished to achieve in the future. Golden Gate Park was a symbol of that future. It was a feature of civic infrastructure that declared the city's world-class pretensions. In retrospect, it reflected a sense of importance that is best understood in relative terms.

San Francisco was not the filthiest, most crowded, most dynamic, or most industrial of American cities. It was neither the largest nor the wealthiest. San

Francisco was not New York, Brooklyn, or Philadelphia. It scarcely approached Chicago or St. Louis. But when considered regionally, the weight of San Francisco's industry was important. The city produced 60 percent of the West Coast's manufactured goods, and its workshops employed one-quarter of all of California's industrial workers in 1860 and half of them in 1870. Over the same decade, the city's total population almost tripled—a growth rate exceeding that of New York, Philadelphia, Chicago, or St. Louis in the same period. Because of its prime location, abundance of capital, and historic good fortune, San Francisco stood out as the economic engine of the entire West. Although by virtue of timing, the city's gradual industrialization probably had a greater impact on the long-term shape of Golden Gate Park than on its inception, by 1880 San Francisco had more factories with more employees, greater capitalization, and higher product value than all other far western cities combined.[12] In the vast region from Kansas City west, San Francisco had no peer—neither Denver, nor Salt Lake City, nor Galveston. All of this was in addition to the city's commercial preeminence, unmatched on the Pacific Coast by Seattle, San Diego, or any other potential rival. Consequently, depending on one's frame of reference, San Francisco projected one of two competing images, both of which persist to some extent even today—one of an accidentally overblown market town, and the other of a world city.

In 1875, the British visitor Anthony Trollope ardently espoused the former view, with a nod to the future potential of the new park:

> I do not know that in all my travels I have ever visited a city less interesting to the ordinary tourist, who, as a rule, does not care to investigate the ways of trade or to employ himself in ascertaining how the people around him earn their bread. There is almost nothing to see in San Francisco that is worth seeing. There is a new park in which you may drive for six or seven miles on a well made road, and which, as a park for the use of a city, will, when complete have many excellencies. There is also the biggest hotel in the world [William Ralston's Palace Hotel], so the people of San Francisco say, which has cost a million sterling—five millions of dollars—and is intended to swallow up all the other hotels. It was just finished but not opened when I was there. There is an inferior menagerie of wild beasts, and a place called the Cliff House to which strangers are taken to hear seals bark. . . . I think I may say that strangers will generally desire to get out of San Francisco as quickly as they can. . . . There is little or nothing to see, and life at the hotels is not comfortable.[13]

Seul Rock in 1870, as Anthony Trollope would have seen it. Courtesy of the San Francisco History Center, San Francisco Public Library.

While Trollope lamented San Francisco's dearth of cultural and historical attractions, he noted with fascination the city's ardent pursuit of commerce and wealth—"the trade of the place, the way in which money is won and lost," and the "demoniac" fury of the Stock Exchange. These were, in fact, the qualities that underlay San Francisco's presumption of greatness. Too young to have produced the sort of civilization expected by an urban European, San Francisco stood nonetheless at the center of a significant economic universe. Historian Fernand Braudel once wrote of an earlier European model, "A world-economy always has an urban center of gravity, a city, as the logistic heart of its activity. News, merchandise, capital, credit, people, instructions, correspondence all flow into and out of the city. . . . At varying and respectful distances around the center will be found other towns, sometimes playing the role of associate or accomplice, but more usually resigned to their second class role. Their activities are governed by those of the metropolis: they stand guard around it, direct the flow of business toward it, redistribute or pass on the goods it sends them, live off its credit or suffer its rule." This described very well San Francisco's role as the American Pacific's main conduit for goods, information and capital, as well as its relationship to subsidiary cities like Sacramento, Stockton, and Oakland. Ever since gold rush days, San Francisco stood out—a colonial city set down in the middle of nowhere, creating its own countryside, promoting the development of its hinterland. As inhabitants of a city without equal anywhere in the American West, San Franciscans were justified in assuming a future of significance. An 1865 petition to the city's board of supervisors expressed this sense of importance explicitly: "The great cities of our own country, as well as of Europe, have found it necessary at some period of their growth, to provide large parks. . . . No city in the world needs such grounds more than San Francisco."[14] Clearly, the park was not a response to the city's problems so much as to its assets. Yet the birth of such a park was by no means assured. The process confronted a series of material and ideological hurdles. The city had to negotiate with private owners over land use; citizens argued over who should reap the material benefits of a park; San Franciscans discovered that they did not all share the same notions of what constituted recreation; and, most notably, San Francisco's effort to construct a rendition of nature was fraught with concerns over what sort of nature was befitting of a great city.

From the time of San Francisco's founding, observers found the city site's natural endowments to be aesthetically displeasing. Reverend John Todd described San Francisco as "a city built on and among the most dreary sand hills . . . no spot could be more uninviting."[15] In the early 1850s, Frank Soulé admitted as well the "sad drawbacks . . . of the place on the land side" and added that human action was failing to improve the site toward any end other than monetary gain. "Over all these square miles of contemplated thoroughfares, there seems to be no provision . . . for a public park. . . . This is a strange mistake, and can only be attributed to the jealous avarice of the city projectors in turning every square vara of the site into an available building lot." Soulé went on to portray both the nascent city and its plan for growth as an assault on the senses: "Indeed the eye is wearied, and the imagination quite stupefied, in looking over the numberless square—all *square*—building blocks. . . . Not only is there no public park or garden, but there is not even a circus, oval, open terrace, broad avenue, . . . or verdant space of any kind . . . except in patches where stagnant water collects and ditch weeds grow."[16] Over a decade later, and only fifteen weeks after General Lee's surrender at Appomattox ended the bloody horrors of civil war, Soulé's more prosaic peacetime concerns were revived by George Fitch, editor of the *Daily Evening Bulletin*. Fitch shared Soulé's earlier park advocacy, this time not in the service of pure aestheticism but in the context of San Francisco's contention for "world city" status.[17] Ten days later, on August

4, 1865, the *Bulletin* published a thoughtful reply from Frederick Law Olmsted, Central Park's designer and leading landscape architect. Olmsted's proposals and San Francisco's ultimately negative response to them spoke volumes to the city leaders' emerging sense of environmental inferiority.

Although Frederick Law Olmsted did not stay in California for long, his personal transition in middle age represented somewhat that of the city of San Francisco. As a Connecticut Yankee, his northeastern origins were shared by many of the city's inhabitants. As a very belated "49er," his short stint as manager of a Mariposa gold mine during the last two years of the Civil War ended in failure when the depleted mine heralded the end of one San Francisco era and the beginning of another. Then forty-three years old, Olmsted adapted to changing times by plying his landscaping trade to the private estates and public institutions that symbolized the spread of urbane civilization throughout the Bay Area as the nineteenth century progressed. His greatest success was the enthusiastic support he received from the directors of Oakland's Mountain View Cemetery, which in August 1865 became in all respects a scaled-down Central Park for the dead. Olmsted was less confident of his ability to produce an equivalent park for San Francisco's living, but he was utterly convinced that the city required some natural relief from the social and environmental pressures of unmitigated urbanism. Grasping the dreams of his audience and the ripeness of the historical moment, and bolstered by his park-building experience in the East, Olmsted ardently promoted the financial, healthful, and social benefits of urban parklands. Yet he could not conceive of the Golden Gate Park that city authorities finally decided to produce: "It must . . . be acknowledged that neither in beauty of greensward nor in great umbrageous trees, do [the] conditions . . . of San Francisco allow us to hope that any pleasure ground it can acquire will ever compare in the most distant degree with those of New York or London. There is not a full-grown tree of beautiful proportions near San Francisco . . . It would not be wise or safe to undertake to form a park upon any plan which assumed as a certainty that trees which would delight the eye can be made to grow."[18]

Olmsted's sensitivity to the potential and limits of San Francisco's natural setting marks him as a truly astute environmental observer and as an insightful urban planner. In retrospect, it is worth noting the generational context of his work. He was the product of an American half century that gave us a number of environmental luminaries. While Olmsted was planning New York's Central Park, his fellow New Englander and contemporary Henry David Thoreau was still busy struggling to find an ideal balance between civilization and wilderness in the face of an ever-urbanizing and industrializing society. A year before

Olmsted's letter appeared in the San Francisco *Bulletin*, George Perkins Marsh, twenty years Olmsted's senior, published his treatise *Man and Nature*, in which he warned of the consequences of unbridled disregard for nature's balances. And very soon afterward, the young John Muir began his sojourns in the Yosemite high country, setting the stage for the preservationist campaigns of the turn of the century. What distinguished Olmsted from these others, though, was that he was a craftsman rather than a critic, a practitioner rather than a prophet. His pragmatism fueled his determination to build countryside in the city at a time when urbanites' access to "real nature" was less and less assured. It also informed his design of "invented nature," which he hoped in its mature state would present the illusion of having always been as it was. "Cities are now grown so great that hours are consumed in gaining the 'country,' and when the fields are reached, entrance is forbidden. Accordingly, it becomes necessary to acquire, for the free use and enjoyment of all, such neighboring fields, woods, pond-sides, river-banks, valleys, or hills as may present, or may be made to present, fine scenery of one type or another."[19] On the basis of these central principles, Olmsted diligently applied himself to developing a schema for a park that would take maximum advantage of what San Francisco's setting could offer, while enhancing that setting with an arguably more pleasing rendition of nature than the ages had produced on their own.

Olmsted proposed a Pleasure Ground for San Francisco that consisted of a set of irregular spaces, each of defined function, connected by linear promenades. The largest portion of the project would have been a two-hundred-acre Rural Ground centered near today's Duboce Park, on the immediate edge of the developed portion of the city. The situation of the Rural Ground conformed cleverly to natural topographic features. It was sheltered to the west by elevations of three hundred to five hundred feet—now Corona Heights and Buena Vista Park—and its valley location ensured that it would be adequately watered. Olmsted envisioned a large square extension abutting the north side of Market Street from roughly Guerrero to Fifteenth streets, which would have included a playground and parade ground, and two sylvan fingers of trees and shrubbery along and uphill from Castro Street, and then again along Oak and Fell streets toward the current placement of the Golden Gate Park Panhandle.

In conformity with Olmsted's overall vision for invented nature, the pastoral grassy sections of the valley and the wooded and vine-covered fingers that followed the contours of the surrounding hillsides could be completely believable as natural landscapes within the confines of their carefully chosen setting. The entire "rural" expanse was connected on the blueprint to the built-up city by a promenade parallel to and two thousand feet north of Market Street, which then joined another longer such parkway. The latter extended southward at Eddy Street to Market and Eighth streets, through today's Civic Center Park, and northward from Eddy along the entire length of Van Ness Avenue to a proposed Marine-Parade and Saluting Ground at the juncture of Fort Mason Center and Aquatic Park. The promenades were designed to shelter their users from the city's northwesterly winds and to provide some visual relief from the cityscape with compact but striking plantings. The emphasis on focused points of horti-cultural interest as opposed to broad views was an inevitable compromise with the spatial limitations, topography, climate, and weather conditions that inspired the unique aspects of Olmsted's San Francisco plan in the first place. Olmsted suggested a 390-foot-wide swath along Van Ness Avenue, with fifty-five feet on either side allocated to streets. The remaining 280-foot-wide promenade was to be set down in a twenty-foot-deep cut with sloping landscaped sides. At the cen-ter of the cut was a pedestrian mall twenty-four feet in width with manicured borders and a horse and carriage roadway at each side. The land and slopes beyond these were to be planted, in sequence of elevation, with lawns, flower beds, shrubs, small trees, and finally evergreens along the top as a sight, wind, and sound barrier to what lay beyond.[20]

Olmsted's plan, although very well conceived, faced a number of obstacles. First, he was already in New York working on Brooklyn's Prospect Park when the San Francisco Board of Supervisors reviewed his proposal in the spring of 1866. Second, the costs of the project were too great for the city to undertake without state support, and the California legislature was out of session. And, finally, the time lag between design and implementation was sufficient for oppo-sition to mobilize and promote an alternate vision. Many opponents took the lead of *Bulletin* editor George Fitch, whose model for San Francisco's future had always been New York. Why, they wondered, should San Francisco settle for a relatively small, oddly shaped set of pleasure grounds when New York had a sin-gle, large park? The very thought of it offended the sensibilities of those eager aspirants to world-city fame. Olmsted's admonition that their park would never "compare in the most distant degree to those of New York or London," was a vir-tual clarion call to uphold the dignity of San Francisco. Even Olmsted's obvious reluctance to ever use the word "park" when referring to his San Francisco pro-posal was fraught with potent cultural meaning. The city knew something of pleasure grounds, and these were not the stuff of grandeur. The city needed a genuine park. But given Olmsted's judicious and pragmatic approach to land-scaping, there was a good deal of irony in San Francisco's eventual rejection of

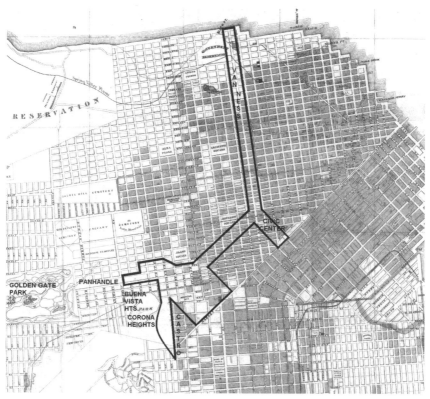

Olmsted's Pleasure Ground, in closely approximated outline, on an 1873 map of San Francisco. Van Ness Avenue and Castro Street are denoted in boldface, as are today's civic center, the Golden Pate Park Panhandle, the eastern portion of the park, Buena Vista, and Corona Heights. Map courtesy of the David Rumsey Map Collection, www.davidrumsey.com. Outline of the Pleasure Ground and boldface landmarks have been superimposed by the author.

the Olmsted plan in favor of one that seemed completely impractical from an environmental standpoint—a New York in the dunes.

By early summer 1866, the park issue had become a contest between competing neighborhood groups from North Beach and the Mission District hoping to benefit from the likely rise in property values that a park would bring. The backdrop for this was the feverish land speculation gripping San Francisco's real estate market through the 1860s. In 1868, both factions lost when Mayor Frank McCoppin and the city's board of supervisors decided on a western location instead. The area in which the park was to be located was a ten-thousand-acre expanse of sand dunes beyond the city's charter line. These Outside Lands, which today include the Richmond and Sunset districts, were subjects of a property dispute between San Francisco and the government of the United States. As land prices within the city limits continued to rise dramatically, some speculators gambled on presumed federal ownership of the Outside Lands to establish tentative homesteads there that they hoped to later resell at substantial profit. These "squatters," as they were known, scored a legislative victory in 1866 when two California Republicans in Washington, Senator John Conness and Representative John Bidwell, secured congressional passage of a bill that abandoned federal claims to the Outside Lands, while requiring that the city cede the land to the squatters. The bill contained an important exception to the general rule of privatization—the city could secure, by unspecified methods, those portions of the Outside Lands that might be needed for municipal purposes, such as a public park.[21]

This turn of events is what shifted city leaders' attention from potential Mission District and Presidio park sites to the western dunes. Aside from the likely role that the squatters played in shaping political events, Mayor McCoppin was hardly a disinterested party. As the largest shareholder in the San Francisco Grading Company, he expected to turn a profit of his own by leveling the dunes on the park site and hauling the sand away to fill the Mission District's tidelands. By 1869, the city, the Outside Land holders, and the state government—whose legal responsibility was to keep the city's debt within prescribed limits—reached an agreement on the disposition of the precious real estate. San Francisco acquired roughly 10 percent of the Outside Lands, including a rectangular swath of slightly over one thousand acres extending westward toward the ocean. Golden Gate Park was to emerge on this rectangle, ignoring the natural contours of the land, but maximizing potential street frontage without interfering with the lot lines of a projected urban grid. Aside from the potential financial benefits of its geometry to future surrounding neighborhoods, the fact that its proportions were very similar to those of New York's Central Park was not an accident. The intersection of narrow private interests and visions of a greater public good had produced a park site that, at least theoretically, could propel San Francisco forward into the lofty ranks of elite metropolises. But faith and good wishes notwithstanding, it remained to be seen how a Central Park, nurtured by the proto-European environmental conditions of the East Coast, could be replicated in the shifting sands of western San Francisco.[22]

It is difficult today to conceive of how unwelcoming the park site was in 1870. Its windswept expanse was as far removed as one can imagine from the sylvan and pastoral idyll that contemporary planners sought in creating urban retreats. Whether on foot or on horseback, passage was arduous, and, in any case, the terrain offered little of value or interest to do. Absent any powerful motivation, a visitor could hardly be expected to take off westward from the inhabited city to the end of the closest streetcar line and trudge for miles through a dunescape for the pleasure of inhaling gusts of sand. It is no wonder that Frederick Olmsted, with his inclination to create landscapes rooted in the intrinsic qualities of their natural settings, gave no consideration whatever to the park prospects of the Outside Lands. In retrospect, it is equally logical that San Francisco, whose existence was made possible by reengineering nature in the gold and silver regions to the east, would turn to the mining engineer William Hammond Hall to conjure a wood from a desert.

Recently returned from a stint in the silver districts of Nevada, Hall was Golden Gate Park's planner and steward from 1870 to 1876 and again from 1886 to 1889. By the end of Hall's first tenure, even Olmsted marveled at the emerging greensward that he had "not hitherto thought reasonable to expect under the circumstances."[23] Despite the constant sand drifts, some areas of the park site had some development potential. The eastern end, adjoining today's Haight Ashbury district, consisted of an arable soil of decomposed leaf mold and rock. In the same vicinity, the water table was readily accessible at ten yards or so below a substantial clay deposit and could be tapped for irrigation. Out toward the western end of the reserve, a series of natural lakes pooled to the east of a ridge that separated them from the ocean. Hall called these lakes into service as well to irrigate the Avenue or Panhandle section of the park that was closest to the built-up city. The lake environment provided rare punctuation to the unbroken expanses of sand and scrub grasses, as tules, lupines, and willow trees dotted the lakeshores. A few ridges east of the lakes, including Strawberry Hill and Prayerbook Cross Hill, also added floral variety with their coverings of wild strawberry, native lupine, scrub oaks, and California cherry. But none of these surface features interested Hall as much as subsurface water for irrigation and clay for roadway foundations. His inclination was to view the rest as blank canvas.

Hall worked assiduously for several years to produce a terrain of romantic beauty. Although Hall's engineering approach to the received landscape differed with Olmsted's, he shared the same ultimate goals. Hall placed great hope in the humanitarian service that a woodland park would provide to urbanites seeking "relief from . . . disturbing city-like influences." He also believed quite firmly that such relief could only be assured if the park appeared to be "a work of nature."[24] While the eastern portions of the park reserve were at least marginally suited to such development, over three-quarters of the park were unusable without first stabilizing its dunes. Hall was lucky to have had some help in this regard.

Dune grading on the site of Golden Gate Park. Courtesy of the San Francisco History Center, San Francisco Public Library.

First, Hall relied on the precedent established during the Civil War by General Barton Alexander, who researched French, Belgian, Dutch, and British sand reclamation methods so he could secure Union gun emplacements on San Francisco's Pacific shore. Second, one of the Outside Land holders, a Frenchman named Paul Rousset, supported Hall's hope that time-tested and inexpensive French techniques for keeping coastal sands at bay could be applied to San Francisco. Hall consequently experimented with an induced and conflated version of plant succession by which the seeds of shrubs and trees were sown simultaneously in the expectation that each in sequence would stabilize the sand and guarantee eventual tree growth. When an initial mixture of yellow broom and coastal pine failed to take, Hall added native lupine, the seeds of which could readily be collected from the existing stock of plants that nature had provided in the park.[25]

When the pine seedlings died, a now legendary twist of fate solved Hall's problem. While Hall and party were camping on site, one of their horses spilled its feed of barley, which in the early winter rains soon sprouted into a green mat covering yards of sand. Hall turned the accident into a plan, and by 1874 he and his workers had stabilized hundreds of acres of once-shifting dunes by sowing them with a mixture of barley, lupine, broom, and maritime pine. The quick-sprouting barley held the ground in the first winter and spring rain, allowing enough time for the lupine to grow and hold the sand for the summer and next winter. After two rainy seasons, the broom had established its permanence, providing enough binding for the tree seedlings to root. Hall further improved on this system by establishing a plant nursery in the park and growing the pines under sheltered conditions before planting them out on the dunes. Hall also brought several other tree species into the burgeoning park environment in an effort to produce the visual effect of a humid-climate retreat. Maples, sycamores, cottonwoods, poplars, and yews all failed to survive, but eucalyptus trees, cedars, and redwoods fared better. Despite continuing problems with drifting sand from neighboring properties whose speculative owners were not inclined to "waste" money on reclamation, and despite the enormity of the landscaping task at hand in the western reaches of the park reserve, by 1875 Hall had led a successful effort to hold down the park's dunes, provide irrigation for its plantings, macadamize miles of roadway, create picnic grounds and rustic shelters, and provide a semblance of forested tranquility for prospective users.[26]

On December 12, 1875, San Francisco's *Daily Morning Call* expressed the enthusiasm of many leading citizens for Hall's accomplishment when it proclaimed, "Every metropolis of consequence now boasts it public pleasure grounds, which even the poorest are privileged to enter. Paris has its Bois de Boulogne . . . , Berlin has its 'Under the Lindens' . . . , London has its St. James' and Regent's parks, New York City its Central Park, Chicago its Lincoln Park . . . , and San Francisco has its Golden Gate Park."[27] The *Call*'s editorial, though propagandistic, is thought-provoking in hindsight. Its reference to the city's "poorest" should remind us that their voices, as well as those of other working-class people, were distinctly absent from the park debates. In fact, until William Hammond Hall gave living shape to what had first been just a dream, public discussions regarding the creation of Golden Gate Park were heavily imbued with the immediate and relatively narrow concerns of property holders and municipal authorities who wanted to fill their pockets and satisfy their personal ambitions by promoting San Francisco's growth. Much as the expansion of the city over made land in prior decades seemed to emerge from a consensus on the benefits of growth, an implicit consensus drove the park forward as well. Yet there were fundamental linked and unexamined social and environmental assumptions underlying these ambitions that were potentially threatening to the least affluent San Franciscans.

The birth and development of a city is a contentious process by which human uses of nature change from one cultural basis to another. A principal source of conflict is the de-ruralization of space that transforms actual or potential farmland, pasture, and hunting grounds into commercial, industrial, and residential real estate. This spatial change is accompanied by a progressively expanding market system in which economic dependency and interdependency become the norm, while the prospects for subsistence and self-reliance diminish and then disappear. On the most basic level, one can no longer imagine putting one's own food into one's own mouth. While this becomes second nature to habitués of

Trees planted in the dunes, looking southwest from Strawberry Hill near the center of Golden Gate Park, as late as 1880. The glaring white expanse at the top left is the as yet undeveloped Sunset district, and the Pacific is at the top right. Courtesy of the San Francisco History Center, San Francisco Public Library, collection of Roy D. Graves.

urban civilization over time, it was not always so, and the transition in use is rarely painless.

In San Francisco, just as the steam paddy of the 1850s had engineered a succession of landscapes from sand hills and wetlands to market gardens to commercial and industrial neighborhoods, the decision to create park space west of the built-up city transformed the land in ways that foreclosed other uses. In most cities, including those cited by the *Call*, an often class-based human contest accompanied this sort of urban environmental change. For example, in New York almost two thousand people were actively using nature for their livelihoods on the future site of Central Park at the time of its planning. These included shanty dwellers, laborers, gardeners, domestics, keepers of pigs and goats, and a few grocers and butchers. Most of them were recent immigrants from Ireland or Germany, and many others were African Americans, including runaway slaves. They drew scorn from the mainstream press, which described them as "vagabonds and scoundrels of every description." Because it served the interests of development, New York's park engineer Egbert Viele reviled them as well, referring to pre-park occupants as "squatters . . . living off the refuse of the city."[28]

The contrast with San Francisco was striking. With rare exception, even the word "squatter" had completely different connotations in San Francisco, where almost all of these were absentee real estate speculators whom Hall described as a "coterie of resourceful and powerful men." San Francisco's squatters neither occupied the future site of Golden Gate Park nor depended on it for their living. While New York's park dwellers were working-class people on the fringes of the market economy, San Francisco's Outside Land holders were capitalists. The one recorded exception proves the rule. Hall reported his surprise at having once encountered "an old, heavily whiskered hermit-like man . . . with several dogs for companions. Chickens and ducks which he raised there, and large frogs which he caught in the ponds out towards the beach and sold to the French restaurants, yielded him a livelihood." The old man was almost completely alone. The only other references that San Francisco planners made to prior occupants did not apply to the park reserve itself, but rather to the unpaved and undeveloped districts just beyond the edges of the built-up city, where undesirable characters and cast-offs from Vigilance Committee days might have intimidated decent citizens on their way to the park.[29]

For the most part, in human terms the future Golden Gate Park was a blank slate. This was partly due to the youthfulness of the city, but it was also a function of the park site's natural environment, which never really had any significant use value to human beings. The native Yelamu had passed it over in favor of the greener lands and milder climes of the peninsula's bay side and for the Tennessee Hollow watershed near the Golden Gate. The eighteenth-century missionaries came to an identical conclusion when they planted themselves in with the Yelamu in Mission Valley, as did the soldiers at the Presidio. The Mexican rancheros made exactly the same environmental choices, as did the founders of Yerba Buena. In the Outside Lands, park builders had to conquer nonhuman nature, but not the resistance of prior human users of the landscape. This meant that one of the classic contests of urbanization—that between existing uses of land for sustenance and emerging uses of land for profit—was absent from the Golden Gate Park story. Instead, the two paradoxical and very modern perspectives on land use that the park shared with its New York counterpart went unchallenged. The first of these was the premise that the natural beauty of the park would create profit for surrounding landholders by transforming their "wastelands" into urban real estate. In other words, the park would build the city. The second was the idea that the park would provide a natural-feeling escape from the very life it was bound to support and promote beyond its gates. In its role as city builder, the park's nature was intimately tied to its perceived antithesis.

The fact that Golden Gate Park made use of a largely uncontested environment is further strengthened in comparison to its principal European reference point, the Bois de Boulogne. The famed Parisian woods had a long history of continuous use and were placed under the supervision of a forestry administration, the *forestii*, as early as the seventh century. The Bois that eventually became the grand urban park of late-nineteenth-century Paris had served as the hunting grounds of French kings for the millennium spanning Chilperic III to Louis XVI. The Bois provided the royals with game, waterfowl, and fish. Its trees yielded firewood for nobles and peasants alike and timber for buildings and military fortifications. Defending and invading armies bivouacked there during the Hundred Years' War, the Revolution, the Napoleonic Wars, and the Franco-Prussian War, and the woods were many times despoiled. When in 1852, Baron Haussmann integrated the Bois into his massive redesign of Paris that included the now-famed boulevards, he presaged Olmsted's Central Park by only five years and Hall's Golden Gate Park by a decade and a half. But France's turbulent history did not permit a rapid and linear transformation of the Parisian woods into urban recreational space. While William Hammond Hall was peacefully experimenting with dune stabilization in 1870 and 1871, France's war with Prussia and the subsequent garrisoning of the capital under the Commune forced Parisians back into a subsistence relationship with the Bois, from which they took carp and deer for food and wood for fires and barricades. One patriotic writer commented, "If the trees that gave beauty to Auteuil pond have been cut, it is consoling to think that we sacrificed them ourselves in necessary defense against the enemy. A poet would say that these old oaks fell selflessly to French axes to defend the soil of the motherland." Because of centuries of traditional peacetime use, punctuated by more intense exploitation in time of war, it took at least a decade beyond the Commune to firmly establish the Bois de Boulogne as a site characterized by its aesthetic and recreational value and largely devoid of direct economic function. By comparison, Golden Gate Park achieved its designated purpose with remarkable speed.[30]

Golden Gate Park's unusual situation as uncontested nature is linked to the secondary issue of its social impact as engineered recreational space. The park embodied the idea that the highest use value for a substantial plot of nature in the city could be exclusively recreational and never productive. Though not original to nineteenth-century San Francisco, the notion that a portion—in fact a man-made representation—of nature was to be shielded from human labor, becoming a site for the practice of nonwork or anti-work, raised the question of what exactly recreation was and how it was to be carried out. Why was a facsimile of nature necessary for proper recreation in much the same way as a factory or office was for proper work? As the proposed principal recreation ground for San Franciscans, Golden Gate Park risked being dragged into a struggle over the meaning of work, the meaning of leisure, and the locus of these human activities within nature. Consequently, not only did the park have the aforementioned potential to fuel economic competition over land use, but it might have become embroiled in a second intersecting axis of urban conflict—the contest that often accompanied the modernization of popular habits and social behavior. Historians of working and laboring classes often refer to this as the emergence of industrial discipline. Whatever one wishes to call it, the fact is that a pre-urban or preindustrial way of being yielded to an urban and industrial one that late nineteenth-century Americans often typified as sober, clean, orderly, and industrious. This change permeated the culture of recreation and work and often made parks hotly contested spaces. Yet in San Francisco, cultural conflicts over recreational uses of nature do not seem to have been any more pronounced than narrowly economic ones. The reasons have a great deal to do with timing and with the rapid succession of conquests that characterized eighteenth- and nineteenth-century California.

The founders of Golden Gate Park were obviously not the progenitors of rest and play. Inhabitants of the San Francisco region, as adequate representatives of their species, had always played. The children of California's first hunter-gatherers played at hunting frogs, at dodging balls made of tule reeds, and at hide-and-seek. Their parents combined play and worship in frequent feasts and dances. In the eighteenth century, the Yelamu neophytes under Franciscan tutelage at Mission Dolores held footraces and ball games, while nineteenth-century Californio pastoralists amused themselves with bullfights, bearbaiting, rodeos, dances, and fiestas. Distinctions between work and recreation within nature were not rigid. In the Mexican era, the game of broncobusting produced the tamed horse that the vaquero employed to ride herd over the ranchero's cattle; the bull that was tormented and turned over by the tail in the game of *colea el toro* could have been a stud of the working ranch; and the roping and subjugation of bears provided some sense of victory over creatures that were otherwise quite fearsome in a natural setting that was still largely wild. Even practical activities like hunting blurred the lines of gamesmanship and work. How does one distinguish between the pleasure of the well-executed and skillful chase and the pleasure of the full stomach or the communal feast?[31]

American conquest and the advent of the gold rush brought an industrializing people and well-developed commercial values to California. The Bay Area's urbanization and Americanization caused the decline of practices that combined economic and recreational functions. The rapid emergence of a cash economy reduced San Franciscans' direct interaction with nature as a source of food, clothing, and shelter and simultaneously separated work and play. As the city rose from the site of erstwhile native villages and Mexican ranchos, urbanization imposed a new geography on human activity. When Yerba Buena became San Francisco, the intensive commercialization of the forty acres around Portsmouth Square banished from the heart of the city any recreation that could not be bought or sold—thus the saloons, brothels, and gambling dens of the Barbary Coast. The construction by steam shovel of the south of Market district had a similar effect, to which industry added the despoliation of potentially attractive natural recreation sites by toxic effluents and organic wastes. The industrialization of meat production, for example, yielded wastes far exceeding the scale of the old ranchos' *matanzas*—slaughters—and the creation through urban concentration of exclusively human habitats pushed away the bears and coyotes that had once acted as garbage collectors. Consequently, the working-class children who swam in Mission Bay in the 1860s and 1870s shared its increasingly stagnant waters with the blood and rotting offal of pigs and cattle. Others fished the foul waters from Long Bridge. From a public health perspective, one can hardly lament the Bay's demise as it was progressively filled with earth from the former sand hills of Market Street. A similar process unfolded in the pastures west of Russian Hill. In a city short of fresh water, a small lake bounded by Octavia, Lombard, Franklin, and Filbert streets served for decades as a communal washbasin. Women's work and social lives converged on washday outings at Laguna Pequeña, later dubbed Washerwoman's Lagoon, which was filled in 1882 when tannery wastes finally made the lake unusable. As these examples illustrate, alterations to the natural landscape caused by urbanization forced changes in household economies and in patterns of work and leisure at one and the same time.[32]

The displacement or elimination of natural recreation sites within the expanding city was accompanied by the emergence of privately owned pleasure gardens. At these private resorts, which were eventually supplanted by Golden Gate Park, San Franciscans sought respite from the routines of commercial and industrial jobs that were more and more divorced from immediate interaction with nature. The pleasure gardens were a unique artifice—a blend of circus, museum, rural dale, and sometimes saloon—found in every nineteenth-century city in the United States and northern Europe. They also represented a transitional form of play that stood somewhere on the road between preindustrial and industrial life. In the late nineteenth century, public park advocates often imagined that the social habits expressed and nurtured in the popular gardens would be replaced

Washerwoman's Lagoon, ca. 1865–67. San Francisco's Marina District now stands largely on the portion of the bay on the right, which was filled in the 1910s to accommodate the Panama Pacific International Exposition. Courtesy of the San Francisco History Center, San Francisco Public Library.

in time by a new set of "genteel" behaviors consistent with retreats of upper-middle-class design like Golden Gate Park. The views of men like Olmsted and Hall made it very clear that perceptions of nature were central to this change. But while Olmsted found a relief in "natural scenery" that he could not achieve from "artificial pleasures such as theatres, parades and promenades,"[33] visitors to nineteenth-century San Francisco's pleasure gardens were hardly conscious of these distinctions or of the tremendous social, economic, and environmental changes they reflected at that moment in time. The frame of reference of workers and businessmen alike was conditioned by their role as transplants building a modern urban order on the blank canvas of the West. This had not been the case in all places at all times.

First of all, it would be incorrect to assume that middle to late nineteenth-century park planners like Olmsted and his colleagues Calvert Vaux and Andrew Jackson Downing were the first Americans to consider the culturally uplifting potential of well-designed public recreational spaces. At least one early nineteenth-century businessman foresaw this possibility and proved as well that even private pleasure gardens could have histories of class conflict. In 1827, a petty entrepreneur by the name of Timothy Crane built a pleasure garden on the north bank of Passaic Falls in New Jersey. Forest Garden served the people of Paterson, a typical factory town of the sort spawned by northeastern industrialism in the decades after the War of 1812. Crane's goal was to provide Patersonians with a balance of nature, art, and entertainment, while turning a profit on his land. He expressly believed that his "improvements" to the natural setting would promote both the material and moral progress of his community, and the *Paterson Intelligencer* agreed, praising Crane's gardens as a place where "the refinements of taste and art combined with the varied and romantic beauties of nature." A precursor to San Francisco's Russ Gardens, Woodward's Gardens, and the Willows, Paterson's Forest Garden was endowed with a number of elements that were ubiquitous to its recreational form. Crane laid down gravel walkways, planted imported bushes and trees, built an ice-cream parlor that also served as a saloon, and provided facilities for circus acts, Indian war dances, and fireworks displays. Lest one have doubted the merits of these diversions, the local paper contrasted them quite favorably to the natural attributes of the neighboring falls: "Take a peep at the awful chasm below—listen for a moment to the tremendous roar of the troubled Passaic, and contrast the scene with your own quietude of mind."[34]

Crane and the editor of the *Intelligencer* had failed to note, however, that the privately owned pleasure garden of 1827 occupied space that had served the needs of free and unorganized public recreation since 1770. The public had always been free to hike the private woods that lined the river, to fish at the base of the falls, and to enjoy the "unimproved" nature of the "troubled Passaic" without impediment. Crane's reordering of nature, and his privatization and systematization of recreation in that redesigned natural setting, unleashed twelve years of class struggle that culminated in Forest Garden's bankruptcy and collapse by 1839. For over a decade, weavers and spinners from Paterson's mills had attacked the park, its employees, and its patrons. They stole liquor at night, defaced property, hurled tables and benches over the falls, threw firecrackers at passing ladies, fired buckshot into windows, chopped down trees and bushes, and generally did their worst to ensure the gardens' demise. San Francisco never contended with anything comparable.[35]

In comparison to Paterson, New Jersey, the apparent lack of serious contests over recreational space in San Francisco can be partly attributed to timing and social succession. The San Franciscans of the 1850s and 1860s had not been around for a half century to establish customary rights in the use of their natural environment. If Paterson's Timothy Crane was a usurper of publicly accessible nature in the minds of many of his neighbors, then San Franciscans were collective usurpers of a nature once used by Californios, and before them by Native

Americans. But in terms of numbers, or in the sense of established right, who was left to contest anything that the new urbanites wished to do? Equally important was the speed at which the gold rush propelled urban growth on a previously marginal pastoral landscape. All of San Francisco's pleasure gardens were built during the city's first two decades in the south of Market and Mission districts, concurrently with the arrival and settlement of the population they served, on land whose prior users were numerically insignificant and who wielded no social power. Consequently, the gardens were uniformly well received.

Yet Crane's problems in New Jersey were not restricted to the fact that he stole someone else's nature and charged admission for something that had once been free. The tireless working-class assaults against Forest Garden were also the result of Crane's social vision. He did not want a clientele of "lazy, idle, rascally, drunken vagabonds." In the words of his chronicler, historian Paul Johnson, he preferred "decorous people who stayed on the walkways and out of the bushes, who conversed politely over brandy and never got drunk, and who contemplated trees without wanting to climb them."[36] He wanted his park to be secure for "ladies." William Hammond Hall echoed these sentiments in San Francisco several decades later when he conceived of Golden Gate Park as a refuge for "eminently respectable and well-behaved groups of people . . . , ladies with their families, children in the charge of nurses . . . , [and] large picnic parties who would enjoy having more freedom." Although Hall also shared to a lesser degree Andrew Jackson Downing's conviction that exposure to nature in public parks and gardens could "soften and humanize the rude," it is evident that such class-conscious appraisals of the uses and effects of engineered nature failed to reflect the realities of San Francisco's development.[37] In San Francisco, the jump from "unimproved nature" to pleasure garden went unchallenged, and the leap from pleasure garden to urban woodland park was far less contentious than in many other places.

In the early years of New York's Central Park, for example, working-class New Yorkers favored the privately owned Jones Wood pleasure grounds on the Upper East Side over their new public park. Even though both were equidistant from their downtown Manhattan neighborhoods, reveling workers, and especially recent immigrants, could enjoy activities at Jones Wood that were discouraged in Central Park. Ironically, these were exactly the sort of activities that had been offered at Paterson's Forest Garden in the 1820s—magic shows, dancing, fireworks, boxing matches, beer fests, and choral performances. Although Jones Wood provided a forum for recreation that had endured for generations, Horace Greeley's *Tribune*, one voice of "respectable" New York, complained bitterly that the pleasure ground attracted thieves, pickpockets, tricksters, lewd women, and rowdy men. While thirty years earlier the *Paterson Intelligencer* had found Timothy Crane's structured recreation preferable to the raw nature of "troubled" Passaic Falls, the *Tribune* yearned for an artistically landscaped park in which a tame nature would provide solace to the soul. The New York paper often criticized the pleasure ground's vernacular contrivances and novelties— grottos, circus rings, and topiary—as vulgar and pedestrian. But Jones Wood was much like the earlier Forest Garden, and both were quite a lot like San Francisco's pleasure grounds. In the latter city, their purported vulgarity did not draw as much negative attention.[38]

San Francisco's experience with private pleasure gardens was different from that of Paterson and New York because of a different frame of reference regarding nature. San Francisco did not have Paterson's dense oak and evergreen woods or its thunderous falls. By eastern standards, Mission Creek paled in comparison to the Passaic River. In the dry, yellow, dusty, almost treeless expanse of San Francisco, a new city thronging with easterners and northern Europeans readily saw any verdant space with lawns, shade trees, and roses as an improvement over a reticent nature. While Patersonians rebelled against the enclosure of a riverbank, San Franciscans rejoiced at the reclamation of a barren. And in comparison to midcentury New York, young San Francisco was an overwhelmingly male boomtown where drinking, gambling, and whoring were not simply unfortunate aspects of urban life; they were the principal forms of recreation. It was no wonder that in 1855, the city government sought to ban "noisy and barbarous amusements" on the Sabbath, and it was no surprise that the law had little effect.[39] Under these circumstances from the city's earliest days, pleasure gardens were seen as suburban retreats that could offer wholesome and family-oriented entertainment in a natural setting removed from the violence and degradation of the Barbary Coast. In that sense, San Francisco's Golden Gate Park was more properly a linear descendant of the pleasure gardens than their antithesis.

San Francisco's first private resorts were Russ Gardens at Sixth and Harrison streets and the Willows between Mission and Valencia and Eighteenth and Nineteenth streets. The former was only one mile from downtown and the latter only twice that distance—and after 1860 accessible by a ten-minute, ten-cent steam train ride on the Market Street Railroad. Despite this proximity to the city, San Franciscans of that day understood the gardens as country retreats. Charles Warren Stoddard recalled, "The Willows and Russ Gardens had their day, and it was a jolly day. They were good for the people those rural resorts; they were rest for the weary, refreshment for the hungry and thirsty—and now they have gone."[40]

Russ Gardens, which was owned by the German immigrant Emanuel Christian Charles Russ, was a beer garden planted with imported fruit trees that was popular with the thousands of San Francisco Germans who used it to celebrate May Day and to put on the athletic performances of their Turnverein societies. The Willows, taken over by Frenchman Francois Pioche in 1861, served a broader clientele with a shooting gallery, a small menagerie, and even the prospect of champagne lunches under the willow trees. Over time, the natural beauty of the grounds dissipated from neglect, and the new Woodward's Gardens that opened at Fourteenth and Mission streets in 1868 came to overshadow both of the earlier resorts.[41]

On just five acres of land, Rhode Islander Robert Woodward provided his guests with gardens and fountains; a lake; flowering plants; shrubs and trees; caverns; statuary; a library; a conservatory; a museum; an aquarium; a five-thousand-seat pavilion for theater, dancing, and acrobatic performances; and a racetrack for Roman chariot races. Woodward stocked a zoo with monkeys, ostriches, lions, tigers, bears, and camels and offered balloon rides, donkey rides, and boat rides, all for a twenty-five-cent admission price. The incredible density of attractions on the site was offset by equally dense plantings, specifically designed to convey an eastern, humid-climate atmosphere in opposition to the sandy city outside Woodward's gates. Aside from its larger size, Woodward's Gardens distinguished itself from its predecessors by serving no alcohol—a measure that in the 1870s seemed to have no negative repercussion on ticket sales and made the resort very appealing to middle-class families and for the May Day outings of thousands of schoolchildren.[42]

Unlike early Golden Gate Park, Woodward's Gardens had no pretension of mimicking true nature. It is ironic then that Woodward's Gardens with its picnic grounds and boat rides, its landscaped walks and collections of exotic plants, its museums of art and natural history, and its concerts and athletic events contained on a more compact scale all of those things that characterize Golden Gate Park today. It is notable as well that the Gardens' demise in the 1880s was directly correlated to the opening of Golden Gate Park and the latter's improved accessibility as the city grew toward the park and as streetcar and train service improved. The ease with which San Franciscans made the transition from one recreational setting to another was also remarkable. Woodward's temperance was genuine and deeply held, but San Franciscans did not make his dry resort part of a grand social struggle against the alcohol-serving Russ Gardens and Willows. Woodward's enterprise may have attracted many citizens who preferred sober recreation, but it succeeded primarily because it was larger and greener and offered more attractions than its competitors, thereby drawing larger crowds. Insofar as its natural offerings were concerned, Woodward's resort also provides some insight into popular expectations of nature that would have at first limited any contention over Golden Gate Park's form, and later profoundly influenced its design.

In the spring of 1877, the actress Miriam Squier of New York, who had become the journalist Mrs. Frank Leslie, visited Woodward's Gardens on a trip to California with her husband. Mrs. Leslie described the resort as "a terrestrial Paradise . . . [of] shady groves, verdant lawns, flowery bouquets, lakes, streams and waterfalls. . . . Such a garden is only possible where frost is unknown, and the Summer's growth is never nipped by Winter's snows. Why does not human nature carry out the rule of inanimate nature, and why are not the persons who have never known sorrow, or a want, or a cloud upon their day, by no means the sweetest, the fairest or most perfect?"[43] Mrs. Leslie's experience of the gardens was no doubt colored by her class status and her romanticism, but her remarks did have an element of universality. Every pleasure garden owner from Emanuel Russ onward seemed to understand that customers would be attracted by lawns, trees, and water. If not, why go to the expense of landscaping at all? Because the substantial attendance at Russ Gardens and its competitors and successors comprised to various degrees a cross-class clientele, it stands to reason that the desire for greenery was not exclusive to the upper middle class. Of course, it hardly seems sensible that San Franciscans of any class would have gone to the trouble of paying admission to be penned up in privately owned corrals, which is what largely unimproved grounds would have looked like in the city's natural environment, so someone had to go about creating a nature that customers would readily use. Mrs. Leslie waxed poetic about Woodward's paradisiacal gardens and correctly ascribed their existence to the city's marine-tempered frost-free climate. Yet she was also describing an island on the land that everyone knew was exceptional, because it was so different from—and "better" than—the natural environment in which it had been built. No one gave a second thought to the price of their pleasures, and accounts indicate that adults and children alike were as entertained by Woodward's zoo as Mrs. Leslie: "The most amusing feature of all was the bear-pit; tall poles were erected in the middle with little platforms on top [so] that Bruin might pretend to himself that he was climbing in a tree and resting in the branches." A reflective Bruin might have mused: "The funniest thing of all was the garden. Shade trees and flowering bushes were planted, paths graded and paved, water pumped through improvised channels and made to flow into an artificial lake so that Homo might pretend to himself that he was hiking through the countryside of Connecticut."

The popularity of invented nature, which contemporary urbanites share with nineteenth-century San Franciscans, is no crime, but it nonetheless reflects

A crowd watches a performing bear at Woodward's Gardens in 1875— perhaps Mrs. Leslie's actual "Bruin." Courtesy of the San Francisco History Center, San Francisco Public Library.

something very unsettling about what nature becomes in an urbanizing world. By 1870, when William Hammond Hall was building his greensward in the dunes, San Franciscans were already quite comfortable with natures of their own invention. Woodward's suburban paradise depended on San Francisco's essential nature of mild winters and the water table of Mission Valley, but it also redrew it in unrecognizable ways. And, as no environment could really escape the grasp of an increasingly dominant urban civilization, a similar process began to affect the city's hinterlands as well, as San Franciscans and other Americans set out to reinvent "wilderness."

In 1864, the United States Congress granted California the Yosemite Valley as the first tract of American "wild" land ever set aside as a park "for public use, resort and recreation." The founding of the new wilderness park was connected in many ways with the emerging urban park movement. Horace Greeley of the *New York Tribune*, who had promoted the virtues of Central Park over Jones Wood, was an early publicist for Yosemite. After an August 1859 visit, he described the valley as a "unique and majestic" wonder, thereby contributing to its sudden national prominence. Like Golden Gate Park, Yosemite's lands were at one time claimed by squatters. James Lamon, an argonaut from Virginia, settled in the valley in 1859 and planted a fruit orchard in the hope of serving summer guests. James Mason Hutchings, an unabashed California booster and editor of *Hutchings' California Magazine*, staked out over one hundred acres from which he expected to gain future tourism revenue. Both men claimed preemption rights that they hoped would eventually gain federal recognition once the United States had surveyed the land. Senator John Conness of California, who had played a central role in the legal compromise over San Francisco's Outside Lands, was equally important in this case, although to a different end. It was Conness's bill that became the Yosemite Park Act, signed into law by President Lincoln on June 30, 1864. The act granted the squatters and other authorized private parties the right to renewable ten-year leases, but not to clear title. Instead, Yosemite Valley and the Mariposa Grove of great sequoias were granted to the state of California for public use—on terms that essentially made the state a trustee—and were to be "inalienable forever." This dramatic upholding of public right was unsuccessfully challenged by the California legislature and by the squatters, with the support of the U.S. House of Representatives, but was reaffirmed by the U.S. Senate in 1868 and by the U.S. Supreme Court in *Hutchings v. Low*, 1873.[44]

Once the park had been established under Conness's political leadership, California governor Frederick F. Low placed the Yosemite preserve under the stewardship of the new Yosemite Park Commission, to which he appointed as chairman none other than Frederick Law Olmsted. In August 1865, just a few days after his first commentary on San Francisco's proposed public pleasure grounds appeared in George Fitch's *Daily Evening Bulletin*, Olmsted filed his initial report with the Yosemite Commission. Olmsted noted, quite in character, that the public interest in Yosemite Valley rested entirely "in its natural scenery." He went on to insist, "The first point to be kept in mind then, is the preservation and maintenance as exactly as possible of the natural scenery," with construction of structures to be contained "within the narrowest limits consistent with the necessary accommodation of visitors." As if the Fates were rehearsing for San Francisco's rejection of Olmsted's urban park plan, the commission suppressed Olmsted's report and prevented it from ever reaching the state legislature. Back in New York to work on Central Park, Olmsted resigned from the Yosemite Park Commission at the end of October 1866.[45]

With Olmsted's uncompromisingly preservationist influence out of the way, Yosemite Valley's future development began to resemble that of Golden Gate Park and even to some extent that of Woodward's Gardens. While much of the original philosophical basis for urban woodland parks like Golden Gate Park had been to provide serene escapes from urbanism, the older pleasure garden model intruded itself into the vacuum of unadorned nature quite rapidly. By the 1890s, San Francisco's park had incorporated many of the recreational features of Woodward's resort—a carousel, boat and donkey rides, an animal menagerie, an aviary, a conservatory, concert pavilions, a casino, and the extravaganza of the 1894 California Midwinter International Exposition. Yosemite's development was not identical but did include significant adaptations of the landscape to promote and accommodate tourists, as well as to allow the private use of meadows as pasture. William Hammond Hall presided over many of these changes. Hall encouraged construction necessary to the "promotion of the use of the valley," such as "hotels, dwellings, stores, shops and other structures." He advocated "a hotel . . . with a wide portico and a great reception room, fireplaces each as big as an ordinary boudoir." And under his leadership, as overgrazing caused the meadows to deteriorate and forest and shrub to encroach on the valley floor, Hall called for "apply[ing] the axe right freely."[46] It is sometimes hard to imagine how such cool pragmatism could emerge only two decades after the *Mariposa Democrat*'s Warren Baer had penned: "As though the enchantress of the woods had suddenly waved her magic wand o'er the mountains, was this fair scenery opened to our view. Thrilling sensations of awe pervaded our senses, which, as we approached, gradually subsided into pleasurable emotions of wonder and delight . . . while before us . . . spread the verdant Valley of the Yosemite."[47]

Though the difficulty in maintaining a kind of pure nature is evident in the case of both San Francisco's urban and hinterland parks, the Yosemite experiment holds an element of immediate poignancy when considered from the perspective of its pre-park occupants. While one can claim within reason that Golden Gate Park's site was uncontested nature, the same cannot be said of Yosemite. In 1851, the Mariposa Battalion—one of many state militia units organized during the gold rush to free California from the "nuisance" of Indians—launched the initial drive to expel from Yosemite the Ahwahneechee Indians who had used the land for centuries. Subsequent militia incursions over the next two years forced the native inhabitants' removal to the Fresno River reservation, but the Ahwahneechee quietly trickled back into Yosemite Valley by the time it had become a park. They and other Yosemite Indians adapted themselves to their former land's new status by working in the hotels, serving as guides, selling fish and berries to tourists, and by turning their songs and dances into marketable commodities. Much as along the coast in the Spanish colonial era, the arrival of newcomers constricted the traditional native economy and constrained collective self-sufficiency. Echoing the earlier contact period, park authorities banned the Ahwahneechee burning practices that former militiaman Lafayette

Bunnell noted had given the Yosemite Valley in 1851 "the appearance of a well kept park." Tourism and grazing replaced Chief Tenaya's fires with William Hammond Hall's axes.[48]

Ultimately, one of the most curious aspects of this whole process of park building was the way in which nature in both its human and nonhuman forms became objectified. Even Frederick Olmsted fell prey to this way of thinking when he argued that the Yosemite Commission's task should be to maintain Yosemite Park "as a museum of natural science."[49] If the park presumably existed in an unmitigated state of nature and this nature was a museum, were trees, wildflowers, granite escarpments, rivers, falls, and even the Ahwah-neechee its exhibits? In their relationship to nature, were most human beings then to be consigned either the role of visitor or curator? This certainly seemed to be the case. Consequently, people tended to see Yosemite as a very distinct environment from their own homes—a truer nature and a remote place of wonder.[50] On the other hand, Yosemite Park shared a very important attribute with Golden Gate Park and Woodward's Gardens and every other pleasure ground of the time—it was an invention of urban folks to whom nature had become an artifact. Functionally, there was no difference between the native sequoia in Yosemite and the nursery-raised coastal pines in Golden Gate Park. No line of distinction separated the tourist shows of native ritual put on by the Ahwah-neechee from Robert Woodward's 1872 "Indian Show," in which Warm Springs Indians fresh from the battlefields of the Modoc War danced and chanted for awed San Franciscans.[51] Nature was always exogenous. It was a thing that could be presented, viewed, experienced, and then retreated from. As wonderful and beautiful as parks were, they were also hallmarks of an urbanizing people's sense that "nature is what and where I am not."

It may seem logical that urbanism would have fostered a growing sense of separation between human beings and the rest of the nature, but it is another irony of history that this split was strengthened by a parks movement that wished to restore to people some of their natural birthright. In the process of doing so, the creation of idealized natures led to remarkable acts of environmental engineering. Golden Gate Park, for example, required tremendous amounts of irrigation water to maintain the desired illusion of a humid-climate countryside and wood. As early as 1875, with only its easternmost regions landscaped, Golden Gate Park already consumed fourteen million gallons per year of water.[52] In a city with a short supply, it was inevitable that one day the needs of the people, their industries, and their park would tax environmental limits. Just a few decades after William Hammond Hall's successful experiment with plant succession on the

A gathering of Indians at Yosemite in 1872. Courtesy of the National Park Service, Yosemite National Park, Morning Council on the Merced, *photographed by Eadweard Muybridge, RL-14,217.*

sand dunes of the Outside Lands, San Franciscans began to consider tapping the rivers of their "natural museum" in the Sierras to quench the thirst of their growing city—a thirst that was aggravated by Golden Gate Park. As San Franciscans moved to transfer the most essential stuff of life from the nature of the mountains to the nature of their city and its urban park, they also proved their utter material dependency on that exogenous world, which in the course of their ordinary lives, they either ignored or idealized. Water became the crux of a new and unanticipated debate over the city's place in nature and over the essence of human needs.

CHAPTER 4

WATER

Any visitor who has experienced a San Francisco winter would be incredulous when told that the city has a dearth of water. The seasonal rains that fall with their greatest intensity from December to March can sometimes evoke the imagery of a biblical deluge. A few months of Pacific storms can deliver two feet of water, while a confluence of warm ocean temperatures with a sagging jet stream may produce over twice that amount. Yet even forty inches of rain in one short season might leave the city high and dry if not for human intervention. On the far eastern side of the present urban site, clay soils quickly reach their saturation point, forcing rainwater to run off into the brackish bay, where it is lost to human consumption. On the sandy soil that predominates in most of the northern peninsula, the rains percolate downward into seasonal subsurface streams, inaccessible for easy use. And but for fog, the rest of the year is dry. Thus, from the very outset, an emergent urban San Francisco was forced into creative development of its water resources. San Franciscans accomplished this in ways that drew upon both the internal landscape of their city and its hinterlands.

In the city's earliest days, San Franciscans drew their water from a few small springs and from wells they dug on private lots. Considering the town's miniscule population before the gold rush, this conventional pre-urban method had much to recommend it, not the least of which was the absence of public cost. However, the 1849 population boom that accompanied the discovery of gold put tremendous pressure on these limited sources of supply. At the same time, an inadequate system of drinking water delivery, coupled with poor sanitation, aggravated disease rates when the young city's rise coincided with the cholera pandemic of 1849–50. On the one hand, the disease migrated with its human hosts across the Pacific from Asia, across the Atlantic from Europe, along navigable rivers from the East, and along the trans-Mississippi western trails to California's goldfields to Sacramento and San Francisco. On the other hand, conditions in San Francisco were sadly conducive to its spread. The same rainy season that washed the first wave of argonauts from their diggings in the fall and winter of 1849–50 turned San Francisco's primitive streets into seas of impassable mud and exposed the city's wells and springs to torrents of effluent from hastily constructed privy pits. The results were gruesome. Although the city's mortality statistics for that time are difficult to reconstruct, it appears that about 5 percent of the population may have died of cholera in 1850. Perhaps five hundred deaths in a floating population of ten thousand seems inconsequential when measured against the great plagues of history, but the ravages of cholera must have evoked tremendous fear in the context of gold-driven dreams of happiness and prosperity. Victims of cholera suffered from violent diarrhea and gushes of vomiting that left them severely dehydrated. Their unquenchable thirst was an outward symptom of the desiccation of their cells—a bacterial assault on their bodies that left them pallid, shrunken, hollow-cheeked, and sunken-eyed. Within hours, sufferers turned violet blue and, in half of all cases, died.

Three decades before the germ theory of disease, medical doctors and others knew enough to place at least part of the blame for such outbreaks on environmental conditions. And although such an analysis is only partly accurate, it must be said that early boomtown San Francisco was well placed to be a center of sickness, both by virtue of its damp climate and especially the recklessness of its human occupants. One witness to the city's environmental degradation, the French journalist Étienne Derbec, described San Francisco as he saw it in 1850. In acerbic Gallic fashion, Derbec noted that the city was "narrow, revoltingly dirty, its squares filled with filth and the remains of animals." As if this were insufficient cause for revulsion, Derbec returned months later to chronicle a town that reeked of "a stinking odor, caused by the slime and by all kinds of filth coming from the interior of the city." One can well imagine the effects of all of this on the healthfulness of the water supply.[1]

While the worst of this first cholera epidemic had passed by 1851, San Francisco's potable-water needs were only exacerbated by continued population growth over subsequent years and decades. In retrospect, disease might have provided a short-term impetus to develop initial sources of clean drinking water, but it was the simple mechanics of urban expansion itself that carried this need well into the future. Already by 1851, personal wells had become inadequate, and businessmen great and small sought to profit from the city's thirst by developing commercial artesian wells, drawing water from outlying springs and lakes and delivering it by cask and cart, and by importing water by barge from Marin County.

By 1855, there were 175 wells in San Francisco, some artesian and others driven by windmills. Unfortunately, because most were on private land and destined to produce private profit, their proliferation led to land speculation and competition, which in turn increased production costs and cut into gains. The wells also began to tax the aquifer, causing the water table to fall, thereby requiring additional expenses for yet deeper excavation and drilling. Since much of the fresh water to the east of Yerba Buena cove was situated under the sand dunes, excavation was further complicated by the unconsolidated quality of the soil.[2] An artesian well on public land at Portsmouth Plaza caused a hopeful stir in August 1851, expressed here by one writer for the *Evening Picayune*, who exclaimed, "We have water on the Plaza! On taking our accustomed survey of that classic spot, yesterday morning, our eyes were dazzled by sundry bright beams, which proved to be reflected from a jet of water which was sputtering from the ground in the vicinity of the famous Artesian well. . . . We chased the water down a few rods and overtook it just before it had reached the cistern, into which it emptied itself at the rate of a gallon and three-fourth per minute." By December, the enthusiasm that accompanied even that paltry flow had cooled: "Will [the well] ever be made to answer the latc watery but dissipated expectations of its projectors? . . . This inverse monument of wealth, wisdom and perseverance . . . its base resting on a block of wood, and its cap bringing up against a rock near a hundred and fifty feet below, still 'holds its own,' though very little else. The city is not able to prosecute the work . . . so why not some enterprising genius get permission of the City Fathers and complete it? . . . Why not possible in San Francisco, as well as in the heart of Paris?"[3]

The *Picayune*'s intimation that mid-nineteenth century San Francisco might be comparable in some way to Paris was even more comical than its initial response to the gurgling stream reluctantly emitted by the Plaza. (It may be helpful to note that a single conventional modern bathtub would take twenty minutes to fill at the Plaza well's rate of flow.) Yet, as it turned out, San Franciscans did discover fairly quickly that their most effective providers of water would be the water carriers who were in fact ubiquitous in Paris and who became prominent figures in early San Francisco's streets. Purportedly, the city's first water carrier was the Basque Juan Miguel Aguirre, whose donkey carried two barrels from which Aguirre dispensed water to his customers at $1 per bucket in 1849. Aguirre and his fellow petty entrepreneurs tapped springs, streams, and lakes that were close to the city but not on private land. Among the most favored sources were the El Polin spring and Mountain Lake, both near the Presidio. Because the trip from the city to acquire outlying water could amount to several miles in each direction, carriers soon adopted horse-drawn water carts as their principal conveyances. By 1854, more than sixty-five water carriers plied their routes in service of the thirsty San Franciscans.[4]

Although the water carriers filled an important transitional niche between the city's village phase and its fully urban period, there is some perspective to be gained by examining the *Picayune*'s Parisian analogy. Seventy years earlier, on the eve of the French Revolution, Paris was served by twenty thousand water carriers—over three hundred times as many as San Francisco. The enormity of this gap should reinforce our image of San Francisco as a very small place indeed, but it should also be noted that San Francisco's received environment could never have yielded enough water for twenty thousand carriers to distribute. If there is any consolation in this, it is that water from El Polin and Mountain Lake was far purer and better tasting than water from the muddy and already-polluted Seine.[5]

The paucity of local resources that placed natural limits on the number of water carriers in San Francisco also promoted early efforts to import water from the city's hinterland. William Richardson, already noted as the first resident of Mexican Yerba Buena, expanded his transbay shipping business in 1850 to include water. Richardson, who for a decade and a half had carried the products of San Francisco Bay ranchos to the port at Yerba Buena/San Francisco, joined with his son-in-law Manuel Torres to operate the Sausalito Water and Steam Tug Company, which carried water to the city by barge from the springs of his Rancho Sausalito. In a rough boomtown whose leading citizens seemed eager to draw hopeful, if distorted, analogies between their little polis and more civilized places, no one thought of remarking that Richardson and Torres had their counterparts in Venice. Another city with limited access to fresh water, Venice had its *acquaroli*, who filled their boats daily in the Brenta to serve the people of a city too dependent on shallow rainwater tanks and too readily salinated by the slightest storm. Richardson, the great *acquarolo* of San Francisco, conducted his rancho's water down to beachfront tanks at Sausalito, from which it was pumped into barges, towed by tug, and then pumped again into distribution tanks on ships moored in the port of San Francisco. Richardson's bankruptcy and death in 1855 led to the eventual collapse of his water business, as did the land-based carriers' consolidation into a defensive monopoly in 1856. None of these efforts proved wholly adequate, however, and San Franciscans continually bridled at their limitations, especially in regards to the series of fires that repeatedly destroyed much of the town in the 1850s.[6]

The young city's thirst, and especially the fire of May 4, 1851, prompted the Common Council to consider permanent systematic methods of water delivery. In June of that year, the council approved a proposal made in March by Azro Merrifield to pipe water into the city from the same Mountain Lake from which the water carriers derived much of their own supply. The city gave Merrifield's Mountain Lake Water Company a twenty-year grant in return for which the municipality would receive free water and the right to appoint three of the five members of a rate commission.[7] Merrifield expected that water sales for private use would more than cover the expense of the city's free share as well as the cost of infrastructure development. He was wrong. But in the initial climate of enthusiasm that accompanied many of the fledgling city's growth and development efforts, the *Alta California* could not refrain from yet another Old World allusion, referring to the "beautiful little sheet of water" that Merrifield hoped to tap as "a Lake of Como in miniature."[8] Just as comparisons between Paris and San Francisco in the 1850s defied reason, the idea that the pond by the Presidio might be analogous to Lake Como, the third largest subalpine lake in northern Italy, was ludicrous at best. Perhaps an editor at the *Alta* saw himself as a latter-day Virgil and imagined that San Francisco's little Mountain Lake could bless the city with a historical legacy as grand as the one that the poet Virgil conferred on the lakes of Lombardy. But even fine poetry could not compensate for the fact that the water resources of Mountain Lake could not have sustained a growing city for very long and that their development would prove excessively expensive.

Romanticism aside, Merrifield and the city leaders envisioned a water system whose practical elements mirrored those of New York City's Croton aqueduct and reservoir, which had been placed in service in 1842. The brainchild of New York governor DeWitt Clinton, the Croton system was expected to bring the city twenty million gallons of water per day from the Croton River, forty miles north of city hall in Westchester County. After completion of a granite masonry dam and brick-lined masonry conduits, the New York system brought water to reservoirs in Central Park and Bryant Park and ultimately provided ninety-five million gallons per day by 1881. The *Alta* projected Mountain Lake's contribution to San Francisco at twenty-five million gallons per day.[9]

When Merrifield left San Francisco soon after his grant was awarded, a group of local investors purchased his franchise and set about surveying prospective pipeline routes from the lake to the city. They settled on a course that would follow the shoreline past Fort Point and end at a reservoir in North Beach. The conduit would consist of a cast-iron main, thirty inches in diameter, which would feed into a sixteen-inch diameter pipe carried over trestles into the heart of the city. The company estimated costs of almost $400,000, half of which covered piping and a quarter of which covered labor. Planners optimistically calculated profits at $360,000 serving three thousand houses in 1852, and $600,000 serving five thousand houses in 1853.

Unfortunately, no profits were to be had in either year, as construction only began in 1853. The company abandoned its initial plans for the main line and decided instead to build a 650-foot tunnel through the hillside on which Mountain Lake was perched in order to tap the lake sixteen feet below its surface.

Mountain Lake, ca.1890. Courtesy of the San Francisco History Center, San Francisco Public Library.

Although the Common Council extended completion deadlines three times in 1853 and 1854, the cost and difficulty of building the tunnel paralyzed the company's progress, and in 1857, with no water in sight, the city of San Francisco revoked its franchise. On January 1, 1857, John Bensley's San Francisco Water Company, also referred to simply as the Bensley Company, took over the franchise. Bensley gave up on the idea of tapping the "miniature Lake Como" and adopted a plan more consistent with that of New York, albeit of lesser scale and flow, which was to dam nearby Lobos Creek and direct its water along the same route originally foreseen by his failed predecessors. The Bensley Company started construction in early 1857 on a fairly primitive stone-and-earth dam across Lobos Creek and on a redwood flume to follow the path of Merrifield's never-built cast-iron pipeline. Crews also began work on a North Beach pumping station and a Russian Hill reservoir from which water would eventually flow by gravity into urban mains. The whole system was completed quickly, and on July 16, 1858, the first water from Lobos Creek entered the flume on its journey northward toward the Golden Gate and then eastward along the shore of the bay to Black Point. The steam-operated pumping station was situated there, in today's Fort Mason, and lifted close to one and a half million gallons of water a day up to an eight-million-gallon dirt-and-rock reservoir on Francisco and Hyde streets. Finally, the city would have its water.[10]

Black Point in 1864, showing the Bensley flume snaking around the bluff in the right foreground, with San Francisco Woolen Mills on the left. Courtesy of the San Francisco History Center, San Francisco Public Library.

Bensley's redwood flume—a rectangular trough a yard wide, four feet high, and several miles long—resembled an enormous, snaking miner's sluice and was certainly the one element of the new San Francisco water system that had the most visible impact on the landscape. In addition to its unsightly imposition on the peninsula's shoreline, an aqueduct made of wood—even with the rot-resistant properties of redwood—was hardly a testament to the permanence and presumed future grandiosity of the urban civilization it served. In these latter respects, the Bensley system not only compared unfavorably with New York's Croton system but was much shoddier than almost all of its Old World antecedents as well. The aqueducts of ancient Rome, of Istanbul, and of medieval and early modern Genoa, Paris, and Lisbon were all built with an eye to eternity that was hardly reflected in San Francisco's slipshod wooden millipede. San Franciscans soon discovered that water in a hurry was not the same thing as water forever. The long-term costs of throwing together an urban version of a here today, gone tomorrow, gold-country trough were greater than anticipated, as the natural setting conspired against technological simplicity.

Winter storms battered and damaged the Bensley flume annually, contaminating the water with mud and debris and bringing numerous complaints from customers. After heavy damage in the winter of 1861–62, the company responded to the problem by constructing two masonry tunnels through the hills most prone to mudslides—one through Fort Point hill above the Golden Gate and the other near the terminus and pumping station at Black Point. At a combined length of over one and a quarter mile, the tunnels, though essential to maintaining service, forced the company to assume substantial construction costs that were compounded by the decision to add a new 3,600,000-gallon reservoir at Hyde and Greenwich streets in 1861 and additional steam engines at the pumping station in 1864. Apparently, the increased cost of operations became especially burdensome when the company's chief engineer, Alexis Waldemar von Schmidt, defected to financier George Ensign's competing company, which brought water northward into the city from Pilarcitos Creek in San Mateo County. Ensign and von Schmidt's new Spring Valley Water Company quickly emerged as the principal threat to its predecessor's survival, so much so that for several months in 1864 a group of Bensley employees apparently saw fit to secretly siphon a million gallons of water per day from the Spring Valley main line into the Bensley system's delivery pipes. With the larcenous employees' arrest and subsequent trial, a progressively weakened Bensley Company, unable to pay damages, was absorbed into the Spring Valley Water Company in 1865. The latter would control the city's water supply for the next half century, until many leading San Franciscans pushed for municipal ownership and launched their now-famous campaign for a permanent, "inexhaustible" supply from the Sierras.[11]

Water is of course a necessity of life, and life is consequently drawn to it. Plants evolve to produce root systems that are adapted to draw water in conformity with the conditions of specific climatic and topographic zones. Animals are instinctively attracted by their thirst to such water as flows through, or pools within, their habitats. Human beings consciously situate themselves as much as possible on or near water, knowing their lives depend upon it. It is no surprise then that every great city of ancient times, and even of the early modern period, was riverine. It is not unusual though, for cities to outgrow the capacities of their immediate fluvial basins. The ancient Romans were not sated by the Tiber, so they built their famous aqueducts to carry water from the surrounding countryside to the city. The Turks later built equally remarkable structures at Istanbul. In Europe, from the fourteenth century onward, old aqueducts were refurbished and new ones were built to serve the cities of Lisbon, Genoa, Paris, and Toledo. The impetus for all of these great waterworks, even as they inevitably reproduced and strengthened the wealth and power of social and political elites, was the ultimate use value of their product— water for drinking, washing, and food production. As such, the most significant distinction between "primitive" water and "civilized" water was the reallocation of human labor from the displacement of people to the displacement of water.

Nineteenth-century San Francisco, though, brought a new element into its water acquisition history that was rooted in the city's economic role as financier and marketer of precious metals from the Sierras. Both Alexis von Schmidt and his successor at Spring Valley, Hermann Schussler, were determined advocates of San Francisco's right to outlying watersheds. Both were engineers, and both played a role in the silver boom. When the restless von Schmidt left the newly enlarged Spring Valley Water Company soon after its acquisition of the Bensley system, Schussler was hired as his replacement. In his former position as a draftsman for the Risdon Iron Works, Schussler had helped design the high-pressure pipes employed in hydraulic mining operations. Over the course of his half-century tenure with Spring Valley, he was largely responsible for guiding most of the water from northern San Mateo County's watersheds up to the city of San Francisco, and perhaps most famously, for the Crystal Springs Dam and Reservoir, visible today as a landmark alongside Interstate 280.[17]

As for von Schmidt, his significance rested in his pioneering plan to harness the waters of the Sierra Nevada for use by the cities, factories, farms, and mines of northern California. Von Schmidt was not only the first to conceive of such a project, but he also served as an exemplary agent of a modern economy's tendency to conflate the commodity value of nature with its intrinsic life-giving qualities. Yes, San Franciscans needed water to drink, but, as it turns out, this was ancillary to water's potentially profitable uses. Much as the technology for San Francisco's famed cable cars was a direct derivative of Andrew Hallidie's cable and skip system for moving Sierra ore, von Schmidt's plan for San Francisco's potable water system derived from his earlier efforts to channel Sierra water to the mines and mills and smelters of the Comstock Lode.

Already in 1863, while von Schmidt was still serving as an engineer for Spring Valley, he also sat on the board of directors of the Lake Tahoe and Nevada Water Company. In that capacity, he proposed to Virginia City's board of aldermen that water from Lake Tahoe could be pumped over the hills at Carson City and through the Washoe Basin to a storage reservoir on Mt. Davidson, from which it could be piped to the towns and mines of the Comstock Lode. The aldermen rejected the proposal on account of the high cost of pumping water to Virginia City's lofty six-thousand-foot elevation, although exactly a decade later, Hermann Schussler actually effected the plan with the backing of "silver king" James Flood of Nob Hill fame. Spurned by Nevada, von Schmidt wasted no time establishing the Lake Tahoe and San Francisco Water Works Company in 1865, with the intent of bringing the mountain lake's water 163 miles across the state to the Bay Area. His plan was nothing if not grandiose. Von Schmidt intended to dam the Truckee River where it flowed out of Lake Tahoe, thereby raising the lake's level by six feet, with each foot supplying an anticipated 137 million gallons of water daily for a possible output of over 800 million gallons a day in wet years. Von Schmidt further foresaw a second diversion dam downstream, from which a canal would branch off to Squaw Valley. Additionally, a tunnel would carry water to a tributary of the North Fork of the American River near Soda Springs and then into another canal to serve the hydraulic mines at Iowa Hill, Michigan Bluffs, and other foothill mining districts. The American River itself would become the conduit to a forty-mile canal linked to a large reservoir at Auburn. From there, the water could serve valley towns and farms as it traveled by pipeline to Sacramento. From Sacramento, the aqueduct would head to Benicia, and under the Carquinez Straits, with branches to Vallejo and Stockton. The main line would continue on through the East Bay to a reservoir in the Oakland hills, and from there along the bottom of the bay to its terminal at Hunters Point for use by the city of San Francisco.[13]

Though ambitious, clever, and technologically feasible, von Schmidt's plan aroused immediate opposition from officials and newspapers in Nevada, who feared that the Truckee River's diversion would destroy any prospect for that state's autonomous industrial and agricultural development. The Nevadans' anxieties were certainly valid when considered against the backdrop of their near-total economic domination by capitalists housed on San Francisco's Nob Hill. Virginia City's *Daily Territorial Enterprise* expressed these fears quite well in the winter of 1870:

> San Francisco speculators have been plundering this state for many years almost without rebuke. They have ruined our best mines, compelled us to feed their extravagance, and played foot-ball with the vital interests of the whole Commonwealth. We have submitted to all this, and shall probably be forced to submit to it for some time to come; but our water supplies from Lake Tahoe must not be tampered with by these gentlemen. They may take the gold and silver from our hills, and bind us in vassalage to the caprice of their stock boards, but the pure water that comes to us from Lake Tahoe, that drives our mills and makes glad our waste spaces, is God's exhaustless gift, and the hand of man cannot deprive us of it.[14]

While opposition from Nevada was not surprising, the fact that even many Californians were hostile to the Lake Tahoe water plan warrants explanation. The obstacles that von Schmidt encountered from within his own state derived in small measure from the competing interests of multiple water users and in large part from a public suspicious of government corruption and inclined toward antimonopoly sentiments. On the first score, the California town of Truckee housed a number of anti-diversion advocates. Situated just a dozen miles downstream from its namesake river's outlet from Lake Tahoe, Truckee's factories and mills depended on the river for power and as a means of floating its felled trees to market in Nevada. Because Truckee sat on the east face of the Sierras, its fate was linked far more to that of Nevada than to California. But while Truckee's future might have been of little interest to San Franciscans, the support that several of California's agricultural and commercial valley towns gave to the Lake Tahoe scheme was in some ways more troubling than the opposition raised in timber country. When the *Marysville Union* declared that von Schmidt's project would cause "hundreds and thousands of acres of the dry plains [to] be made into pleasant homes," and the Sacramento *Daily Bee* noted that "If San Francisco gives $10,000,000 to somebody to bring in the waters of Lake Tahoe, they will have to come by our door and we can have them cheap, clear and in abundance," many San Franciscans wondered if their property taxes should subsidize the interest on bonds for a project that would unduly benefit others, and that, some argued, might yield only twice the water of San Mateo County. In a strange inversion of reality, the *Alta* even alluded to San Francisco's sacking at the hands of Sacramento robber barons.[15]

Despite this initial climate of negativity, the San Francisco Board of Supervisors accepted a revised financing proposal from von Schmidt in April 1871. The board agreed to issue $6 million in bonds at 6 percent interest—down from $10 million at 7 percent—to strengthen the Lake Tahoe and San Francisco Water Works Company's credit, and only after water began flowing into the city. Von Schmidt expected to be able to deliver the water within four years. Mayor Thomas Selby vetoed the supervisors' decision, however, due to his concern that the new plan would simply put the city at the mercy of yet another water corporation like the much-despised Spring Valley Company. Selby much preferred that the city own its own water system. When the mayor established a water commission that concluded that peninsular water supplies would be sufficient for San Francisco's use well into the future, von Schmidt's plans suffered yet another blow.

Mayor Selby's hope of one day securing a municipally owned water supply for San Francisco reflected widely held public concerns about the marriage of corrupt legislatures and venal businessmen. Although many conflicts over resource use in nineteenth-century America were rooted in the competition between two or several private exploiters, a growing corps of antimonopolists also saw a larger issue at stake in the conflict between well-organized and well-connected private interests and the general public good. A number of circumstances surrounding the evolution of the Lake Tahoe plan did much to fuel the impression that these larger issues were at play. For example, the well-publicized tendency of the 1870 state legislature to subsidize private enterprises at public expense made many Californians suspicious of bond measures such as those proposed for the water project. Members of the public remained skeptical of their federal representatives as well. A United States senator from California, the Republican Cornelius Cole, took up the cause of von Schmidt's Lake Tahoe and San Francisco Water Company in Washington with Senate bill 572 on February 21, 1870. Senator Cole made a career of linking the economic development of California with federal largesse to private enterprise. Cole kept the Forty-first Congress's Committee on Public Lands very busy with the many land-grant bills he drafted, including Senate bill 186 in March 1869, which sought a federal land subsidy for the Sacramento Irrigation and Navigation Canal Company, and Senate bill 775, which in April 1870 sought to uphold the preemption claims of Yosemite squatters James Hutchings and James Lamon.[16]

From a public relations perspective, the language of S572 was destined to cause a furor. The bill would have provided von Schmidt's company with a right-of-way through federal lands for construction of the aqueduct; free use of all the earth, timber, and stone along the right-of-way; and a substantial land grant of alternate square miles in a checkerboard pattern for twenty miles on both sides of the aqueduct. It was not the bill's novelty that aroused opposition, but rather its disturbing familiarity. It resembled in virtually all respects the Pacific Railway Acts of 1862 and 1864, which had facilitated the construction of the Central Pacific Railroad's trans-Sierra line, propelling California's "Big Four"—Collis Huntington, Leland Stanford, Mark Hopkins, and Charles Crocker—on their path of rising economic and political dominance. No one had forgotten that in his capacity as governor in 1861, Stanford had pushed through a state bond measure to finance his own railroad company, and few astute observers could neglect the fact that intense lobbying by the Central Pacific had, in the second of the federal railway acts, effectively subordinated the public interest to the private by restructuring loans of U.S. Treasury bonds from a first mortgage position to a second.[17]

The ongoing lessons of the Central Pacific (CP) years cast a substantial pall over public attitudes toward the Lake Tahoe and San Francisco Water Company, and it was hardly helpful that the two businesses became entangled in 1871. In 1870, Leland Stanford sought a partnership with the Tahoe Company on construction of a joint water and railroad tunnel through the Sierras that would have substantially reduced the length, grade, and wintertime danger of the railroad line while relieving it of some expense. Von Schmidt and the Tahoe directors were initially resistant to what they feared was a power grab, but they soon gave in under the pressure of litigation. In the spring of 1871, the Donner Boom and Logging Company filed an injunction suit in Placer County against the Lake Tahoe Water Company, arguing that von Schmidt's dam disrupted the flow of the Truckee River and infringed on the Donner Company's extensive water rights. It was no accident that Donner Boom and Logging was a subsidiary of the Central Pacific Railroad, and that in August 1871, it dropped its lawsuit in conjunction with the signing of a tunnel-boring contract between the Tahoe Company and the CP. As fate would have it, the death of George Ensign, a major Tahoe Company investor and former Spring Valley founder, coupled with stockholder complaints of inequitable distribution of the tunneling costs, led to the contract's cancellation before the end of the year.

Alexis von Schmidt spent the next six years revamping and repeatedly resubmitting his water plan to the San Francisco Board of Supervisors, but to no avail. Another decade later, in 1887, rumors that the Tahoe Company faced imminent revival at the hands of silver king James Flood gave the moribund project a brief but entirely chimerical boost. In 1895, von Schmidt's plan was almost resurrected by state assemblyman Calvin Ewing, who proposed a bill that would have established a state-owned water and electric company based on the Lake Tahoe scheme. The bill failed due to constitutional limitations on state bond debt. Nonetheless, Nevadans took California's renewed interest in the lake seriously enough that their senator, William Morris Stewart, attempted to secure congressional approval for a Lake Tahoe National Park in 1900. This bill failed as well but revealed the connection that often linked preservationist means to utilitarian ends in early twentieth-century natural resource management. The most telling and salient section of the bill that would have protected the lake would also have secured much of the Truckee River's water for Nevada's farmers. In the political arena at least, Lake Tahoe had little intrinsic value if left economically unused. The question was rather who would use it—the people and industries of San Francisco or its subordinate market towns; the farmers, miners, or lumbermen of California; or the farmers, miners, or small cities of Nevada? At least in the short run, the political contest between competing users simply preserved the status quo.[18]

When von Schmidt died in May 1906, he had had the misfortune of witnessing the near-total destruction of San Francisco in the last weeks of his life. The great earthquake that leveled the city in April also ruptured the gas mains, and there was not enough Spring Valley water to put out the fires. The conflagration that raged for days finished the job that the temblor had started, and it was just a matter of time before the whole water question took political center stage again. When it did, the late von Schmidt's plan to quench the city with Sierra—although not Tahoe—water had become the only plan in town, although its realization continued to be hampered by dissension and legal obstacles.

While water projects like von Schmidt's operated on the presumption that their rights to essential water were legally defensible, things were rarely so straightforward in practice. Von Schmidt's initial confidence that his company, if so contracted by the state, could secure Lake Tahoe water for the people of California was based on reasonable legal principles. Federal law holds that all navigable rivers, lakes, and streams have been public since time immemorial, and that in colonial British North America, these bodies of water were held in trust for the people by the king. With the birth of the United States, the several states that comprised the new nation each acquired the public-trust ownership once exercised by the monarchy. The U.S. Supreme Court upheld this public trust doctrine several times before California's annexation to the Union, in *Arnold v. Mundy*, 1821; *Martin v. Waddell*, 1842; and *Pollard v. Hagan*, 1845.[19] Given Lake Tahoe's location, two-thirds within California, and the situation of the Truckee River's source on the California side of the lake, the Golden State could arguably claim public-trust ownership of their waters. Yet the evolution of California water law, the state's political and business climate, and the consequences of urbanization in an arid region all conspired to make any water allocation plan a complicated matter. The particular environmental conditions of the American West, and the awkward ways in which its inhabitants sought to adapt their customs and laws to them, cut across all of these factors and compounded the difficulties they presented.

Water law is a good point of departure for understanding these problems. The traditional underpinnings of the U.S. Supreme Court's interpretation of public water rights had a corollary in the nation's system of private water rights as well. Just as English common law provided the basis for treating rivers as the public domain, so did it establish the framework for the riparian laws of the original colonies, and thereafter, the eastern states of the United States. All of these eastern states held that usufructuary water rights attached to properties that were riparian to bodies of water. In other words, a landowner whose property abutted a river, stream, pond, lake, or well-defined underground channel could draw water from that source for reasonable use. The doctrine's origin in the wet climate of the British Isles also meant that riparian rights were seldom quantified.

When California achieved statehood in 1850, this well-established wet-climate doctrine was adopted by the new state legislature.

In practice, however, the gold rush that prompted statehood in the first place also planted a novel and opposing water doctrine on California soil—appropriative rights. The many gold claims that were not situated on the banks of natural streams required diverted sources of water to flush the diggings. Toward this end, miners built flumes and sluices to move water from its source and posted claim notices at the points of diversion. In 1855, the California Supreme Court gave legal recognition to this common practice in *Irwin v. Phillips*. After the gold rush ended, California's growing population of farmers and ranchers needed water as well. As in the other nineteen western states where climate and geography make access to riparian lands far from assured, many of the newcomers depended on water diversion to make their holdings productive. Hence, appropriative rights, or the system of "first in time, first in right" coexisted alongside riparian law in an uneasy arrangement.

In 1886, the California Supreme Court finally affirmed the legal preeminence of riparianism over appropriation in *Lux v. Haggin*. Fifteen years earlier, the cattlemen Henry Miller and Charles Lux had purchased 328,000 acres of land, including portions of the San Joaquin River's banks over a length of 120 miles. Miller also owned land further south on the Kern River, where his rival was James Ben Ali Haggin, a Kentuckian who had risen into the Nob Hill elite. Between 1873 and 1890, Haggin and his partner Lloyd Tevis purchased large tracts of Kern County real estate from the Southern Pacific Railroad and established their own land company with holdings in excess of 410,000 acres. Haggin's Kern County Land Company also benefited from its owners' fraudulent manipulation of the 1877 Desert Land Act through the use of dummy entrymen and false mortgages. To make their land attractive for resale to prospective farmers, Haggin and Tevis took over the Calloway Canal near Bakersfield and built additional canals to irrigate their holdings. In an 1881 state court dispute between the two sets of land speculators, Miller claimed riparian rights and Haggin appropriation rights to the same sources of water. Between the filing of the initial suit and its settlement by the state's supreme court, the controversy roused rural Californians, who quickly took up position as warring factions of riparian ranchers and appropriative farmers. Since farmers were in the majority, a legal battle that was no more or less than a contest between two versions of land grabbing by the wealthy was contorted in the public mind into a struggle between elitism and democracy, with Haggin and appropriation carrying the mantle of democracy. In actuality, the conflict was falsely framed. Both sides practiced irrigation, no one challenged fraudulent land acquisition, and there was no discussion of the fact that appropriation might just as easily serve elite interests by harming populations that were proximate to water by moving the supply to serve a distant few. Additionally, from an environmental perspective, it was notable how readily people presumed at first that the reclamation of arid lands was intrinsically democratic.

The California Supreme Court's decision to uphold Lux and Miller's riparian rights produced a complicated compromise in the state's water law. Any land purchased from the state or situated on a former Mexican land grant was deemed riparian. Any landowner who had taken water from the public domain before 1866 had appropriation rights, with transferability by sale. All grants after 1866 were riparian, and appropriators who drew from the same sources could only use such water by permission of, or be forced to relinquish it on demand from, the riparian owner. Finally, all riparian owners on the same stream had coequal rights. In effect though, the decision to grant Miller and Lux's water rights legal preeminence over those of Haggin and Tevis had fewer consequences to the disputants than one might imagine. Realizing that neither party could employ the full flow of the Kern River, and fearing the property damage that accompanied wet years, the two sides agreed to a division of the river's natural assets and the construction of a shared holding reservoir. While Miller and Lux therefore had continued access to water for the cattle they raised in the valley and processed in their San Francisco Butchertown slaughterhouses, Haggin and Tevis continued to irrigate the lands of the Kern County Land Company. Within a few years, many of the local farmers who had sided with Haggin abandoned their allegiance in despondency as water diverted into the reservoir caused their own ditches to dry up. In Kern County, the illusory dichotomy between riparian and appropriative rights finally evaporated in the face of corporate monopolization of water.[20]

The significance of all of this to San Francisco's own urban water saga is that the city's early water companies, whether actual or only prospective—Bensley, Spring Valley, Lake Tahoe and San Francisco—all had to acquire private rights to water under the same contentious and competitive conditions that prevailed in the rural sections of the state. While rural folk feared and resisted the kind of monopolization of water that was ultimately actualized in Kern County, urbanites like San Franciscans were caught on the horns of a dilemma. Since urban water users in general have no direct access to the resource, either individually or in sufficient quantities for the collectivity, they inevitably become entirely dependent on external sources of supply that require heavy capitalization to exploit. Where water is deemed a private possession, distribution monopolies are both necessary to the provision of effective urban service and an economic threat to the consumers of that service. Furthermore, under prevailing legal conditions in California, the companies' need for riparian lands from which they could extract water for distant appropriative purposes always had the potential to put them at odds with nonurban users. It should be noted that the English riparian model that was imported to the United States and then to California was quite ill-suited for Western urban conditions. In its sheer simplicity, riparianism assumed an abundance of the resource, certainly in relation to population, and was based largely on rural subsistence use. Neither of these circumstances prevailed in San Francisco or anywhere else in the urban West. Consequently, one of the great problems raised by urbanization in relation to nature was magnified in the case of San Francisco. How could a substantial concentration of human beings in an arid setting where water was subject to private property rights access that most essential material of life in a way they deemed just and equitable? And what would be the consequences of their efforts?

One might say with some justification that when it came to California water, nature's aridity aggravated fears of monopolies. But this really is an oversimplification, since California is neither Arizona nor the Sahara. There is plenty of water in California. The problem is that much of it originates as snow high in the mountains where no one would ever build a city or plant a farm, while the most commercially attractive land, from the point of view of urban and agricultural development and ease of transport, lies a couple of hundred miles west of this source. There were consequently two separate factors that became entwined in San Francisco's struggle for water. The first was political, and entailed a gross disaffection with the corruption endemic to nineteenth-century urban machine politics. This political element fueled San Franciscans' hostility to the Spring Valley Company monopoly and its venal allies at city hall throughout the late nineteenth and early twentieth centuries.

The second factor was natural—albeit with economic overtones—and resulted from the fact that San Francisco simply did not have enough local water to sustain the kind of growth that a city with pretensions of greatness required. These two factors together explain much of what happened between the depression years of the mid-1870s, when von Schmidt's company foundered, and the early 1900s, when San Francisco embarked on its tortuous path toward municipalized water. Along the way, a minority railed against the very concept of privatized water, as evident in the debates of the 1878–79 state constitutional convention, where delegate J. S. Hager of San Francisco declared, "That which should be open and free to the world has been reduced to private ownership, a thing never heard of in any country of the world except California, where water, the essential of life, is made the subject of private ownership by individuals and held by them."[21] Delegate Hager's remarks may have evoked modern socialism on the one hand or the ethos of the ancients on the other, but the essential fact remained that for Hager and all others concerned, "the essential of life" was still to be a form of property. Those who sought the public ownership of water would simply have substituted a form of state property over a corporate one. The constitutional convention, not inclined toward too radical a solution to the water problem, framed Article 14, mandating state regulatory control of water rates. In so doing, the representatives of the people of California preserved private property rights in water but recognized as well that water ultimately served a public purpose that needed to be protected.

The political treatment of California water as an essential public resource toward the end of the nineteenth century laid the groundwork for the emergence of the urban water systems of the early twentieth, both in San Francisco and Los Angeles. The primacy of these cities, and hence of urbanism itself, in shaping the economic history of the state has already been well established. With regards to California water, the historian William Kahrl has noted: "The impetus for water development on a massive scale originated in the cities, not on the farms, and the particular problems they faced were a consequence of growing up in a state which developed backward and in the wrong direction. . . . For the nation as a whole, the central event distinguishing the nineteenth century from the twentieth was the gradual transition from a predominantly rural to an urban society. But in California this transformation began almost simultaneously with the first major influx of population."[22] Thus framed in an urban political context, the focus on dangerous monopolies, corrupt politicians, and thirsty cities assured that the water question would be addressed in a way that centered exclusively on human consumption. And yet, as the twentieth century opened, San Francisco's efforts to quench its thirst launched a major contest over the limits of that vision—a contest that absorbed the efforts of old-guard machine politicians and progressive reformers, local politicians and federal officials, engineers and business leaders, and the city's own contribution to a growing panoply of national wilderness enthusiasts, the Sierra Club. The battleground was the Hetch Hetchy Valley in Yosemite, which had become a national park in 1890, thanks to the efforts of John Muir and other defenders of wilderness. Before the struggle was over, it developed into one of the most significant episodes in the history of the nascent conservationist and preservationist movements of the early twentieth century.

Just as the engineers Hermann Schussler and Alexis von Schmidt played piv-
otal roles in San Francisco's nineteenth-century water history, their younger
counterparts Marsden Manson and Carl E. Grunsky were its central figures at the
onset of the twentieth. Manson was a West Virginian with science and engineering degrees from the Virginia Military Institute as well a doctorate in physics
and chemistry from the University of California at Berkeley. A resident of California since 1878, Manson devoted decades of his life to various works of civil
and hydraulic engineering and traveled widely in the Sierras as a state consultant on the effects of mining debris on California's river systems. While on his
mountain sojourns, Manson developed a keen interest in both the beauty of the
Sierra Nevada range and its potential as a source of water and hydroelectric
power for the people of his state. An avid outdoorsman who lived and worked in
San Francisco, Manson joined the Sierra Club in 1895, just three years after its
founding. In so doing, he embodied quite well the internal conflicts of a generation of upper-middle-class American city dwellers who were committed to the
development of urban civilization on the one hand and to its antidote of wilderness recreation on the other.

From the mid-1890s until 1912, Marsden Manson was involved in one way
or another with San Francisco politics. His early participation in an engineering
study of problems with the city's drainage system convinced him of the need for
municipalization of utilities and their management by technical experts. This
placed him squarely in the progressive political camp, and when San Francisco
obtained a new charter in 1900 that recognized the need for precisely such a
technocracy, Manson served on the first board of public works as an appointee
of Mayor James D. Phelan. Over the next three years, and again as city engineer
from 1908 to 1912, Manson dedicated himself tirelessly to promoting the cause
of municipally owned Sierra water for the city of San Francisco. Not the least of
his concerns was the Spring Valley monopoly, its stranglehold on proximate supplies, and its undue political influence. Manson saw the 1900 city charter as a
momentous opportunity to replace private water with public water while at the
same time providing efficient and honest government to the city.

City Engineer Carl Grunsky led the San Francisco Board of Public Works on
which Manson served. Grunsky reviewed several proposals for improving the
city's water supplies, including a plan to buy out Spring Valley. Because the
company was not eager to sell at an acceptable price, and the board estimated a
substantial increase in future water demand, Grunsky quickly began to consider
plans for alternate sources that could supply as much as sixty million gallons a
day. Several possibilities existed, including once again Lake Tahoe, Mount

Shasta, or even the Sacramento River. Mayor Phelan directed Grunsky to consider as well the option of tapping Clear Lake, the San Joaquin River, and the famed gold country streams—the Stanislaus, Yuba, Feather, and American rivers. However, the board of public works found all of these lacking in some way, either because of inadequate water quality, competing legal claims, or technical obstacles to storage.[23]

By process of elimination, San Francisco settled on the Tuolumne River in Yosemite National Park as the most likely candidate to provide the city with an abundant, pure, inexpensive, and municipally owned supply of water into the indefinite future. The decision, as controversial as it would become, was based on sound technical and legal foundations. From a technical standpoint, the Tuolumne had three principal assets. First, it carried a substantial amount of the Sierra Nevada's runoff. With its source in a perpetual glacier on thirteen-thousand-foot-high Mount Lyell and a watershed of 652 square miles, the Tuolumne could certainly be counted on for steady production. Second, at Hetch Hetchy meadows, it flowed through a channel flanked by impermeable half-mile-high granite walls that offered an ideal dam site. And finally, the valley floor's 3,500-foot elevation meant that virtually no pumping would be required to deliver the river's water to San Francisco. In addition to these natural assets, from a legal standpoint Grunsky and other city officials saw the Tuolumne's situation on federal lands as an advantage rather than a limitation. With no extant competing private claims to the water, the city's task of access would presumably be simplified. On this latter score, San Francisco's position compared favorably at that moment in history with Los Angeles's, at least in theory.[24]

One should remember that even San Francisco's temporary role as America's principal Pacific metropolis was not assured by its natural setting so much as created by active human intervention and environmental rearrangement. Other Pacific cities were blessed and hindered by their own landscapes and transformed more or less adequately by their own human occupants under circumstances not entirely of their choosing. In San Francisco's earliest days, the grand natural harbor provided by its bay, coupled with the accident of the gold rush and the fact that the fluvial highways of gold country flowed toward that bay, gave the city a tremendous initial boost. In the 1870s, years after the end of the gold rush, some of San Francisco's most prominent capitalists labored to preserve their city's primacy over an ascendant prospective southern rival with a great natural harbor of its own—San Diego. The Central Pacific's Big Four—Stanford, Huntington, Crocker, and Hopkins—laid the groundwork for Los Angeles's future growth by connecting the sleepy agricultural hamlet to the Cen-

Hetch Hetchy Valley before the dam. Courtesy of the National Park Service, Yosemite Park, Hetch Hetchy valley early 1900s, *RL-15,688.*

tral Pacific trunk line to San Francisco and transforming L.A. into the southern terminus of their transcontinental railroad. Their primary motive was to promote the commercial development of Los Angeles at the expense of a potentially more competitive San Diego.

It should be noted that San Diego did face its own environmental obstacles to growth. The city had no potentially rich agricultural hinterland comparable to San Francisco's proximate Central Valley, nor did its surrounding landscape offer particularly good rail access for transcontinental shipping. In 1852, the Army Corps of Engineers had rejected Jacumba Pass and other access routes from the east, and the remaining options—the San Gorgonio and Cajon passes— pointed more logically to a Los Angeles terminal. In addition, the beautiful natural harbor that had served San Diego so well in the days of the hide and tallow trade, if left unimproved, would eventually have been as deficient as a modern port as Yerba Buena cove had once been. It was not until the late nineteenth and early twentieth centuries that politically engaged civic leaders engineered San Diego's modern port into existence. Nonetheless, in the economic and technological context of the 1870s and 1880s, the Big Four understood the power of mobilized capital and political will well enough to imagine a San Diego threat—

so much so that Charles Crocker declared that he and his colleagues "would blot San Diego out of existence if we could, but as we can't do that we shall keep it back as long as we can." The inland village of Los Angeles seemed far less dangerous to the interests of the state's preeminent shipping magnates.[25] As historian Robert Fogelson has noted of L.A. at this critical juncture in its history, "The town's cardinal deficiency—its inadequate and unprotected port—was its saving grace."[26]

Deficient as a port, early Los Angeles, despite the aridity of its climate, was not deficient in water, at least from the perspective of a preindustrial farming community. Unlike San Francisco, it at least had a river and occupied a seat on a broad swath of cultivable land. When the first governor of California, Felipe de Neve, authorized the construction of the Los Angeles pueblo in 1781, he selected a site that was ideally situated in relation to its water supply. North of the pueblo, the Los Angeles River, or Rio de Porciúncula, is pushed to the surface from its subterranean source by the ridge that forms the Santa Monica Mountains, assuring plenty of water even during the dry summer months. The pueblo's habitations were built on a terrace above the river's expected flood level, and fields were anticipated in the bottomlands along its banks. Thanks to the Los Angeles River, as late as the 1870s, prior to the arrival of the Central Pacific, Los Angeles was one of the nation's richest agricultural basins and appeared to visitors as a garden paradise in the desert. In 1849, not long after the pueblo passed over to United States sovereignty, U.S. Army Lieutenant Edward Ord became one of the first of many American arrivals to sing the region's praises: "Rising the slope . . . we see the city of Los Angeles. Someone points across the plain to a thin line of green some 15 miles off. Where are the houses? Oh, they are surrounded by trees and vineyards. . . . By and by we rode between willow hedges, and zanjas . . . of flowing water went perling along the roads and thro the fields of corn and the long rows of vines, the almond and orange groves. All around us was a refreshing green, so grateful to the eyes and nose after the arid brown and yellow of the hot plains."[27]

When Americans inherited Los Angeles from the Mexicans, they also acquired the water rights that had made the land green. Consequently, again unlike San Francisco, American Los Angeles was founded on a system of pueblo rights to water. As the successor to a Spanish pueblo, the city of Los Angeles possessed from the outset a "paramount right to the beneficial use of all needed, naturally occurring surface and subsurface water from the entire watershed of the stream flowing through the original pueblo." Under California law, the quantity of water available under this system of rights increases with population and with land annexations, limited only by the vague restriction that its use be reasonable and beneficial. One can readily imagine how, from the completion of the Central Pacific link onward, development in the Los Angeles basin quickly outstripped available supplies of water. Even the proliferation of artesian wells from the late 1870s onward failed to keep pace with growth, which in turn further depleted the local aquifers. With the intensifying pace of urbanization that pushed Los Angeles's population over one hundred thousand in 1900 and over three hundred thousand in 1910, L.A. and San Francisco found themselves contemporary competitors in a search for external water sources that would promote their own local development and the collective self-interest of Angelenos on the one hand or San Franciscans on the other.

One-time mayor, longtime city engineer, and Los Angeles City Water Company boss Fred Eaton had been pushing a plan for a canal from the southern Sierras since 1892. In 1907, after a period of drought, Los Angeles officials finally agreed and announced their plans to draw on the resources of the Owens Valley, where city engineers subsequently tapped the Owens River and channeled it into a 223-mile-long aqueduct that brought its first water to Los Angeles and the San Fernando Valley in 1913. While the enormity of contemporary Los Angeles is unimaginable without the aqueduct, many of the water acquisition methods employed by the city's water company—later the Los Angeles Department of Water and Power—aroused the ire of those country folks who saw their lands dry up to serve the needs of distant urbanites, commercial farmers, and land speculators. More than once, their anger erupted into violence, including dynamite attacks on the aqueduct in 1927. While the Los Angeles project proved to be a greater success than San Francisco's in terms of its size, the speed of its completion, and its lower cost, its biggest problem was the conflict it generated with smaller private claimants of water. Although the shooting wars of the 1920s could not have been anticipated in the early 1900s, San Francisco's designs on Yosemite Park's Tuolumne were geared to avoid all of the legal machinations and possible difficulties that might have arisen if the city had put itself on Los Angeles's course.[28] Yet, while San Franciscans escaped one form of conflict, they were forced to confront another as the city became embroiled in a national debate over resource conservation and wilderness preservation. The outcome would reveal much about Americans' attitudes toward nature in the early twentieth century.

In 1901, subsequent to City Engineer Grunsky's investigations, Mayor Phelan, acting as a private citizen, applied to the Department of the Interior for water rights in the Hetch Hetchy Valley. The city's interest, and the deliberations that preceded Phelan's application, were kept secret for fear of competition, although Phelan later assigned his claim to the city in 1903. The subterfuge arose from the events of a quarter century earlier. In 1874, San Francisco had sought to operate outside its arrangements with the Spring Valley Water Company by trying to purchase independent sources in Alameda County's Calaveras Valley, only to find the private water company buying out those rights before the city could act on its own. Phelan had no desire to set the stage for a repetition of this scenario. Unfortunately for him, obstacles immediately emerged at both the local and national levels.

Locally, the Democratic mayor's use of city police to break a strike of teamsters and longshoremen in 1901 alienated many of his traditionally Democratic working-class supporters. Consequently, in 1902 he was turned out of office by Eugene Schmitz, the candidate of an upstart third-party movement that capitalized opportunistically on labor's disenchantment under the apt label of Union Labor Party (ULP). The ULP proved to be a poor champion of the worker, but an excellent example of an old-fashioned corrupt political machine. Schmitz, his partisan colleagues on the board of supervisors, and their party's boss, Abraham Ruef, were more interested in a personally lucrative deal with the Bay Cities Water Company than in Phelan's Hetch Hetchy plan. Bay Cities, once associated with Alexis von Schmidt, owned water rights on the tributaries of the American and Cosumnes rivers. More importantly, the company quietly offered Ruef a $1 million kickback out of an estimated profit of $3 million from the sale of its holdings to the city. In 1906, the board of supervisors resolved to drop the Hetch Hetchy plan altogether and might have succeeded in killing it permanently if not for the graft prosecutions that brought down the ULP administration in 1907.[29]

On the national level, former Mayor Phelan and other supporters of the Hetch Hetchy plan were disappointed by the initial failure of the Roosevelt administration to lend San Francisco the support necessary to draw water from federal lands. Despite the passage of Stockton representative Marion DeVries's Right of Way bill in 1901, which would have paved the legal road to aqueduct construction, the Interior Department was loath to grant the city's permit. In January 1903, Secretary of the Interior Ethan Allen Hitchcock weighed the merits of San Francisco's case against his own obligations under the Yosemite Park Act of 1890. Hitchcock ruled that the Yosemite Act in fact required him to protect the park's natural endowments while the Right of Way Act merely permitted him to authorize the construction of aqueducts and dams. In the balance, therefore, he felt compelled to place the integrity of Yosemite Park and the office of the Interior Secretary over the interests of the city of San Francisco. The city's application was denied.

In 1904, as former city engineer Grunsky left San Francisco to join the Isthmian Canal Commission, Marsden Manson—no longer on the board of public works—became the city's chief promoter of the Hetch Hetchy project. On a trip to Washington, D.C., in 1905, rather than trying to sway Secretary Hitchcock, Manson circumvented him and took his arguments to what he hoped would be the more sympathetic ears of wise-use advocate Gifford Pinchot, Theodore Roosevelt's close friend and U.S. Chief Forester. Manson also approached James Garfield, director of the Bureau of Corporations and future Interior Secretary, and eventually sought out the president himself. When Attorney General W. H. Moody advised President Roosevelt that the 1901 Rights of Way Act empowered the Interior Secretary with the right of executive judgment in matters such as the Hetch Hetchy proposition (meaning that the secretary's hands were not tied by the Yosemite Park Act), Manson revived San Francisco's rejected application hoping that the president would move it forward. Despite these advances, upon his return to San Francisco, Manson continued to confront the obstructionism of the ULP-led city administration. Mayor Schmitz and the board of supervisors did put Manson to work on a new water committee but directed him to evaluate only proposals that did not include the Hetch Hetchy scheme.

Manson did his best to take advantage of this limited situation to draft negative reports on the proposals of the Bay Cities Water Company as well as on a plan to tap the Mokelumne River—used today, incidentally, by the East Bay Municipal Utilities District that serves Oakland and Berkeley. Frustrated, Manson and other proponents of a Hetch Hetchy dam finally saw their opportunities reopened in the aftermath of the 1906 earthquake and fire and the graft prosecution of Schmitz and sixteen San Francisco supervisors. By that time, Manson's earlier efforts had begun to bear fruit, as the Hetch Hetchy plan began to take shape as part of a larger national drive toward efficient and regulated resource use. San Francisco municipal water advocates finally found a propitious political climate that would place their efforts squarely in the context of a rising technocratic conservation movement whose principal national figure was, arguably, none other than Chief Forester Pinchot himself.

Those San Franciscans who thought of their home as a significant metropolis could perhaps compliment themselves with the fact that a city of fewer than four hundred thousand inhabitants in the early 1900s temporarily played a central role in an issue of great national importance. Forty years later, reflecting back on the rise of conservationism, Gifford Pinchot remarked that "launching the Conservation movement was the most significant achievement of the T. R. administration. . . . It seems altogether probable that it will also be the achievement for which he will be longest and most gratefully remembered."[30] In fact, had it not been for the nation's particular moment in its history, for the political capital that the Roosevelt administration was actively investing in conservationism, and for the ways that San Francisco's water needs tied in to these circumstances, the city's acquisition of Hetch Hetchy might have followed an even more tortuous path than it did.

Chief Forester Pinchot's ideas did not emerge in a historical vacuum. By the end of the nineteenth century, thoughtful Americans were considering the consequences of the liberal land policies implemented by the federal government from the Civil War onward. The famed Homestead Act of 1862, and the subsequent Timber Culture Act, Timber and Stone Act, and Desert Land Act had all been politically popular efforts at roughly democratic land allocations in the American West. With grants limited—with the exception of the Desert Land Act—to smallholdings of one-quarter square mile per household, the expectation was for broad distribution of the nation's natural economic assets and the promotion of a time-honored American ideal of a society of hardy and personally independent petty producers. While the laws failed in many respects, and economic development of the West occurred as much if not more in the breach of the laws' intent rather than in their strict observance, the result was profound. By 1900, individuals and especially business corporations had almost entirely claimed and developed the West's natural wealth in land and resources. As already noted by the historian Frederick Jackson Turner in 1893, the frontier had closed, and "never again [would] such gifts of free land offer themselves."[31]

Awakened by the integration of the vast West into the larger national economy, some Americans abandoned their parents' and grandparents' perceptions of the country's seeming natural abundance and turned instead to a concern about destruction, waste, and inefficiency. As noted earlier, George Perkins Marsh, although hardly noticed as a prophet in his own time, wrote as early as 1864 that "man has too long forgotten that the earth was given to him for usufruct alone, not for consumption, still less for profligate waste."[32] Warning that the United States might suffer the fate of the ancient deforested civilizations of the Mediterranean, Marsh's fears found their parallels in the concerns of late-century associations like the Appalachian Mountain Club (1876), the Boone and Crockett Club (1885), the New York Audubon Society (1886), San Francisco's own Sierra Club (1892), and numerous other local and national associations of hikers, sportsmen, birders, women reformers, and nature lovers of all stripes.

Pinchot's immediate antecedent, both in position and in intellectual orientation, was the first chief of the Department of Agriculture's Division of Forestry, the

German-born Bernhard Fernow. Fernow brought well-established German forest husbandry principles to his job in the U.S. government, and in 1902 he challenged the prevailing nineteenth-century doctrine of laissez-faire capitalism in his book *Economics of Forestry*. Rather than allowing the free market alone to govern the disposition of the nation's natural resources, Fernow argued for a government-driven policy of *faire-marcher*, or "make it work," by which experts would guide economic development through conservation. This idea fit well within the governing framework of twentieth-century political progressives who put a premium on efficiency and planning to promote social welfare. From the perspective of humankind's relationship with nature, conservation was also highly utilitarian in that it promoted functionality above all other values. Conservationists revived and expanded on the utilitarianism of the eighteenth- and nineteenth-century British philosophers Jeremy Bentham and John Stuart Mill, who had proposed the "utility" of promoting public happiness by the principle of "the greatest good for the greatest number." When Pinchot took over the reins of forest management from Fernow, he was deeply influenced, by his own admission, by the thinking of the geologist and philosopher W. J. McGee, "who defined [conservationism] as the use of the natural resources for the greatest good of the greatest number for the longest time." "It was McGee who made me see," wrote Pinchot, "at long last and after much argument, that monopoly of natural resources was only less dangerous to the public welfare than their actual destruction."[33]

Although Pinchot's expertise and purview were with timberlands, his faith in the expansive powers of government over resources in general was stoked by President Roosevelt's support of Nevada senator Francis Newlands's ideas regarding western water management. Newlands's bill drew from an unpopular 1878 study by John Wesley Powell, who had classified western lands by their aridity and consequent optimal economic use.[34] The lesson that Newlands drew from Powell was the need for federal water projects to support agricultural development in the arid and semi-arid states. In 1902, the Reclamation Act did just that by setting up a fund from the sale of public lands to finance irrigation projects in the West. But if Pinchot saw this as progress, and derived much of his conservationist ideology from McGee's invocation of the dangers of resource monopolization, many other Americans saw conservation itself as a governmental monopoly and as a threat to individual rights. There was some justification to this argument. For example, when the National Lumber Manufacturers Association convened the first American Forest Congress in 1905, the assembled representatives of the large timber corporations praised Gifford Pinchot for his scientific managerial wisdom. And when federal forest reserves were on the national agenda, it was the smaller firms, fearing they would be shut out of the competition for remaining woods, who most opposed conservation. Businessman and free market advocate George L. Knapp effectively represented the anti-conservation, antigovernment views of Pinchot's opponents:

> I propose to speak for those exiles in sin who hold that a large part of the present "conservation" movement is unadulterated humbug. That the modern Jeremiahs are as sincere as was the older one, I do not question. But I count their prophecies to be baseless vaporings, and their vaunted remedy worse than the fancied disease. . . . I am one who does not shiver for the future at the sight of a load of coal, nor view a steel-mill as the arch-robber of posterity. I am one who does not believe in a power trust, past, present, or to come; and who, if he were a capitalist seeking to form such a trust, would ask nothing better than just the present conservation scheme to help him. I believe that a government bureau is the worst imaginable landlord. . . . Our success in doing the things already accomplished has been exactly proportioned to our freedom from governmental "guidance."[35]

It was precisely attacks of this sort that attracted President Roosevelt and Chief Forester Pinchot to San Francisco's cause. Of course, by the fall of 1906, the city still basked in a certain amount of national sympathy deriving from its destruction by earthquake and fire in April, and Hetch Hetchy advocates had played the water card in this regard. But a more important consideration for the president and Pinchot was their plan to convene a White House Conference on the Conservation of Natural Resources within a year. The conference, they hoped, would create a positive public relations environment for the administration's policies and would lay the critics' arguments to rest by emphasizing that federal conservation was not about preservation but about resource development and public use. The resignation of Interior Secretary Hitchcock in March 1907 gave Roosevelt the opportunity to replace the man who upheld the letter of the Yosemite Park Act with James Garfield, the former chief of the Bureau of Corporations and an advocate of utilitarianism. Further, a positive federal response to San Francisco's Hetch Hetchy application presented the administration with an unparalleled chance to demonstrate that, even in the national parks, efficient resource use in the public interest was the primary function of conservation. On July 22, 1907, immediately after the ouster of the ULP city government, the new San Francisco Board of Supervisors reinstated their application for a Yosemite reservoir. Five days later, on July 27, Secretary Garfield came to town to hear arguments on both sides of the issue. After several months of energetic work by

Marsden Manson, newly appointed as city engineer, San Francisco reached a compromise over the future allocation of Tuolumne waters with Central Valley irrigators, and on May 11, 1908, two days before the White House conservation congress convened, Secretary of the Interior James Garfield issued the long-awaited permit allowing San Francisco to begin construction of its dam in the national park and its aqueduct to city. Opposition arose immediately, with the Sierra Club leading the charge.[36]

John Muir served as president of the Sierra Club from its founding in 1892 until his death in 1914. The legendary nature lover—to his admirers a visionary activist and to his detractors an eccentric tramp—was one of the two men most responsible for the extension of federal protection to Yosemite Park in the first place. In 1868, a year after he was temporarily blinded in an industrial accident and then stricken with malaria from a trip across the Gulf of Mexico, Muir first visited the Sierra high country. Awed by the region's beauty and dismayed by the impact of overgrazing by sheep, Muir spent the next two decades writing and lecturing on behalf of government control and protection of wilderness. After failed efforts to attract federal support for parks at Kings River and Mount Shasta, Muir met Robert Underwood Johnson, the associate editor of *Century*, the nation's foremost literary monthly. In the summer of 1889, following a trip to the high country above Yosemite Valley, Muir and Johnson resolved to launch a campaign to create a doughnut-shaped national park in the highlands surrounding the state preserve that had already included the valley floor since 1864. In the fall of 1890, Muir wrote two illustrated articles for *Century* that described the extraordinary qualities of the Sierra landscape and advanced the importance of preserving it both as watershed and for its intrinsic appeal as wilderness. At the same time, with the support of the Southern Pacific Railroad, which imagined a lucrative traffic in tourism, Johnson lobbied Congress for a 1,500-square-mile park along the lines envisioned by his new friend and colleague Muir. On September 30, 1890, Muir and Johnson scored an early victory for preservation as Congress passed the new Yosemite Act, which was signed into law by President Benjamin Harrison on October 1.[37]

On the heels of this great accomplishment, Johnson suggested the need for long-term public oversight of protected lands by the establishment of a civic association to defend Yosemite and the earlier Yellowstone Park from future utilitarian threats. Around the same time, a group of academicians led by J. Henry Senger of the University of California were planning to form an alpine club dedicated to the recreational use of the Yosemite region. Thus inspired, John Muir joined with professors Senger, Joseph LeConte, and Cornelius Beach Bradley, Stanford University president David Starr Jordan, the artist William Keith, and

San Francisco attorney Warren Olney in forming the Sierra Club on May 28, 1892. Muir was elected its first president. The club's stated purpose was "to explore, enjoy, and render accessible the mountain regions of the Pacific Coast; to publish authentic information concerning them, and to enlist the support and cooperation of the people and government in preserving the forests and other natural features of the Sierra Nevada."[38] At first, neither John Muir nor the other 182 charter members seemed to consider the possibility that two of the club's goals—accessibility and preservation—might be inherently contradictory. The later struggle over Hetch Hetchy, however, would bear this out.

For several years prior to Interior Secretary Garfield's decision to grant San Francisco's reservoir permit, Muir and the Sierra Club had devoted their energies almost entirely to convincing the California legislature to cede Yosemite Valley back to the federal government for inclusion in the national park. In one of the club's first political victories, the state approved transfer of the valley in 1905, and President Roosevelt signed the federal law incorporating it into Yosemite National Park in 1906. Buoyed by this achievement and thus far certain of the president's support for the preservationist agenda, Muir and his allies were distressed and disheartened by the turn of events from 1907 on. Determined to stave off Pinchot and Garfield's support for San Francisco's ambitions in the Sierra, the Sierra Club spent the next six years fighting the proposed Hetch Hetchy dam. The presidency of Roosevelt's successor William Howard Taft, the changing of the guard at Interior Department—where Richard Ballinger took over from James Garfield—and the firing of Gifford Pinchot after his dispute with Ballinger over conservation policy in Alaskan coalfields all contributed to prolonging the Hetch Hetchy debates and clouding their outcome. But even more than shifting political winds, two factors from within the nascent conservation movement did more than anything else to shape the course of events. First, with something as fundamental as drinking water at issue rather than trees and coalfields, the split between advocates of careful resource use and supporters of wilderness preservation deepened. Second, the arguments used by the preservationists to make their case seemed in many respects to be no less utilitarian than those of the wise-use advocates.

On the first score, the evolving relationship between Muir and Pinchot provides a good example of the eventual bifurcation of early conservationism. In 1896, five years after Congress passed the Forest Reserve Act that created what we now call the National Forests, Muir and Pinchot collaborated in producing a landmark U.S. Forestry Commission Report. The report led to the 1897 Forest Management Act, signed into law by President William McKinley, which made it clear, to Muir's dismay, that there would be no preservationist aspect to federal policy. From that point on, Muir and Pinchot represented the poles of what at first had seemed a common movement of concern for humans' relationship to the rest of nature, with Pinchot carrying the mantle of "conservation" or utilitarianism, and Muir that of "preservation" or romanticism (although these terms are somewhat reductionist). But by the summer of 1907, because the issue was water, even the Sierra Club faced internal dissension over the wisdom of following a pure preservation agenda. Warren Olney, a leading member and the host of the club's founding meeting, led a significant pro–Hetch Hetchy dam minority within the Sierra Club, weakening its ability to present a unified opposition to San Francisco's plans.

On the second score, it is remarkable that Muir, noted for his religious or mystical devotion to wilderness, and the Society for the Preservation of National Parks, which he helped to create in 1909 to lead the preservationist struggle, did nothing to promote the idea that Yosemite's nature had any intrinsic value other than what could be measured in terms of human use. Instead, quite a bit in the Olmsted tradition, the society focused almost exclusively on the recreational uses of nature and their benefits to the physical and mental well-being of people. In November 1909, Muir and the society produced a pamphlet entitled "Let Everyone Help to Save the Famous Hetch Hetchy Valley and Stop the Commercial Destruction Which Threatens Our National Parks."[39] On the first page, Muir wrote, "Let all those who believe that our great national wonderlands should be preserved unmarred as *places of rest and recreation* for the use of all the people, now enter their protests." This emphasis on recreation produced a series of significant unexamined contradictions throughout the text. The pamphlet later described Yosemite National Park as the "most wonderful national *playground* in California." The Hetch Hetchy Valley was said to be "a wonderfully exact counterpart of the great Yosemite, not only in its crystal river, sublime cliffs and waterfalls, but in the gardens, groves, and meadows of its *flowery park-like floor.* This park-like floor is especially adapted for *pleasure camping*." While the pamphlet went on to argue that Yosemite was to be "preserved in wildness for all time," nowhere did it address the meaning of "wildness" or the potential effects on the landscape of "its use as a public playground," or the impact of proclaiming of Hetch Hetchy: " IT IS A PARADISE FOR CAMPERS AND CAN ACCOMMODATE THOUSANDS." In the same vein, almost all of the organizations that the pamphlet listed as opposing the flooding of Hetch Hetchy Valley were essentially upper-middle-class hiking and recreational clubs, including the American Alpine Club, the Sierra Club of California, the

Appalachian Mountain Club of Boston, the Mazamas of Portland, the Mountaineers of Seattle, the Saturday Walking Club of Chicago, and the Playground Association of America.

Aside from its defense of "nature parks," the "preservation as recreation" argument put forward in "Let Everyone Help" was also intentionally crafted so as not to appear foolishly opposed to the human right to drinking water. *Century*'s Robert Underwood Johnson remarked, in fact, that "we hold human life more sacred than scenery, than even great natural wonderlands." The issue, then, was not just a matter of natural playgrounds versus drinking water, but, as the pamphlet went on to say, that San Francisco could easily get its water elsewhere and leave the national park alone. One essential point that was immediately manifest was that in describing the nation's "great natural wonderlands" as "scenery," these were automatically cast as objects of human invention and consumption, for what is scenery if not an image and experience produced in the mind of a transient observer? The preservationists' inclination to be just as human as anyone else, and just as much a product of an urban, industrial society—to be "visitors to nature"—was reflected as well in their discussion of San Francisco's alternatives to Hetch Hetchy among the "several large rivers . . . North and South of San Francisco [that] *waste* their waters into the ocean." Who was prepared to determine which rivers would continue to flow through their ancient channels and which would be diverted rather than "wasted"? And what superior justification could be offered in one case as opposed to another? Could one argue that the Stanislaus, Eel, and San Joaquin rivers were less worthy of preservation than the Tuolumne? "Let Everyone Help" did just that.

Given the nature of these arguments, one is compelled to ask whether the case that the preservationists made against San Francisco's acquisition of a Hetch Hetchy reservoir site was principled but inconsistent or whether it was in some ways disingenuous, elitist, and opportunistic. On the one hand, Muir and his allies deserve credit for far greater political realism than their detractors granted them. Just as the supposedly sentimental preservationists were willing to make common cause with the Southern Pacific Railroad in establishing Yosemite Park in the first place and, as it turned out, with the Spring Valley Water Company in opposing municipal ownership of Hetch Hetchy, they were also cognizant of the fact that they would never succeed in gaining general public support for leaving Hetch Hetchy Valley untouched if they appeared unconcerned about the development of water resources for urban use. If their alliances with unpopular corporations and their advocacy of engineered water systems were opportunistic, then this was the normal sort of opportunism that almost always characterizes political struggles in electoral democracies. On the other hand, the way in which the Society for the Preservation of National Parks touted the apparent mass recreational value of Hetch Hetchy must be seen either as naïve, since it threatened many of the preservationists' own views of wilderness as something unchanged by human effort, or simply as disingenuous.

John Muir, for example, had once echoed Henry David Thoreau's idealization of "unaltered nature" by remarking that "in God's wildness lies the hope of the world—the great fresh, unblighted, unredeemed wilderness."[40] But Muir's personal journeys through the Sierras reflected and shaped his views of what wilderness was. As the historian Kenneth Olwig has noted: "Muir . . . was emphatically a cliff and cascade man who climbed the valley's walls alone and preferred the view from the top down." Commenting on the Sierra Club and other upper-middle-class alpinists who shared Muir's passions, Olwig continued, "The elite who followed in his singular footsteps traditionally have looked down on the hoi polloi flocked below, and the two differing points of view have made of the park contested territory. As a club member wrote in 1919, 'to a Sierran bound for the high mountains the human noise and dust of Yosemite [Valley] seem desecration of primitive nature.'"[41] Consequently, while it may have been politically necessary to advertise Hetch Hetchy as a campground for the thousands in order to save it, it is doubtful that most preservationists believed this use of the valley to be either possible or desirable.

Martin S. Vilas, an opponent of the preservationists and a supporter of the 1913 Raker Act that finally authorized San Francisco's reservoir and dam, noted the physical qualities that distinguished Hetch Hetchy from the more readily accessible and famous Yosemite Valley.

Hetch Hetchy Valley is separated from the Yosemite Valley by a mountain range having a mean elevation of over 8,500 feet, and distant from that valley about thirty-five miles by mountain trail. . . . It is surrounded by steep cliffs, out of which extend deep gorges. . . . The sides of the valley are very steep and precipitous. . . . The area tributary to [it] is very rough. Edmund A. Whitman, a lawyer of Boston and president of the Society for the Preservation of National Parks . . . stated [before Congress]: "I cannot attempt to describe to you the character of the country. It is some of the roughest God ever made. . . . The largest part of the country is the roughest sort, where camping is as impossible as it would be on the top of this table." Hetch Hetchy Valley is difficult of access. Thus while 6,000 or 7,000 people visit Yosemite Valley each year, less than 300 visit Hetch Hetchy Valley."[42]

Although one could be rightfully suspicious of Vilas's descriptions due to his motive as a dam supporter, the accuracy of his representations was corroborated both by the cited testimony of preservationist Edmund Whitman and by the experiences of Robert and Dorothy Duryea, newlywed wilderness campers who spent their honeymoon at Hetch Hetchy in 1914. The Duryeas' fathers stood on opposite sides of the dam controversy, with Robert's father Edwin, a hydraulic engineer, on the pro-dam side, and Dorothy's father John Stillman, a Stanford chemist and hiking enthusiast, on the anti-dam side. The Duryeas' account of their unusual honeymoon included descriptions of beautiful and prolific flora and fauna, as well as arduous conditions, difficult overland travel, mosquito swarms, cold June weather, and solitude.[43] While the Duryeas concluded that San Francisco's proposed dam was a worthy enterprise—although Dorothy did so with greater ambivalence than her husband—the young couple were good representatives of the class and sort of person typically engaged in early twentieth-century mountaineering. They were in fact quite like the hundreds of Sierra Club members who, beginning in 1901, took part in the club's annual monthlong High Trip. Even though the club made efforts to control the expense of such excursions, their long duration would have precluded the participation of ordinary workers, while the Sierra Club's membership of professionals and intellectuals had a tendency to be self-reproducing. Consequently, when San Francisco's most aggressive dam advocates, like Marsden Manson, accused preservationists of elitism, their criticisms were not entirely unfounded.

As an institution of the professional and intellectual elite, the Sierra Club, like the other preservationist and recreational associations across the nation, was handicapped in its ability to promote a broad and democratic sort of environmental consciousness. More correctly, it was handicapped by its moment in history, insofar as few Americans could have shared in the class-bound experiences and perceptions of the Sierrans. Perhaps grasping this, the club and other preservationists negotiated an awkward road between touting the aesthetic qualities of untouched wilderness and defending its recreational use value, between the real need for resource use and the real need to draw some line of containment around rampant commercialism, and between their own communal enjoyment of nature and their proffering of the same to the masses, who in their numbers could only destroy its pristine solitude. When these same masses in San Francisco were polled on their willingness to bear the expense of flooding beautiful Hetch Hetchy Valley with millions of gallons of drinking-water-to-be, their answer was consequently quite affirmative. In May 1908, when San Francisco voters were asked if they would pay $5.2 million for a public water supply, 93 percent voted "yes." No district had a majority of fewer than 87 percent in favor. In a second ballot in November, 86 percent voted to authorize the Hetch Hetchy project specifically and to allocate $600,000 to purchase rights and claims to lands adjoining the valley. Much later, years and decades after Congress authorized the project by passing the Raker Act, San Franciscans repeatedly approved bond measures to finance the Hetch Hetchy system. In 1924, 1928, and 1947, voters supported another $59 million in bonds for tunneling, expansion, and a second pipeline by majorities of 95, 90, and 78 percent respectively. By any measure, it would be fair to say that public support for clean and abundant municipal water was very high.[44]

By the end of the Taft presidency, John Muir and the Society for the Preservation of the National Parks had seemingly failed to garner the support of San Franciscans, but they continued their battle in the nation's capital. However, the election of Woodrow Wilson in 1912 and his appointment of dam advocate and former San Francisco City attorney Franklin Lane as Secretary of the Interior did not bode well for the preservationists. Soon thereafter, California representative John E. Raker authored a bill approving the Hetch Hetchy grant, and the House Committee on Public Lands initiated a series of hearings on the merits of the city's case. One of the key members of the committee who was instrumental in shaping the outcome of the Hetch Hetchy debates was the United States congressman from Marin County, William Kent. Kent, an independently wealthy man who was drawn to reformist politics, first in Chicago and then in Marin County, had impeccable pro-nature credentials. Unlike Muir's mysticism, however, Kent's sentiments derived in large part from an intensely masculine strain of conservation ideology that saw wilderness as the fuel of virility. Kent, an avid hunter who described his life as one "largely spent outdoors . . . [riding] the prairies, the mountains and the desert," saw man's engagement with the wild as a way of reclaiming a healthy level of one's natural predatory instinct: "It's good to be a barbarian. . . . You know that if you are a barbarian, you are at any rate a man." On this point, he echoed former President Roosevelt's disdain for the "unhealthy softening . . . of fiber that tends to accompany civilization" and his praise for wildlands as places to promote "hardihood, resolution, and scorn of discomfort."[45]

In 1903, Kent purchased hundreds of acres of virgin redwood forest on Marin County's Mount Tamalpais to protect it from logging. Ironically, in light of the later Hetch Hetchy episode, Kent soon found himself at odds with a water company. In 1907, the North Coast Water Company in Mill Valley sought additional water for Sausalito by pursuing condemnation of Redwood Canyon, situated in

Kent's newly acquired woods, to build a dam and reservoir. In December of that year, Kent preempted the North Coast Company's move by transferring his land to the federal government under the terms of the Antiquities Act. At Kent's request, on January 9, 1908, President Roosevelt officially proclaimed that the grant would be known as Muir Woods National Monument.

Admired and praised by Muir, the Sierra Club, and preservationists far and wide, Kent nonetheless became one of Congress's leading supporters of San Francisco's Hetch Hetchy plans. While recognizing the value of Hetch Hetchy's wilderness and its special status as federal park land, William Kent was concerned about what would happen to it if San Francisco did not claim it as a font of municipalized water. Much as the North Coast Water Company had tried to take Redwood Canyon as its own, the powerful Pacific Gas and Electric Company (PG&E) had designs on Hetch Hetchy as a part of its plan to dominate California's hydroelectric resources. For progressive reformers like Kent, PG&E occupied a space in California's pantheon of dangerous monopolies that was roughly equal in significance to that filled by the Southern Pacific Company. All else being equal, Kent and the progressives believed firmly that municipal water was a better alternative than corporate water. Since Kent was widely known for both his admiration of John Muir and his apparently selfless grant of the national monument in Marin County, his decision to support the Raker Act had substantial influence on other members of Congress. Kent's letter-writing campaign to his colleagues may have been one of the crowning blows to the preservationist side of the Hetch Hetchy issue. One of his letters described Muir as "a man entirely without social sense," while another to Gifford Pinchot labeled the dam opponents as "misinformed nature lovers." Kent's support for San Francisco also provides significant evidence that the issue cannot be neatly cast as a battle between the friends and enemies of nature. During the whole Hetch Hetchy contest, Kent continued to solicit Pinchot's support for a state park on Mount Tamalpais, and after the passage of the Raker Act, he went on to help create the National Park Service and the Save-the-Redwoods League and to grant additional land to Muir Woods.[46]

William Kent's defection from Muir and the ranks of the "nature purists," however, does not alone explain Congress's passage of the Raker Act in the fall of 1913. Another contributor to the preservationists' defeat was the way in which they framed their side of the debate. By placing so much emphasis on the scenic and recreational value of Hetch Hetchy Valley, the preservationists left themselves vulnerable to the predictable counterargument that the dam and reservoir would either enhance or not impinge upon these uses. The most thorough presentation of this counterargument appeared in the pages of the Freeman Report, published in July 1912. To make its case in Congress and before the public, the City of San Francisco commissioned John Ripley Freeman, a world-renowned hydraulic engineer and M.I.T. graduate who had advised Boston and New York on their water systems. In addition to refuting the viability of any other source of water for San Francisco besides the Tuolumne River and of any other reservoir site other than Hetch Hetchy Valley, the Freeman Report also included an entire well-illustrated section describing the scenic and recreational attributes of reservoir sites around the world. A brief list of the captions below the attractive illustrations will capture the gist of Freeman's compelling argument:

A picnic group on the park road around Boston's Middlesex Fells Reservoir
A Sunday afternoon stroll along the shore of Boston's main distributing reservoir
An inviting foot path bordering Boston's Chestnut Hill reservoir
Highways and pleasure drives around Croton Lake [New York]
On the public highway in the catchment of Lake Thirlmere [England]
The Stronachlacher Hotel on the shore of Lake Katrine [Glasgow, Scotland]
Tourist steamboat crossing Lake Katrine
The beautiful Craig Gôch Dam, Elan River, Wales
The Hetch Hetchy Scenic Road would present a view much like this [Oifjord Lake, Norway][47]

This partial list, and the visually appealing scenes it described, helps to explain in part why the conventional prospective consumer of public parkland might, thus edified, have found San Francisco's project at least inoffensive and perhaps even pleasing.

The Freeman Report consequently undermined the Hetch Hetchy protection effort of the Society for the Preservation of National Parks just as the San Francisco city administration had intended. Yet what may have been a gross strategic error on the part of Muir and his allies can also be understood as rooted in ambivalence and uncertainty, even among nature lovers, as to what nature really was. For example, when John Muir described the pro-dam forces as "temple destroyers, devotees of ravaging commercialism, [who] seem to have a perfect contempt for Nature, and, instead of lifting their eyes to the God of the mountains, lift them to the Almighty Dollar,"[48] he was speaking for the face of preservationism that tended to view landscapes as natural only if they were devoid of

Oifjord Lake, Norway, one of several attractive pro-reservoir images from the Freeman Report.

the traces of human labor. Muir's own hunger for "any place that is wild,"[49] and his preference for solitary treks through the high country reflected his need for what he imagined to be pristine spaces, uncorrupted by the hand of humankind.

Yet solitude in nature had never been a typical human condition; it was a yearning understandable only as the counterpoint or antidote to what Muir called "the galling harness of civilization." The problem with this desire, however, is that it conflicted with the reality that landscapes are not just natural, but cultural as well. Recall that the park-like atmosphere that so captivated Lafayette Bunnell upon his entry to Yosemite Valley in 1851 was the product of Native American burning practices (see chapter 3). When these were banned after the creation of the park, it was necessary to use axes to maintain the valley in some semblance of its "natural" state. When the Ahwahneechee occupants were divorced from their traditional land uses and became a well-managed sideshow for tourists, urban visitors were unknowingly put in an odd position. They could experience both the natives and the park as natural artifacts, imagining them as somehow frozen in time and fortuitously bypassed by the historical forces that had elsewhere produced urban civilization. A visit to Yosemite thereby fostered a comforting ignorance of the relationship that binds all people to nature through their labor and compels them to make choices about how they use the external world. By 1894, because traditional Indian work on the land had long been extinguished, the extent of clear, open meadow in Yosemite Valley was only one-quarter of what it had been four decades earlier. When Totuya, the granddaughter of Chief Tenaya, returned home to this foreign cultural landscape in 1929 after an absence of 78 years, she remarked, "Too dirty; too much bushy."[50]

Like the native Totuya, the preservationist Muir had very clear ideas about what nature should look like. In his battle to protect Yosemite from "hooved locusts" in 1895, Muir clearly exhibited the link between culture and nature when he declared that "one soldier in the woods, armed with authority and a gun, would be more effective in preservation than millions of forbidding notices." Muir praised the army because "the sheep having been rigidly excluded, a luxuriant cover has sprung up on the desolate forest floor."[51] Totuya and Muir both knew that the job of human beings was to manage land. The difference between them was that for Totuya, the task was second nature; for Muir—who probably suffered no less confusion about nature than any modern man—it was self-conscious and fraught with contradictions. These contradictions were endemic to the preservationist movement's efforts on behalf of Hetch Hetchy Valley, which, all pretensions to the contrary, was inevitably cast as a cultural landscape as well. The cultural function of the valley was well-established by the defenders of its nature—it was to be an awesome and visually splendid recreational retreat. The most interesting thing about this preservationist proposition is how utilitarian it was in its own way and how deeply connected to the evolving values of urban life.[52]

It should not be surprising that early twentieth-century San Francisco—with its typically urban dependency on the nature of its hinterlands as an economic resource—stood at the heart of a debate that centered so focally on the proper function and treatment of that nature. Yet this gave all sides of the issue a metropolitan bent. From an environmental perspective, the leading historical role of cities like San Francisco produced the contradictions that characterized preservationist thought. In the specific case of San Francisco, the issue was how people should use Hetch Hetchy Valley. In effect, the whole debate over the fate of that corner of wilderness was about two different kinds of consumption, both of which depended on the idea that cities are not integrated into nature. Would Hetch Hetchy be used to quench San Franciscans' thirst, since they could not provide water for themselves, or would it be used to provide them with an occasional natural retreat, since presumably they did not live in nature at home? These questions were not bad questions, but if they are taken to indicate the existence of an unbridgeable divide between utilitarian conservation and preservationist conservation, they clearly fail to do so.

The crucial distinction between the two positions—the former promoting economic and thereby transformative use and the latter arguing for aesthetic or experiential use—failed to arouse the many people who in this case were just thinking about getting water, the essential stuff of life. It was also too early for the kind of ecological perspective that has since placed human beings within a larger network of living interdependencies rather than alone at the terminal end of a consumption chain. If even preservationists, in their self-assigned roles as the nation's nature educators, found it difficult to produce a distinct and compelling argument for leaving Hetch Hetchy alone, what could be expected of ordinary folks? When President Woodrow Wilson signed the Raker Act into law on December 19, 1913, he weighed, as did Congress, and as did several times the voters of San Francisco, the merits of two competing utilitarian visions. Coming down on the side of an urban water system, the president declared, "The bill was opposed by so many public-spirited men . . . that I have naturally sought to scrutinize it very closely. I take the liberty of thinking that their fears were not well founded."[53]

It took another two decades for San Francisco's Hetch Hetchy water supply system to become operational—much longer than its equivalent in Los Angeles.

O'Shaughnessy Dam at Hetch Hetchy in its fourth year of operation, 1938. Courtesy of the National Park Service, Yosemite Park, O'Shaughnessy Dam, October 27, 1938, *photographed by Ralph Anderson, RL-7278.*

And although Los Angeles's growth far outpaced that of San Francisco in the intervening period, shifting California's urban center of gravity southward, the Hetch Hetchy aqueduct was no less important than the Owens aqueduct in promoting the state's urbanization. John Freeman had foreseen and contributed to these developments in his 1912 report. In an effort to quash all political support that may have existed for water sources other than the Tuolumne, Freeman used his report to advocate a four-hundred-million-gallon-per-day system, rather than the promised sixty-million-gallon one, with massive hydroelectric capabilities, that could only be built on the basis of the Hetch Hetchy plan. In defense of his apparent farsightedness, Freeman produced population projections for the San Francisco Bay Area through the end of the twentieth century. Although his sense of how that population would be geographically distributed was incorrect, he was not far off the mark on overall growth rates. Based on the experience of other major cities around the country, San Francisco was forecast at a population of 1.2 million by the year 2000, almost twice its actual size today. But this overestimation was compensated for by an underestimation of growth rates in San Mateo, Santa Clara, Alameda, and Contra Costa counties. Overall, Freeman estimated a metropolitan Bay Area population of just over 3.6 million by 2000, compared with 773,000 in the year 1910, a forecast which actually fell short by about two million people.[54] Freeman's projections, once considered plausible but extraordinary, have been met and exceeded, with an abundant supply of Sierra water as the cause. While it is true that the Hetch Hetchy system does not serve the entire Bay Area, the process of its development set into motion other similar projects, such as the East Bay Municipal Utilities District system, which draws, as mentioned, from San Francisco's rejected Mokelumne.

After its completion during the Great Depression in 1934, the Hetch Hetchy project launched a new phase in San Francisco's history. San Francisco, at one time a city whose political boundaries conformed to visible demarcations separating urban and non-urban landscapes, was becoming the heart of a much vaster metropolitan region that was barely interrupted by occasional pockets of seemingly nonurbanized space. As the Bay Area became more metropolitan, the environmental issues it confronted changed. The attitudes of its people toward questions that affected their quality of life evolved in tandem. By midcentury, the seeds of contemporary environmentalism had been sown. At this point, beyond question, urbanites were its driving force. How would they reinvent nature this time?

CHAPTER 5

THE QUEST
FOR LIVABILITY

The Hetch Hetchy controversy of the early 1900s provides a useful tool for understanding urbanites' responses to the challenges of metropolitan growth over the entire course of the twentieth century. Certainly, the activist minority in the Sierra Club adopted both an organizational form and an ideological position that is familiar today, and the debates they fostered over water and wilderness are easy for us to recognize as antecedents of the modern environmental movement. But beyond this, the controversy illustrated an important aspect of the nature/human nexus—the absolute impossibility of separating human perspectives on the environment from human needs.

The Hetch Hetchy debate proved that the most significant human-driven variable in the relationship between people and their external world is how human needs are felt and defined. In San Francisco's formative stages, the perceived needs of its people were often reflected in business leaders' active transformation of space toward commercial ends and workers' more tacit cooperation with this process, from which they hoped to gain as well. By the late nineteenth and early twentieth centuries, as evident in the discussions surrounding Golden Gate Park, Yosemite, and Hetch Hetchy, at least some San Franciscans were beginning to argue that an urban civilization needed to satisfy human needs beyond those of production and distribution. The contest between these views was not precisely binary though, as it involved competition between fluid public constituencies defending a variety of aesthetic forms and a variety of economic functions. Yet, throughout the twentieth century, the recognition that human beings "did not live by bread alone" emerged as a persistent correlate to urban growth and its tendency to produce periodic environmental crises. It was a manifestation of what historian Samuel Hays—referring most pointedly to its prevalence in post–Second World War America—has dubbed "environmental culture," and it was rooted in a set of beliefs that he has described as "environmental values."[1] These values, in conflict, competition, or concordance with others, shaped public engagement with an external world that people sought to improve for what they imagined to be the better. In an urban setting, "better" was shorthand for a complex of only partially objective variables that included the achievement of viable work, health, and comfort; aesthetic satisfaction; and social cohesion—in short, what we have come to describe as "livability."

The effort to achieve a better urban environment was always colored by the class basis of society since civic leaders, urban planners, and technical experts usually emerged from the middle and upper classes, and because a modicum of livability could be purchased by persons of means who could remove themselves physically from the most unpleasant aspects of unregulated city life. Yet it is evident that portions of the social elite were also driven by civic virtue to seek general betterment rather than merely private refuge. For example, at the same time that San Franciscans were arguing over the merits of the Hetch Hetchy project, they were also considering implementation of the Burnham Plan, an especially remarkable experiment in urban planning. Like Hetch Hetchy, the Burnham Plan was given a big boost by the earthquake of 1906, but unlike the city's big water project, it barely approached even partial fruition. Insofar as urban livability is a compromise in the contest between various aesthetic forms and economic functions of space, the contrast between the two outcomes is instructive.

If we did not have the benefit of a photographic record, it would be hard to imagine the devastation wrought on San Francisco by the earthquake of April 18, 1906, and the resultant fires. It has been noted that the latter were far more destructive than the temblor itself, as at least those portions of the city built on the rock substrate of the hills shook less vigorously than the made-land districts that occupied onetime marshes. All told, the combined effect destroyed over five hundred blocks, killed as many as three thousand people, and left a quarter million homeless. One cannot presume the reasons for San Franciscans' collective resilience, and their willingness to reestablish themselves on a site fated to suffer again in the future the severe consequences of nature's minor adjustments. But if the events of 1906 are measured against the numerous fires of the 1850s, one readily sees that the long-term value of San Francisco's spot of ground consistently exceeded by far any cost of reconstruction. By 1906, the enormous capital and the countless livelihoods invested in the city made rebuilding, and doing it quickly, the inevitable order of the day. The question was not if, or even when, but how and according to what plan?

Ironically, the devastation of 1906, for all its attendant misery, had presented San Franciscans with a blank canvas on which to paint the city of their dreams. Rarely do cities have a chance to reinvent themselves. The cautious, the safety-conscious, and especially those who live in cities not prone to natural disasters, might ask whether San Franciscans should have reshaped their city to accommodate itself more humbly to the irrepressible tectonic forces over which it lies. In fact, as regards reconstruction, similar questions will be raised about New Orleans in the aftermath of Hurricane Katrina and the floods of 2005, additionally informed by an ecological consciousness that did not exist a century ago. But caution and humility had no place in the discussions of 1906, as business and civic leaders in particular were primarily concerned with economic growth and interurban competition. As in the Golden Gate Park debates of the 1860s and 1870s, a principal rationale for urban improvement was the preservation of San Francisco's position as the nation's preeminent Pacific metropolis, with a marriage of infrastructure and aesthetics as the vehicle for achieving this. And as the history of the period shows, when aesthetic concerns were largely motivated by the drive to accumulate capital, the subjective qualities of beauty could be made to compromise with the quantifiable measures of the balance sheet.

When San Francisco burned to the ground, it already had behind it the decade-long legacy of an active neighborhood-based civic improvement movement. Local clubs, with a membership consisting largely of local business leaders, advocated on behalf of street paving and lighting, sewer construction, municipal water, and public buildings. In addition, more prominent San Franciscans did their part toward urban beautification in the San Francisco Art Association, whose president in 1894 and 1895 was none other than future mayor James Phelan. As manager of California's exhibit at the famed 1893 World's Columbian Exposition in Chicago, Phelan became an ardent devotee of the emerging City Beautiful movement and joined a growing list of business leaders dedicated to urban adornment. In support of an 1899 bond measure to improve the city's infrastructure, Phelan declared that "by making San Francisco beautiful and attractive the outlay will be repaid many times by increasing population, flow of visitors, and a happy contented people."[2] Andrea Sbarboro, head of the Italian-American Bank, agreed: "Beautifying a city pays enormous returns on the expenditure . . . [as] demonstrated in the case of Paris."[3] Sbarboro's by now familiar and oft-repeated allusion would be made again and again in support of assuring San Francisco's development into a "great and beautiful and attractive city where men and women of civilized tastes and wants will desire to live, [rather than] a great and ugly and forbidding city which people will shun."[4]

By 1905, San Francisco's urban aesthetes had a design to pin their hopes on—the Burnham Plan. In January 1904, the city's business elite had formed the Association for the Improvement and Adornment of San Francisco (AIASF), dedicated to the construction of an opera house, music conservatory, civic audi-torium, and terraced parks. With James Phelan yet again as president, the AIASF commissioned Daniel Burnham, the urban planner and architect responsible for the design of the Columbian Exposition, to prepare a city plan for San Francisco. Phelan, sugar baron Rudolph Spreckels, the Southern Pacific Railroad, the San Francisco Gas and Electric Company, and others contributed to Burnham's sixteen-thousand-dollar fee. Working from a studio on top of the Twin Peaks, Burnham and his assistant Edward Bennett completed a plan in the late summer of 1905. The final product was a somewhat fanciful proposal to completely rebuild the city's street system into a web of concentric rings traversed by broad diagonal boulevards, with the whole arterial network defining a series of sepa-rate use zones—administrative, economic, and residential—and punctuated with grand public buildings, parks, and playgrounds. Burnham's vision was closely aligned with that of the earlier park advocates—for instance, Olmsted and Vaux—in its attachment to the notion that the character of public space could shape the character of its users. If not an environmental determinist, Burnham was at least a true believer in the moral qualities of space, and he defended his plan as of potentially inestimable positive "influence on the masses."[5] Yet it was telling that people barely figured in his drawings. It was almost as if human beings could, with the greatest ease, be plucked out of and dropped down into environments that existed independently of them—human habitats that emerged with no evolutionary relationship to human use. Despite this conceptual limita-tion, the AIASF delivered the Burnham Plan to Mayor Schmitz and the board of supervisors in September 1905, who, in conjunction with the press, dissemi-nated it to the broader public.

A few months later, disaster struck. In the earthquake's aftermath, AIASF leaders expressed confidence that the Burnham Plan could become the blueprint for the city's reconstruction. Charles Lathrop, rector of the Church of the Advent, echoed Burnham's moral reformism and advocated rebuilding San Francisco in a way to provide "blue sky and fields and out of doors to keep peo-ple healthy and normal in their ideals."[6] Twelve days after the earthquake, James Phelan himself was still promoting the plan, but by July he was beginning to con-sider the need for rapid and cost-effective rebuilding to get the city's businesses back on their feet. The city's new Committee of Reconstruction, made up of business leaders, professionals, and the heads of the Labor Council, Building Trades Council, and Carpenters' Union, could reach no consensus on a rebuild-ing plan. Some saw the blank slate created by the temblor and conflagration as an opportunity to completely reshape the city. One member commented that

Daniel Burnham's "suggested architectural treatment for Telegraph Hill," 1905.
Courtesy of the David Rumsey Map Collection, www.davidrumsey.com.

"ours now are like the chances of youth, which will never come again."[7] Others, including the president of the Merchants' Association, also an AIASF member, were not so certain that the costs and delays of comprehensive planning were justified in light of the pressing economic need to restore function to the downtown business district.

In the face of physical devastation and economic ruin, many downtown merchants and outer-neighborhood small business owners looked at the Burnham Plan and saw little to address immediate concerns such as the harbor, the economy, or the housing stock, and therefore little to guarantee either their short-term livelihoods or the long-term promise that San Francisco would not lose its dominance on the Pacific Coast. These, in their minds, were the greatest needs. In the absence of consensus, piecemeal reconstruction occurred out of necessity, and the Burnham Plan's historical moment slipped away. One could correctly argue on the one hand that the limited, economy-bound vision of some business and labor leaders buried a chance to rethink San Francisco. On the other hand, the only overarching reconstruction plan on the table had problems of its own. Burnham, the idealist, quite explicitly saw his geometric, monumental, and highly systematic design as an instrumental lesson of order that would invoke civic patriotism in—and harmonious relations between—San Franciscans. Pragmatic business owners wondered where the money was to be made. If idealism eventually yielded to pragmatism, it was in part because Burnham's most ardent enthusiasts had not inquired into the human needs served by the organic nature of urban neighborhoods already populated and put to use by real people. In keeping with its time and intellectual origin, the Burnham Plan was an effort to engineer the city's environment toward idealized ends in a similar fashion to the physical engineering of Golden Gate Park or the social engineering of Yosemite Park. The common thread was always to strive to produce a "better nature"—in both the physical and moral senses of the term—that failed to occur on its own. But given the intensity of use to which huge numbers of people put the urban landscape, such engineering was far more daunting in this case. Burnham's proposed urban environment, separated from the experienced need and practical use of its occupants, was divorced from a clear conception of how people would work it. Unlike the Hetch Hetchy project, the Burnham Plan proposed too radical a redefinition of aesthetic form with too little attention to the economic functions that might support it.

Three years after the earthquake, as San Franciscans debated the construction of a new civic center, architect Willis Polk voiced the most practical approach that could be taken to aesthetics from a business point of view by drawing an analogy between San Francisco and Pericles's Athens. Faced with the rivalry of Syracuse, "as a matter of statesmanship, they decided to make Athens more beautiful; not for any inherent love of beauty itself, but purely and simply as a business proposition."[8] While post-Burnham support for beautification continued alongside a largely conventional pattern of reconstruction, the Polk approach carried the day. In 1911, with the impending opening of the Panama Canal, San Francisco defeated New Orleans for the right to hold the Panama Pacific International Exposition that was scheduled for 1915. Soon thereafter, Mayor James Rolph took the opportunity to declare—as had become almost obligatory since the 1860s—that San Francisco would be to America as "Florence is to Italy and Paris is to France."[9] From then on, all efforts toward utopian planning were focused on the upcoming world's fair and deflected from the city itself. By the time of the First World War, San Francisco looked much as it had before, but bigger. Uncoordinated growth had defeated comprehensive planning in the name of need, and, as had been the rule for some time, "need" was largely within the purview of competing groups of business leaders and professionals to define.

While the generation of the Roaring Twenties and the Great Depression therefore inherited a new San Francisco that had adopted much of the physical shape of the old, the earthquake had nonetheless accelerated a major change in the urban environment—an ongoing process of deindustrialization that was turning San Francisco more and more into the commercial, administrative, and financial center of a broader metropolitan region. Although some San Franciscans had mobilized to exile noxious industries from the proximity of their residential neighborhoods as early as the 1870s, industrial flight from the city over subsequent decades was not the result of widespread popular environmental agitation. The most notable example of legislated industrial zoning in the nineteenth century had been the removal of Butchertown to the Hunters Point district. Over time, the butchers' reservation proved to be the seed of an expanding industrial district on the relatively cheap land of neighboring South San Francisco, at the foot of San Bruno Mountain. In the 1890s and 1900s, "South City" became the home of the Union Stockyards, the Whittier-Fuller Paint factory, the Columbia Steel mill, and a growing working-class community. No one in the heart of San Francisco was troubled by the noxious byproducts of industries ten miles away in South City, but wealthy capitalists, including Darius Mills, William Sharon, and William Crocker, were. Concerned about industrial encroachment on their new rural estates at nearby Hillsborough, they blocked the construction of a copper-smelting plant in South City in 1908, and thereby limited the southward march of industry in San Mateo County.[10]

The limited space in San Francisco proper, the resistance of suburbanizing magnates to the despoliation of their retreats, the growing scale of twentieth-century industrial plants, the cost of unionized labor in the city, and the disruption caused by the earthquake and fires all contributed to the industrialization of the East Bay and the relative decline of such activities in San Francisco. This is not to say that nothing was made or processed in the big city. Businesses in North Beach and the south of Market district made shoes, shirts, mattresses, machinery, bread, and beer, and they processed and packed coffee, chocolate, and fruits. But overall, the center of gravity of Bay Area industry shifted to Contra Costa and Alameda counties, which together surpassed San Francisco in manufacturing output by 1910 and in industrial employment by 1920.[11] Many, if not all, of San Francisco's early boomtown industries—mining equipment, workers' clothing, wooden barrels, steam boilers, cast-iron stoves, and leather belting—had but marginal importance in the twentieth-century economy, and more modern industries—petroleum refining, chemicals, and automobiles—developed primarily outside the city limits. Symbolic of San Francisco's shifting regional role, the Standard Oil Company maintained its corporate offices in the city, but its refining and shipping facilities were across the bay in Richmond. H. C. Cutting, who planned the Richmond harbor, explained San Francisco's future role as he saw it: "This growth means as much to San Francisco as though it took place within her own city limits, for financially it is all one. We grow together. An immense development is going to take place here, and San Francisco will always be the main office, the money reservoir where these industries will be financed."[12]

As San Francisco moved further toward administration and finance, Oakland emerged as a significant industrial center and one of the three fastest-growing cities in the nation between 1900 and 1930, with a spillover effect on neighboring Berkeley, Alameda, and Emeryville. In 1930, San Francisco was home to 600,000, closely followed by the east shore of the bay from Richmond to San Leandro, which housed 450,000. The peninsula south of San Francisco held another 77,000 people. Outside of San Francisco proper, growth followed a well-established low-density pattern, and occupants became accustomed to seeing residential blocks carved out of rural spaces. The expanding and increasingly contiguous bands of urban and suburban settlement that characterized all but the northernmost and southernmost bay counties presaged a future not unlike that projected by Hetch Hetchy advocate John Freeman in 1912.[13]

The overall effect of these changes was to produce a vast metropolitan region stretching along the shores of San Francisco Bay. Within the greater metropolis, there were areas like Oakland that maintained some independence from San Francisco capitalists, and other areas—like much of Contra Costa County—that were industrial colonies of the big city. But while the levers of control within the modern metropolis may have varied, an overall physical pattern had emerged by the time of the Great Depression in which the most readily observable environmental costs of industrialization had been exported from the metropolitan core. It remains difficult to assess whether this aspect of industrial decentralization had a conscious effect on the way San Francisco residents experienced their own particular urban environment, but two outcomes are clear. First, from 1930 on, the environmental concerns raised by San Franciscans regarding their own little patch of urban space had less to do with industrial blight than with other qualities of city life, like congestion, noise, and the integrity of residential neighborhoods; and second, as the metropolis became regional, the environmental debates attendant to urbanization and industrialization spread to the inhabitants of the entire Bay Area.

While the Bay Area's stature as a regional metropolis presented numerous environmental problems, the depression of the 1930s at first challenged residents' ability to exercise the sort of environmental values that had surfaced periodically in past efforts at municipal improvement. The collapse of production and employment was a far more pressing concern for most San Franciscans at that time than the shape of the urban landscape. When the first water flowed from Hetch Hetchy into Crystal Springs Reservoir in 1934, even such a long sought accomplishment was overshadowed by the dismal economic climate. The project's completion, in fact, shared the same year as the great San Francisco general strike. With the optimism of the 1910s a distant memory, public attention turned to food, shelter, and work.

As already noted, human beings cannot effectively separate their environmental perspective from their perception of need. One might add that most modern urbanites have neither the time nor inclination to imagine how the environment they occupy assumes its shape, and very few people at any given moment believe that they exercise much control over the barely considered processes that create their habitat. When confronted with a question of immediate survival, as was the case during the Great Depression, urbanites in an industrial society are especially handicapped by the very same environmental alterations that made their city an engine of production, distribution, and capital accumulation in the first place. They cannot farm the paved streets and built-up lots for their own subsistence. Their parks do not sustain game for the hunt or fuel for the hearth. They cannot fulfill their most elemental physical needs without commercial or industrial employment. They are adrift in an environment engineered by human beings who took for granted that the lifelines connecting the city's dependent population to the hinterland of their natural essentials would not break. Those lifelines may nonetheless rupture, either by force of nature, as in the earthquake of 1906, or by the hand of human beings, as in the economic collapse of 1929. When such a breakdown occurs, attention inevitably turns to regenerating economic growth by further intensifying the process of urbanization and industrialization to create work and to strengthen markets. San Francisco's business leaders took this approach in 1906, and Presidents Hoover and Roosevelt did so in the 1930s. Two direct results of this drive for growth were an unsuccessful plan to completely redesign San Francisco Bay and the successful completion of San Francisco's depression-era bridges—the Bay Bridge and the Golden Gate Bridge. Both efforts were conceived in the interest of furthering the metropolitan integration and economic might of the Bay Area, and both succeeded in raising persistent questions about urban quality of life that helped launch the modern environmental movement of the 1960s.

From a storyteller's perspective, the extraordinarily prolonged planning and construction of the Hetch Hetchy system was quite opportune, as it bridged two periods of American history in which environmental management was the order of the day. The project was conceived during the Progressive Era, a time in which resource conservation joined the ranks of the many efficiencies promoted by advocates of technocratic and managerial government. It came to fruition during the New Deal era, just as the leaders of an emerging welfare state began to recognize the relationship between economic prosperity, social stability, and the effective harnessing of the forces of nature. In this new age of federal reforestation projects, soil erosion management, flood control, and rural electrification, government officials worked hard to foster the public's faith that a plural marriage of the people's labor, modern technology, and scientific resource management would restore all that was lost in the Great Depression. Like San Francisco's bridges, many of the most visible manifestations of this marriage and this vision were monumental works of public infrastructure. In an age that gave the nation the Tennessee Valley Authority, the Bonneville Dam, the Boulder Dam, and the Colorado River Project, San Francisco voters' authorization of a bond issue to raise the height of Hetch Hetchy's O'Shaughnessy Dam was a comparatively minor matter. Yet the nation's love affair with dams did produce an odd scheme for San Francisco Bay that received little initial public airing— a plan to conserve fresh water by using dams to partition the bay into a saltwater port at midsection and two freshwater lakes to the north and the south joined by a ship canal.

John Reber, the politically well-connected amateur theatrical producer who authored the plan in 1933, conceived of two huge earth-and-rock barriers stretching across the bay in close proximity to the current locations of the San Francisco–Oakland Bay and Richmond–San Rafael Bridges. In addition to its water conservation function, the southern barrier would have accommodated rail and automobile traffic, while the eastern side of the bay between the two dams was to be filled to provide for industry, airports, and naval bases. If implemented, the landfill plan would have brought Berkeley's shoreline three miles farther west into the bay, with its docks sitting less than a thousand yards from Yerba Buena Island—a scenario which, under future and different circumstances, stoked the Save San Francisco Bay movement of the 1960s. In its ambition, audacity, and faith in engineering, the Reber Plan was a perverse corollary to the Burnham Plan. Where Burnham's urban engineering had an aesthetic and moral dimension at its heart, the core principle of the Reber Plan was its use of engineering toward exclusively utilitarian and economic goals.

Reber may have arrived at his ideas by independent discovery, but similar, if less ambitious, proposals had been made before by C. E. Grunsky, former San Francisco City Engineer, and especially by the Salt Water Barrier Association

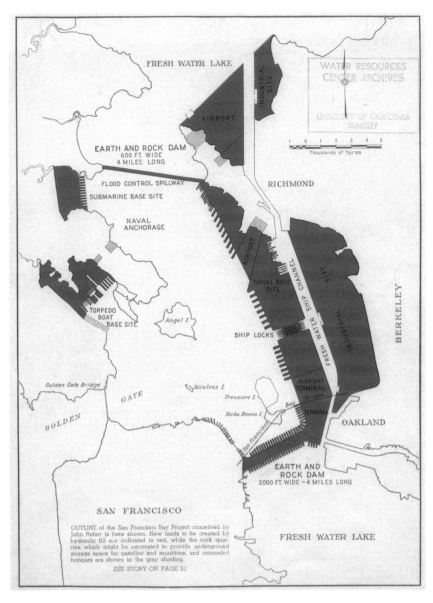

San Francisco Bay Project—The Reber Plan, with proposed landfill shaded. San Francisco Bay Water Barrier Collection, Water Resources Center Archives— University of California, Berkeley.

formed in 1929. This latter organization had the full backing of the Association of Industrial Water Users of Contra Costa and Solano counties, and its efforts and ultimate failure reveal again how debates over matters of significant environmental import were once primarily the provenance of competing groups of business leaders. As early as the 1910s, San Joaquin River valley irrigators and Sacramento River valley rice farmers were drawing so much water out of their river systems that the amount of fresh water reaching the delta and the bay was severely reduced, especially during the dry summer season. Droughts such as occurred in 1920 made matters worse. Aside from harming the health of the estuary's ecosystem, which was of little public interest in that era, the increased salinity produced by agricultural water users presented two risks to the region. First, elevated upstream salt concentrations caused by deeper tidal penetration threatened to make the water unusable for irrigation, and second, the salination of the Carquinez Strait and Suisun Bay hurt the many industries located there, some of which had relocated from San Francisco from the 1870s onward in search of more space and water, and sometimes to escape complaints of pollution.

In 1930, Ben Allen, manager of the Salt Water Barrier Association, emphasized the importance of Contra Costa industry, whose wealth "pour[s] into San Francisco . . . just as surely as the floods of the Sacramento and the San Joaquin run into the Pacific Ocean." What this industry needed was a saltwater barrier that would unlock the "secret of turning water into wealth."[14] On the strait at Crockett, for example, Spreckels' California and Hawaii Sugar Refinery was saddled with the cost of importing fresh water by barge for its industrial processes, while Carl Schedler of the Great Western Electro-Chemical Company of Pittsburgh complained of salt damage to boilers and cooling machinery. Despite these problems, the early consideration given to bay salinity barriers was dropped by 1931 due to their potential impediment to navigation, and because some farmers feared that the cure might be worse than the disease, especially if their levees were breached in flood years by water held behind the dams.

Given the failure of early efforts, it is remarkable that Reber's reinvention of the barrier plan survived a tortuous history of ups and downs well into the early 1960s. The plan's ultimate demise was the result of attacks and concerns from various quarters. The city of Oakland, for example, feared that its harbor would be isolated to the sole benefit of San Francisco; the state's Division of Water Resources concluded in the 1950s that wastes would accumulate behind the barriers, severely polluting the proposed lakes; and in 1963 the Army Corps of Engineers determined that continued depletion of upstream water resources would eventually cause the lakes to fall below sea level, forcing a reversion to pre-dam conditions. While many and probably most people today would consider Reber's vision for San Francisco Bay an abomination, it is notable that for two decades his plan received as much serious attention as it did. Yet the debate, the outcome of which would have radically transformed the function and aesthetic of San Francisco's greatest natural asset, was at first largely confined to a small cadre of civil and military engineers, industrial and agricultural associations, and key state legislative committees.

In 1933, Reber secured the support of former President Hoover, himself an engineer, and by 1936 Reber had tried to convince U.S. Secretary of War George Dern of the military advantages of his plan. In 1940, the Reber Plan received its first broad public airing by way of an exhibit at the Golden Gate International Exposition—San Francisco's world's fair on Treasure Island. Concurrently, the advent of the Second World War provided Reber with a new climate of opinion within which to market his proposal from a national defense perspective. Three weeks before Japan's attack on Pearl Harbor, San Francisco mayor Angelo Rossi and the board of supervisors approved a resolution asking California's U.S. senators Hiram Johnson and Sheridan Downey to initiate a congressional investigation into the merits of the Reber Plan. The resolution emphasized the plan's desire to create "impregnable all-land crossings of San Francisco Bay . . . and an indestructible supply of fresh water." The city leaders further noted that due to "the supreme importance of this Western outpost of the United States, it is imperative that adequate defense be provided . . . and the most feasible solution so far proposed has been advanced in the Reber Project."[15] Two weeks after the Pearl Harbor attack, the exact wording of the San Francisco resolution was repeated in a state senate joint resolution, which additionally touted the Reber Plan's anticipated creation of "a main naval base, submarine and torpedo boat base . . . with added shipbuilding expansion . . . impregnable storage for aviation gasoline . . . [and] underground hangers in solid rock for the safe housing of thousands of fighting planes."[16]

In 1942, Reber seized upon the opportunity created by the war to embellish his proposal in ways that would make it even more attractive to the military and to a security-conscious public. Reber appended the catchphrase "Streamlining California" to his informational releases and added to his proposal a "5-hour military highway and super freeway" linking San Francisco and Los Angeles and flanked by a canal from the delta to the San Joaquin Valley and southern California. Yet despite Reber's apparent political success in the halls of San Francisco and California state government, the military itself was not enthused. At the end of April 1942, U.S. Navy Rear Admiral John W. Greenslade, commandant of the

Twelfth Naval District, protested that the Navy had consistently made the best possible use of "San Francisco Bay . . . always seeking to take full advantage of and to protect the natural features afforded by this wonderful harbor." Arguing that major alterations of the natural features of the bay would harm rather than serve the interests of the U.S. Navy, Greenslade went on to say that if "a salt water barrier [were constructed] across both arms of San Francisco Bay . . . no naval or other vessel could reach the present naval facilities without passing through shiplocks or tidal locks and gates . . . [resulting in] delay and risk to every vessel, including the danger of complete blockade . . . and would mean a very serious dislocation of existing naval facilities. . . . The Commandant does not believe that the military features . . . of the Reber Plan have any merit."[17]

It is the good fortune of today's Bay Area residents that despite the initial enthusiasm of some business, agricultural, and civic organizations, the Reber Plan was ultimately deemed unfeasible by the technical experts in whom so much authority over matters of environmental consequence had been entrusted since the Progressive Era. While Reber received a number of endorsements—including at various times from the San Francisco Board of Supervisors, the California Farm Bureau, the Santa Clara County Farm Bureau, the Saint Francis Kiwanis Club, and both the Shafter County and Madera County chambers of commerce—the negative testimony of prominent engineers stalled the plan's political progress. When World War II ended without implementation of the Reber Plan, its proposal for a second bay crossing that would provide a direct rail link from San Francisco to the mainland had sufficient merit as to prompt hearings before a joint Army-Navy Board in August 1946. At these hearings, even Carl Schedler, an engineer and early proponent of salinity control barriers in his former employ at Pittsburgh's Great Western Electro-Chemical Company, argued that the plan was too expensive, that it might harm the delta, and that it would be ineffective due to water loss through ship locks and evaporation. Schedler reiterated Admiral Greenslade's wartime concerns, noting that the "Reber Plan would concentrate shipping, rail, air facilities, etc., thus making it easier for an enemy to destroy the port of San Francisco in time of war." He stressed the costs to navigation of impediments to shipping, and to industry in the likely need for expensive pumping systems to prevent flooding of waterfront businesses. Schedler also predicted an 85 percent reduction in the tidal prism, resulting in bar formation in the rivers that flowed to the bay and at the Golden Gate, which would need to be dredged continually at an unknown cost. He anticipated that the obstruction of fish spawning beds in the Sacramento and San Joaquin rivers would destroy the commercial fishing industry as well as "the salmon, shad, and striped bass sport fishing industry" at an annual cost of $18 million. And while dismissing conservationists for their insistence "that nothing but water fit to drink be discharged into a stream or bay," Schedler warned that the Reber Plan would cause the "water [to] be quiet in front of the outlets of municipal and factory sewers, resulting in the creation of numerous nuisances."[18]

Compounding the effect of Schedler's concerns, state engineer Edward Hyatt cast doubt on the actual freshwater savings that Reber's plan might produce, while A. M. Barton of the state reclamation board warned that if the plan were implemented, delta levees might not hold during high-water years. B. C. Allin, another consulting engineer, offered equally damning testimony, while leaving open the possibility of pursuing more conventional wetland reclamation: "It is our opinion that the reclamation of tidal flats or swamp areas and the creation of industrial acreage . . . are in no wise dependent upon, nor have anything in common with a system of locks and dams." Because of the military nature of the hearing, Allin concluded his report with an assessment of the national security impact of the Reber Plan. Providing further independent corroboration of Carl Schedler's findings, Allin noted that the "last war demonstrated forcefully that anchorage space for large convoys is . . . vital to the protection of the nation. San Francisco is the main operating base of the Pacific Coast for the United States Navy, [with] large supply bases . . . at Oakland and Stockton . . . and repair bases . . . at Mare Island and Hunter's Point. Aerial attack is a major hazard in future warfare. . . . Should [the system of proposed locks and dams] be bombed . . . all shipping . . . both naval and convoy, would be effectively bottled up. . . . Succinctly stated, San Francisco harbor could never again operate as safely in war as it has in the last decade."[19] Allin, Hyatt, Barton, and Schedler's reservations had their intended effect, and the Army-Navy panel finally rejected the Reber Plan as "economically infeasible . . . [and] untenable from the standpoint of navigation and national interests."[20]

Within a year or two, having failed to turn the security climate of the World War and early cold war period to their advantage, the Reber Plan's advocates shifted back primarily to promoting the plan's assets in the areas of water engineering, land reclamation, and direct rail transportation to San Francisco. The San Francisco Bay Project—the nonprofit corporate form assumed by the plan's advocates—gained two important new adherents. One was Vice Admiral Greenslade, now retired, who reversed himself and joined the project's board of directors; and the other was retired Brigadier General Philip G. Bruton, who in 1948 delivered an important address to the Irrigation Districts Association of California. Bruton touted the plan's projected "increase [in] the amount of water available for transfer to the San Joaquin River Basin as well as . . . for the Santa Clara Valley." Echoing the sentiments of other dam advocates, from the Progressive Era defenders of Los Angeles's Owens Aqueduct to the New Deal–era proponents of damming the Colorado River, Bruton emphasized the inherent value of reducing the annual "wastage" of fresh water through the Golden Gate. Besides this appeal to agricultural interests, the former general also played on San Francisco's decades-old struggle for commercial dominance on the Pacific Coast. In regards to the transportation benefits of the proposed earthen dams, he noted that "in competition with other ports along the Pacific . . . San Francisco Harbor is at a serious disadvantage by being without direct ship-to-transcontinental rail facilities. Seattle has such [connections, as does] Long Beach-Los Angeles Harbor." The San Francisco Bay Project's south mole would have provided a "2,000 ft. wide [link between] the San Francisco peninsula [and] the Alameda mainland [with] ample rights of way for . . . the four railroads of the Bay Area—the Santa Fe, Western Pacific, Southern Pacific, and the Northwestern Pacific." Adding to the roster of economic advantages, the general remarked that the Reber Plan would produce "20,000 acres of newly created land [with] 50 miles of new deep water shoreline," all of which would have been lucrative real estate.

If completed, the entire project would have resulted in a monumental rearrangement of the Bay Area's landscape, requiring, by Bruton's estimate, "750 million cubic yards of hydraulic fill" to be dredged from the bottom of the bay and "20 million cubic yards of rock" to be excavated from the Tiburon peninsula, Candlestick Point, and the East Bay hills. Not surprisingly, Bruton and company gave no consideration to any potential negative consequences of such actions. In fact, the Bay Project's publicity releases and prospectuses consistently displayed tremendous comfort with and assuredness in the merits of large-scale environmental reengineering. When it came to human dominance and control over the external world, doubt and caution were certainly not its trademarks. Bruton even went so far as to suggest that the species destruction that would accompany San Francisco Bay's transformation from a saltwater to a freshwater environment would offer the extra benefit of eliminating "barnacles and marine growths [that] foul ships' bottoms." Clearly, in both science and policy, much has changed since then.[21]

In December 1949, the Public Works Committee of the United States Senate took up the Reber Plan issue at hearings held in San Francisco. Carl Schedler played a major role once again, this time preparing a negative report on the plan for Senator Sheridan Downey. To give even greater credence to his views, the engineer emphasized his former positions as production manager of Dow Chemical Company, chairman of the Industrial Water Users Association of Contra Costa County, and president of the Salt Water Barrier Association. Schedler reiterated and elaborated on his earlier assessments of the San Francisco Bay Project's negative impact on navigation, industry, employment, national defense, and on the cities of Richmond and Oakland.[22] He was joined for the first time by the U.S. Bureau of Reclamation, whose statement to the Pubic Works Committee noted the bureau's cooperation with the state of California in the 1920s in a feasibility study regarding saltwater barriers across the northern portion of San Francisco Bay. The technical findings of the 1920s investigation by Walter R. Young had been published in 1929 by the State Division of Water Resources, which then went on to address cost-effectiveness in a further report in 1931. The conclusion of the federal and state inquiries had been that "a barrier was not justified . . . and that the desired salinity control could be obtained more economically by maintaining adequate outflow from the Delta, utilizing storage reservoirs to be provided within the Central Valley." In defense of its own institutional merits and departmental efficiency, the bureau noted that "Shasta Reservoir which has since been constructed by the Bureau of Reclamation on the Upper Sacramento River has as one of its functions the maintenance of flow into the Delta to repel the saline Bay waters. The reservoir has been successfully operated for this purpose for the past five years." Whether the bureau's judgments were shaped purely by technical and economic efficacy, or informed even in small part by its wish to defend its own prerogatives, its conclusions regarding the Reber Plan were sobering: "Considered from the standpoint of water conservation only, it appears that the Reber Plan would require an appreciable amount of fresh water from storage reservoirs in the Central Valley in order to replace that portion of the evaporation from its large freshwater surfaces which could not be supplied by local run-off into the lakes or by direct precipitation thereon. . . . The Bureau of Reclamation is of the opinion that from a water conservation standpoint, the Reber Plan is objectionable."[23]

In contrast to the negative appraisals offered by independent and federal engineers, San Francisco's superintendent of recreation, Josephine Randall, spoke of the Reber Plan in glowing terms. Reminiscent of the public recreation arguments made by those who supported damming Hetch Hetchy a half century earlier, Randall imagined "the entire population of the . . . Bay Counties, along with countless tourists and visitors, enjoying the splendid beaches, aquatic sports, and swimming facilities that would border the shores of the two giant fresh water lakes." She went on to strike a competitive chord, arguing that "the creation of these . . . lakes . . .

would bring to San Francisco . . . all of the beach and aquatic attractions which our neighbors in Southern California now enjoy and use as a tourist lure. . . . These great . . . lakes would also bring to our Bay Area all of the sportsman enthusiasm for lake boating, sailing and fishing that our northern neighbors of Oregon and Washington enjoy." Invoking New York's Jones Beach, Long Island—"an almost inaccessible sandbar, slough and windswept reef [transformed] into the most popular playground . . . in the world"—Randall either ignored or was unaware of other experts' predictions that the Reber lakes would be fouled by pollution and barren of fish. One doubts that such conditions would have really turned the Bay Area into "the envy of every other vacation spot in the nation."[24]

With differences of opinion abounding, Senator Downey, who had been instrumental in calling the Senate hearings in the first place, did manage to secure a $2 million federal appropriation in the 1950 omnibus Rivers and Harbors Bill for the U.S. Army Corps of Engineers to survey the best way to remodel San Francisco Bay. In the meantime, the San Francisco Bay Project's continual and dogged lobbying efforts seemed to pay off at the state level as well in that year, when the California Assembly's Committee on Tidelands Reclamation succumbed to pressure by engaging yet another consulting engineer, John L. Savage, to conduct yet another independent examination of the Reber Plan. However, while he agreed that the construction of Reber's vision was feasible, Savage argued that the desired practical results of the plan could not be accomplished. Due to evaporation from the artificial freshwater lakes that were to replace the estuarine environments at the north and south ends of the bay, water would be wasted rather than saved. Besides corroborating the negative assessments already registered by Schedler, Allin, Young, Hyatt, Barton, and others, Savage quoted even more extensively from the testimony of military authorities who opposed the plan as destructive to national security: "Headquarters, Sixth Army: 'The Reber Plan would seriously jeopardize the National Defense'; U.S. Pacific Fleet, Air Force, Fleet Air, West Coast: 'The Reber Plan would interfere unacceptably with the operation of naval aircraft'; U.S. Pacific Fleet, Third Reserve Fleet: 'The Reber Plan would affect national defense adversely'; Twelfth Naval District: 'The Reber Plan is totally unacceptable; it would seriously interfere with naval surface and air activities'; Staff Headquarters, Western Sea Frontier: 'The Reber Plan . . . obliterates the fleet anchorage off San Francisco.' "[25] In the political climate of the early cold war, these were certainly very serious reservations.

On November 18, 1950, the *Saturday Evening Post* ran a mostly supportive article on the plan that appears to have been documented largely from the San Francisco Bay Project's press releases. A perusal of the magazine reminds the reader of the world that Americans confronted at that time, with the Reber Plan article appearing back-to-back with another titled "We Won Back Korea—and We're Stuck With It."[26] Given the nature of the moment, military planners in active service remained concerned about preserving the mobility of Pacific Coast defenses, while the retired military men on the Bay Project's board offered their massive proposed southern bay crossing as a way of evacuating San Francisco if it were devastated by an atomic bomb. It remained to be seen which set of fears would prevail.

John Savage's report convinced the Tidelands Reclamation Committee to drop consideration of the Reber Plan, but the plan's supporters kept up the fight. R. Ken Wilhelm, secretary of the Santa Clara County Farm Bureau Board of Directors, took up the struggle in 1952 by demanding that "the Governor appoint a committee [with] representation [from] the Farm Bureau, Grange, Labor, Industry, Business, Parent Teachers' Association, and Irrigation Districts Association . . . charged with [preparing] legislation . . . to effect by qualified experts . . . an unbiased and complete investigation of the San Francisco Bay Project known as the Reber Plan." Wilhelm received additional support from the farming districts a few months later, when the Madera County National Farm Loan Association addressed to Governor Earl Warren their deep concerns "over our water requirement. The future development of our county will make more and greater demands for fresh water. . . . To insure a constant and sure supply . . . a salt water barrier must be built."[27] Prodded by agricultural interests, in 1953 the state legislature passed the Abshire-Kelly Salinity Control Barrier Act. This appeared to be a political victory for Reber and his supporters, but it backfired instead. The law authorized a comprehensive study of potential barriers throughout the bay-delta system, to be conducted under the auspices of California's Division of Water Resources. One of the chief consultants hired by the investigating commission was Cornelius Biemond, a Dutch expert on barriers and reclamation. Adding insult to injury, Biemond concluded that aside from the problem of saline seepage, the man-made lakes in Reber's plan, because of their immunity from tidal action, would become so hopelessly polluted by domestic, agricultural, and industrial wastes as to be completely useless.[28]

In the spring of 1955, California's public water engineers presented the legislature with their final summations of the two-year investigation. Walter Schulz, principal hydraulic engineer of the California Division of Water Resources told the state assembly that while the construction of barriers in the bay did "not offer any unusual problems that could not be solved with present engineering knowledge," the outcome of such barriers would be undesirable and counterproductive.

Schulz emphasized the likely need to rebuild delta levees to hold back floodwaters, and he repeated the oft-cited challenges that the plan would present to shipping and national defense. He also referred to the State Department of Fish and Game's estimate that "95 percent of the striped bass might be eliminated," with equally detrimental consequences to steelhead and salmon. Worst of all, the Reber Plan's promise of a vast new reserve of fresh water was flawed to the point of functional infeasibility. Schulz noted that "a barrier pool in either arm of San Francisco Bay would not be favorably situated from the standpoint of water quality" due to the surrounding area's "intensive urban and industrial development. In addition, a substantial portion of the polluting substances discharged into streams of the Central Valley would eventually enter the barrier pools. . . . In the event of a series of [dry years] . . . salt would accumulate in the pool from return irrigation water of the San Joaquin Valley." Essentially, according to Schulz, it was best to leave well enough alone, as "the average water quality throughout the Delta [was] better than in a [prospective] barrier pool. . . . In any event, the quality [in the pools] would be considerably lower than most of the water presently used in the San Francisco Bay Area."[29]

Although the Reber Plan's political future already looked dim in 1955, its last gasp was a protracted one, as the proposal's implementation ultimately hinged on the results of the Army Corps of Engineers' study that had been authorized by Congress in 1950 at Senator Downey's prompting. The Korean War delayed initiation of the study until 1955, and it was not completed until 1963. The Corps' approach was to build in Sausalito a huge hydraulic scale model of the bay and delta. This impressive project went into operation in 1957 and is still open to visitors today. Among those invited to visit the model during its construction were Clarence Walsh, Ted White, and George Johns of the San Francisco Labor Council, whose opinions of the Reber Plan reflected the outlook and interests of yet another public constituency. Because Ted White served as well on the San Francisco Planning Commission, the labor leaders' views were of some political significance. The unionists expressed great admiration for the Corps' bay model but were reserved in their judgment of the Reber Plan. Secretary Johns remarked that "it would be foolish and wasteful to proceed with any major project without first testing it on the model to determine its effects, costs, and feasibility."[30]

With no expressed interest in the salinity control aspects of the plan, the Labor Council focused entirely on a variation of only one aspect of the Reber proposal—the southern "mole." With a powerful attachment to regional planning and job development, the council stressed the need for "the southerly development of San Francisco . . . and a southern link to the East Bay." "It is vital," George Johns noted, "that transcontinental rail lines be brought directly into San Francisco [and] not halted helplessly on the eastern shore of the Bay. . . . The next Bay crossing must be a southerly one. It must have a terminus south of Hunter's Point so as not to interfere with the needs of that vital naval installation [and] it must be capable of carrying transcontinental railway lines and mass public transit, which means a low-level, fill crossing that can be as wide as necessary [and] will not require a perpetual toll barrier around the city of San Francisco."[31] The Labor Council's highly selective endorsement of only one piece of the Reber Plan, the years of negative assessments by private consulting engineers, the conflicting needs of land-based interest groups like industrial and agricultural water users and water-based interests like the commercial fishing industry, the conflict between potential private-sector economic gain and the United States Navy's need to uphold national security and a viable defense, and the strong reservations of state agencies like the Division of Water Resources and the Department of Fish and Game, with both the public welfare and their own institutional turf to protect, made the Corps of Engineers' study all the more crucial to the final turn of events.

John Reber died in 1960, before any final conclusions were reached, but in 1963 the Corps of Engineers reported that no salinity control barriers save for those in the Carquinez Strait or farther upriver would have any actual utility. The engineers warned that "the lakes created by the Reber Plan would shrink in a matter of years to below mean sea level." Navigation would require "lake levels to be maintained by reversion to present conditions . . . eliminating . . . the functions for which the barriers had been designed."[32] In effect, after all of the expense required to produce the huge earthen dams, shipping channels, and ship locks, all would have been for naught and would have had to be undone. The Reber Plan died in 1963. As intriguing, ambitious, and awful as it was, the Reber Plan reflected at least in part its author's honest desire to manage a precious and essential resource—water—that had been in one way or another at the core of California's efforts at environmental engineering for a century. In that sense, Reber, the eccentric visionary, was in good historical company. It is interesting though that, at midcentury, his proposal did not arouse the same degree of preservationist opposition as the Hetch Hetchy plan of fifty years earlier. Why? Was it that the extraordinarily long and technical process of conducting government inquiries and engineering studies simply encouraged public inattention? Or did the bay somehow not resonate with the public's conception of what constituted worthy and uncorrupted nature? Did Reber's deeply and, one might say, coldly utilitarian views really reflect the people's feelings about their bay? After all, the plan did not die because of an outpouring of resistance over the destruction of a truly magnificent body of water, but because the needs of conflicting resource users could not be reconciled and because it was impractical at a sheer utilitarian level. Yet, in late 1959, the release of a new government report opened a new chapter in the contest over the bay.

While the salinity-control barrier studies were being conducted in Sausalito, the Army Corps was also engaged in a separate investigation of Bay Area development patterns for the U.S. Department of Commerce. In December 1959, the Corps released its report *Future Development of the San Francisco Bay Area, 1960–2020*. In anticipation of unchecked population growth, the Corps predicted that by 2020 the metropolitan region would have achieved maximum use of available space, forcing expansion onto "marginal" lands. The bay would become real estate. The Corps estimated that 325 square miles of San Francisco Bay were shallow enough to make filling economically feasible, and that at the current rate of reclamation, nothing more than a shipping channel would remain within a century. When the *Oakland Tribune* published the Army Corps of Engineers' futuristic map of a bay vastly shrunken by projected landfill, it catalyzed the Save San Francisco Bay drive of the 1960s, an exemplar of the grassroots movements that were to increasingly characterize an emergent environmental age and that would significantly reshape public policy in the latter twentieth century. The phase of sheer utilitarianism had passed.

Mobilized by their concern over the future of the bay, three university wives founded the Save San Francisco Bay Association in 1961. Catherine Kerr, Sylvia McLaughlin, and Esther Gulick were on the one hand "ordinary" homemakers, but they were also socially and politically well-connected on account of their husbands' positions with the University of California, of which Clark Kerr was the president and Donald McLaughlin a regent. The work of the three "tea ladies," as they were called, harkened back to a long tradition of upper-middle-class female activism in the United States, while it launched an opening salvo in a modern era of urban environmentalism in the San Francisco Bay Area. The local movement was not an isolated occurrence. It developed in a nationwide context of mounting environmental awareness that was linked to a general increase in disposable incomes, the popularization of leisure, and the consequent desire for intangible amenities beyond the basic necessities of life. Like subsequent efforts to reverse the degradation of the Chesapeake Bay, the Great Lakes, the Long Island Sound, and other bodies of water, the Save the Bay movement arose in an era of contestation between conventional uses of urban water-

San Francisco Bay today, looking west toward San Francisco from the Oakland hills. The Reber Plan would have filled in the bay from the east shore roughly up to the white horizontal line. Photograph by the author.

ways for navigation and sewage disposal and emergent recreational uses. As noted by historian Samuel Hays, this contest was heightened by the fact that "cities with varied land- and waterscapes fostered a much sharper sense of environmental image and hence of urban identity."[33] Consistent with this analysis, San Francisco's dramatic setting played an inevitable role in shaping the environmental consciousness of its occupants, and, precisely because of this, an important novelty surrounded this particular preservation effort—its activists' simple attachment to beauty.

Of course, it would be foolish to say that the founders of the Save San Francisco Bay Association were the first to discover natural beauty or to tout the merits of beauty in an urban setting. Nonetheless, their environmental impulse held important and distinctive attributes. For example, John Muir and other early twentieth-century preservationists used the beauty of Hetch Hetchy Valley in its defense, but they also explicitly linked the valley's aesthetic qualities to its remote, rugged, mountainous, wild, pristine, unadulterated, uncorrupted, and consequently "fully natural" essence. Endowed with a beauty thus far unblemished by man—their argument went—Hetch Hetchy deserved to be maintained as a refuge from the unending march of civilization, to nourish the souls of those lovers of nature who might venture there. The wilderness focus of this earlier struggle even continued to shape the perspective of the Sierra Club long thereafter. In fact, the club's David Brower, who attended one of the early meetings of the Save the Bay Association at Esther Gulick's home, was supportive of the bay activists' goals but noted that the Sierra Club's expertise was primarily in wilderness and trails rather than in urbanized environments. Later, as Save the Bay's mounting success enabled alliances with other organizations, Dwight Steele, the chairman of the Sierra Club's newly constituted San Francisco Bay Committee, remarked that it was "the first time in the Sierra Club's 76-year history that the environment of a major urban area [received] the club's special attention."[34]

Of course, as far as the promotion of urban beauty was concerned, San Francisco did have the precedents of both the parks movement and the City Beautiful movement of the nineteenth and early twentieth centuries. Yet there were substantial differences here as well. First, both of these earlier drives were at least partly dependent on material ambition, whether toward the collective goal of an enhanced competitive position for San Francisco vis-à-vis other great cities or toward the individual goal of enhanced property values for some urban landowners. Second, the construction of Golden Gate Park and the consideration given to the Burnham Plan both involved the radical transformation of an existing landscape by human design. The former aimed at producing a more aesthetic nature, and the latter, a more aesthetic urban infrastructure. Neither sought to protect an existing landscape, anthropogenic or not. Third, the most socially minded progenitors of these other movements developed or depended on detailed theories regarding the moral qualities of space that provided an intellectual justification for their desire to achieve beauty, as if it were impermissible to argue in favor of the immeasurable and subjective yearning for loveliness alone. In an age of objective engineering and rational thought, perhaps it was.

As opposed to all of this, the tea ladies of Berkeley and their early allies simply felt the beauty of San Francisco Bay and unabashedly went about defending it from destruction. It mattered little that it was not remote and wild or designed to perfection—it was a compelling natural feature of the San Francisco urban environment that the metropolis had not entirely swallowed up, and it was all the more precious for it. The bay imparted sensual pleasure by its presence and made the Bay Area worth living in. Some fellow travelers like local environmental writer Harold Gilliam displayed attitudes somewhat different than those of the wilderness advocates of an earlier generation. For Gilliam, the bay need not have been divorced from human history to merit preservation. Rather, that history itself added weight to the experience of its beauty: "[At] that initial moment when the great Bay was first spread out before you, fresh and new and shining . . . you became a member of that company of explorers, pioneers, Argonauts, and empire builders who came to the edge of the New World when the land was young, and, like you, felt a sudden blaze of exhilaration."[35] The persistence of this magnificent body of water at the heart of a metropolis linked the modern inhabitants of its shores to the drama and beauty of the region's human past.

Looking back in 1985, Catherine Kerr remembered her "concern about the Bay [as] the result of [her] appreciation of the beauty of the Bay, or the beauty of water." She recalled driving around the Berkeley hills in her husband's graduate school days, dreaming of a future home "with a view of the Bay." Having achieved their dream in 1949, the Kerrs witnessed the gradual destruction of the bay from their living room windows: "Where there had been a nice wooded cove at Point Isabel, we watched the bulldozers knock off the trees, and level the area, and fill in the little harbor. We watched the garbage fill at Albany."[36] Sylvia McLaughlin was similarly motivated, recounting, "I came from Colorado . . . a semi-arid type of country. I thought that San Francisco Bay was the greatest thing I had ever seen. I felt so fortunate that the gentleman I married in 1948 lived here, and he already had a home that was halfway up the hill. It had a view of the Bay. My concern grew out of my appreciation of the Bay, of its beauty." What held true for McLaughlin was equally so for Esther Gulick: "As a young child [I] went down to live in Fresno in the San Joaquin Valley, where we also had the same kind of arid conditions that Sylvia mentioned. But when we came up to San Francisco . . . it was always a big moment . . . when we saw the Bay . . . from our car."[37] She recalled as well that Jan Konecny, a chemical engineer who served as the first president of Save the Bay and swam in the bay daily, "had a good view of the Bay from his house . . . liked the beauty, and didn't want to see it spoiled."[38] A Czech citizen with a Swiss wife, he "expected San Francisco Bay to resemble the beautiful lakes of Europe."[39]

The bay activists' initial, unexamined, but powerfully instinctive attraction to the beauty of San Francisco Bay was undoubtedly based on the same immeasurable human impulses as an earlier generation of alpinists' love of Hetch Hetchy and the Sierras. Yet the fact that a coterie of wilderness enthusiasts found Hetch Hetchy to be intrinsically beautiful had not been enough to save it. In fact, even dam advocates like John Freeman had discovered that they could manipulate aesthetic concerns to their advantage by offering the public both an abundance of water for urban growth and the man-made beauty of a landscaped reservoir in place of limited growth and the unmodified physical qualities of the "wild." In the absence of a definable, a broadly held, and—especially—a politically defensible definition of environmental beauty, aesthetics alone had proven to be a weak basis for a preservation movement. Politics in the modern industrial world offers a poor forum for whatever it is that drives the human need for some sort of aesthetic satisfaction in nature, some kind of sensually satisfying experience of being of the world. Determined and politically astute, Kerr, McLaughlin, and Gulick understood very well the challenges that they faced, and they set about meeting these by assembling as strong an empirical defense of the bay as possible. As Harold Gilliam has noted: "Unlike a good many well-intentioned but ineffective conservationists who feel that indignation is enough, the Save-the-Bay people did their homework: they consulted economists about the feasibility of the proposed fill; they talked to engineers, city planners, and sociologists; and they confronted the Berkeley city council with an impressive array of hard facts."[40] They were greatly aided in this by the proximity of a community of sympathetic university scholars.

Among those academicians who assisted the fledgling Save the Bay Association was the retired professor of economics and business administration William Leonard Crum, who submitted a critical evaluation of Berkeley's waterfront plan to Mayor Claude Hutchinson, himself as former dean of the School of Agriculture. Catherine Kerr has noted the good fortune of having an academic mayor who could read and grasp Professor Crum's dense prose. Other professors, including economists Fred Balderston, Charles Gulick, and Lovell "Tu" Jarvis, and political scientists Eugene Lee and Tom Blaisdell, were very supportive as well.[41] The technical assistance and professional cachet they imparted to Save the Bay's arguments before the Berkeley City Council suggested a shift in the locus of politically respectable expertise from where it had been in the 1930s and 1940s. Save the Bay's professorial spokesmen were given credence to make authoritative public attestations that a generation earlier had been the provenance of private consulting engineers. In the new postwar era, universities were effectively carving out a niche as repositories of socially valuable knowledge and as the home of the experts who could apply it. This phenomenon was further demonstrated by the alliance between the leaders of the Save the Bay Association and the University of California's Institute of Governmental Studies, whose assistant director was Professor Eugene Lee.

Save the Bay labored assiduously and successfully to convince the Berkeley City Council to give up the city's waterfront landfill plan, which it did by December 1963. Determined as well to carry the larger battle for long-term protection of the bay to the state legislature, Catherine Kerr convinced the Institute of Governmental Studies at the University of California, Berkeley, to produce a comprehensive analysis of the bay and its history, uses, and problems. In the late spring of 1961, the institute engaged city planning expert Mel Scott—also president of Citizens for Regional Recreation and Parks, which was later known as People for Open Space—to author this detailed report, which was released in September 1963 as *The Future of San Francisco Bay*. Eugene Lee's foreword emphasized the report's multifocal approach, arguing that continued neglect of the bay would "result only in further attrition of [its] economic, scenic and recreational value." Mel Scott, certainly aware of the political arena in which his report would have to stand scrutiny, did not merely argue for San Francisco Bay's preservation as an object of beauty but, as Lee noted, identified "the economic resources that may be jeopardized by further unplanned and uncontrolled filling; the increasing need to use the bay for the disposal of waste and flood waters, and the potential conflict between these requirements and demands for various filling projects; the great potential of the bay for meeting regional recreational needs; and the political choices and decisions facing the people of the Bay Area as they seek to safeguard the bay for present and future generations." Nonetheless, despite his eminently practical approach, Scott launched his discussion in a critical anti-utilitarian tone: "To the man who owns a sailboat the bay may be an aquatic paradise and to the visitor from New York . . . a magnificent scenic attraction, but to attorneys, developers, title insurance companies, land companies, manufacturers of salt and cement, innumerable government officials, members of the state legislature, and many others it is some of the most valuable real estate in California."[42]

The idea that the bay was real estate was not a new one, as Scott pointed out in the opening pages of his study. In the immediate aftermath of the U.S. conquest of San Francisco in 1847, Brigadier General Stephen Kearny granted to the town hundreds of underwater lots in Yerba Buena cove that were sold at public auction. In 1853, Governor John Bigler declared that the state held title not only to the shores of the bay but to wholly submerged lands as well. In 1868, the state surveyor general authorized the sale to companies and individuals of thousands of acres of property in San Francisco Bay that were not tidelands as defined in the law, but that were submerged to a depth of six to eighteen feet. In that same year, the legislature created a Board of Tide Land Commissioners, empowered to dispose of all "salt marsh and tide lands belonging to the state" within San Francisco south of Second Street, to "a point not beyond twenty-four feet of water at . . . lowest . . . tide." In 1880, the state's title and right to dispose of such lands was sustained by the California Supreme Court as well in *Le Roy v. Dunkerley*. Throughout the twentieth century, California made numerous and abundant grants of tidal and underwater lands to the various municipalities surrounding the bay. In short, what shocked and alarmed the Save the Bay activists was the exercise, past midcentury, of a public and private property right that had, without their full understanding, been around for a long time. As Mel Scott declared, "for eleven decades the state government has tended to regard the bay as property rather than as a great natural resource to be safeguarded." This historical course is what the activists of the 1960s dedicated themselves to change.[43]

Scott's study provided much of the ammunition that the Save the Bay Association employed in its legislative lobbying and public relations battles. Though the initial and most powerful impulse driving the movement's public was a love of the bay's beauty, the report on which supporters pinned their political success shared the pragmatism of the various utilitarian reports made by public agencies and private engineers that had finally buried the Reber Plan. It was, however, a novel, thoughtful, and environmentally conscious pragmatism that sought to wed three functions of the bay—its economic use as the site of "bay-appropriate" production, its semi-economic use as a recreational asset, and its largely noneconomic right to exist as a living object of nature. In other words, in addressing the proper relationship of people to what was already a thoroughly anthropized environment, Scott neither ceded ground to the primacy of technical efficiency and private profit nor relied on the sort of wilderness advocacy that divorces human labor from pure nature. Instead, he presumed that production and nature could be compatible but that human beings would have to set viable terms for their coexistence.

Scott's central goal was to promote regional planning based on the idea of using the "bay as bay." He expressed confidence that the federal government would always ensure the navigational functions of the bay by maintaining deepwater ports and shipping channels, even in the face of reclamation, but he was not sanguine that other important uses would be safeguarded without state and regional intervention. Scott noted, for example, the bay's ten-million-dollar-per-year solar salt industry. This industry produced one-third of the world's solar salt and virtually all of the salt consumed in the Pacific states, Idaho, and Nevada. It provided salt at under 60 percent of the cost of alternative supplies for a whole range of processes including the manufacture of ammonia, soaps and detergents, solvents, water sterilizers and softeners, pulp and paper products, petroleum and plastics, and hides and leather, in addition to its use in meatpacking and produce packing. Salt production—as well as the dredging of blue clay and oyster shell deposits used in the cement industry—was dependent on the continued existence of the bay's shallow tidelands that were most susceptible to reclamation for real estate.[44]

Besides its mineral resources, San Francisco Bay was also replete with living resources of substantial value. Although overfishing and pollution had taken their toll on the bay's fisheries, sport fishing still generated annual revenue in excess of $32 million—a sum that could increase with more effective pollution controls. In addition, the bay served as the breeding and nursery ground for many ocean fish and was the habitat of the mysid shrimps, branchiopods, and amphipods consumed by fish higher on the food chain. The bay's wetlands were home to waterfowl, which, like the fish, had a multimillion-dollar value in terms of recreational hunting. While stressing the economic importance of hunting and fishing, though, Scott did not reduce the bay's wildlife to a mere accounting factor. The natural areas of the bay, Scott remarked, were "worthy of conservation because of their importance to wildlife . . . [and their] value for ecological research and nature recreation. Shallow bays are spawning and nursery grounds for various species of commercial and sport fish. Intertidal mudflats are the habitats of small invertebrate animals on which shore-birds, terns, ducks, and gulls feed. Saltmarshes and natural bay shores include plants which are essential to many kinds of birds and small mammals."[45] Scott's report was a lesson in ecological interdependencies that made the survival of the "living bay" the core principle in achieving the satisfaction of multiple human needs.

Scott followed his appraisal of the linked economic, ecological, and recreational merits of the "bay as bay" with a sobering assessment of San Francisco Bay's role as the region's great sewer. Noting both significant advances in waste treatment since the Second World War and the steady increase in pollution that nonetheless accompanied residential and industrial growth, Scott asked, "Do the people of the Bay Area . . . wish to eliminate all hazards to health, all pollution, and all nuisances whatsoever in the entire estuarial system? Do they wish to be able to enjoy water-contact sports in every part of the bay, and to encourage maximum development of the fishery resources of the bay? Or if not this, are they willing to sacrifice some of the beneficial uses of the water in certain parts of the bay and to permit . . . various discharges that do pollute the bay?"[46] Turning the matter over to "the residents of the metropolitan region . . . collectively," Scott emphasized the urgency of regional coordination, policy-making, and long-range planning. Scott addressed the problem of bay-front sanitary landfills in the same way, and even offered a forward-looking alternative to dumping and incineration that is now commonplace—citywide and countywide recycling and composting of household wastes.[47]

While avoiding explicit environmental policy advocacy, Scott used his report to publicize a thorough analysis of the history, uses, and condition of San Francisco Bay, and to promote regional planning through the establishment of a Bay Conservation and Development Commission. Most importantly, he demonstrated a powerful faith that the open, public, and democratic processes underlying such planning would produce a healthier bay environment of enduring beauty. Certain of the general public's ultimate will, Scott challenged his plan's potential critics to "leave no doubt that your proposal will give the people of the Bay Area an effective voice in decisions of the state and federal governments affecting the bay. Above all, satisfy our desire for a bay that will express our pride in the region, our belief in the right of every man to enjoy his natural heritage, our reverence for wonders and beauties that are beyond the power of man to create." Scott's report represented an important new direction in environmental activism especially suited to cities, where the most transformative consequences of human activity sometimes meet persisting elements of a pre-urban nature. The San Francisco region was particular blessed by such an encounter, with "hills and mountains lift[ing] serenely above enclosed waters." Scott effectively summarized the challenge facing modern urbanites: "What matters is the continuity of Nature's best enhanced by man's most creative response."[48]

By April 1963, just a few months before the release of Scott's study, the bay conservation issue was taken up by Oakland assemblyman Nicholas Petris, who sponsored a bill prohibiting any further filling until a state commission could be established to consider an overall shoreline plan. Well-intentioned but lacking political clout, Petris failed several times over the next year to secure legislative support for any meaningful moratorium. Catherine Kerr then drew upon her vast social connections and approached San Francisco's state senator Eugene McAteer, who was a tough and influential member of the California Senate's "insiders club." McAteer was hardly a conservationist, and had even supported a northern bay crossing that would have destroyed Telegraph Hill in San Francisco. He did, however, burn with ambition, and he had his eyes on the city's mayoralty. McAteer may have sensed the potential future political significance of environmentalism and pursued the opportunity to break legislative ground. In any case, by May 1964, he had managed to secure a small appropriation to set up a temporary San Francisco Bay Conservation Study Commission, entrusted with the task of determining "what effects the further filling of San Francisco Bay will have upon navigation, fish and wildlife, air and water pollution, and all of the regional needs of the future population of the bay region." With former *Examiner* reporter Joseph Bodovitz at the helm, the commission held a dozen televised hearings that did much to generate public interest in the fate of the bay.

When the 1965 legislative session opened, the commission presented the state's lawmakers with a sixty-four-page study that included seven pages of findings and recommendations, all of which were consistent with the earlier university-sponsored Scott study. The commission declared that the public interest would best be served by "a politically responsible, democratic process by which the bay and its shoreline can be analyzed, planned and regulated as a unit . . . [with] creation of a governmental mechanism . . . to guide [its] conservation and development." The McAteer commission recommended the establishment of a San Francisco Bay Conservation and Development Commission (BCDC)—the exact title recommended earlier by Mel Scott—that would be empowered to prepare a "comprehensive and enforceable" bay plan and to issue or deny permits for any proposed landfill project. Soon after the release of these findings, McAteer and Petris cosponsored implementing legislation. McAteer spared no effort to secure the necessary support for passage, including seeking out the help of the popular San Francisco disc jockey, Don Sherwood, who used his morning radio program to mobilize listeners into a very successful letter-writing campaign. As a dramatic indication of the now-aroused general public's affection for their bay, legislators received thousands of letters and telegrams urging them to pass the BCDC bill.

McAteer's hard work in the state senate and Petris's in the assembly, backed up by the extensive public support that was generated by the Save San Francisco Bay Association and the media, resulted in passage of the McAteer-Petris Act in June 1965. Shortly after SB309 became law, McAteer acknowledged his debt to Mel Scott in a personal letter praising his "superb book, *The Future of San Francisco Bay* . . . [which] was the single most important medium involved in arousing the effective interest of thousands of Bay Area residents in the problems of unrestricted filling of San Francisco Bay."[49] He might well have also noted that it was the influence of the tea ladies that had led to the Scott study in the first place and that, in fact, had even brought McAteer himself on board. For all their own efforts, Catherine Kerr, Sylvia McLaughlin, and Esther Gulick did not find SB309 to be perfect. As McLaughlin recalled in 1985, "we wanted Bay fill stopped."[50] In order to secure passage, the politically savvy McAteer had been forced to make two important concessions—one excluding lands not subject to tidal action (that is, the salt ponds, from BCDC jurisdiction) and the other excluding projects already under way before formation of the BCDC. These politically necessary amendments, though less than ideal from a conservationist standpoint, facilitated the battle against the powerful myriad corporate and municipal lobbyists arrayed against the bill.

When all was said and done, the BCDC was born on September 17, 1965, and comprised twenty-seven members—one representative each from the Army Corps of Engineers, the Department of Health, Education and Welfare, and each of the nine area counties; one member each of the state's Resources Agency, State Lands Commission, San Francisco Bay Regional Water Pollution Control Board, and Bay Area Transportation Study Commission; the state's highway administrator; the state planning officer; three city representatives; and seven representatives of the general public. There was, by design, no direct representation of special interests like bay-front landowners, developers, or port agencies. Instead, the BCDC solicited opinions from beyond its varied and presumably disinterested body of lay commissioners through the vehicle of a citizen's advisory committee without enforcement power, which was mandated by law to consist of representatives of conservation and recreation organizations; one representative each of a public harbor agency, an airport agency, and an industrial development board; and a biologist, a sociologist, a geologist, an architect, a landscape architect, and a private landowner. Engaging multiple contending voices and perspectives strengthened the authority of the commission, which was given until the start of the 1969 legislative session to complete its bay plan.[51]

The 1969 San Francisco Bay Plan opened with words "San Francisco Bay is an irreplaceable gift of nature." The BCDC declared the plan's goal as maintenance of "a magnificent body of water that helps sustain the economy of the western United States, provides great opportunities for recreation, moderates the climate, combats air pollution, nourishes fish and wildlife, affords scenic enjoyment, and in countless other ways helps to enrich man's life."[52] A substantial victory for the rising environmental movement, the BCDC and its plan yielded mixed results over time, as one might expect from an effort to manage such a hotly contested landscape. On the one hand, San Francisco Bay's urban context made it impossible for the BCDC to pursue complete prevention of landfill and shoreline development for transportation, industrial, and residential purposes. On the other hand, despite the approval of most development permits between 1974 and 1983, the BCDC's sanctioning of a limited amount of filling was balanced by its insistence that, in exchange, developers restore wetlands and provide public access to the bay front. The net effect over that ten-year period was a gain of 625 acres of open water.[53]

Another problem faced by the BCDC was an alarming increase over the years in toxic pollutants from storm drains and oil refineries, as well as from agricultural pesticides and fertilizers from regions beyond its jurisdiction. Sadly, ongoing pollution has been extraordinarily deleterious to the bay as a living environment, to the extent that human consumption of bay fish is considered a health hazard today. However, it is a testament to the determined anti-fill advocacy of the three women who launched the Save the Bay movement that the BCDC's 1969 manifesto introduced explicit ecological considerations in an enforceable public document regarding San Francisco Bay. The Bay Plan stated that "filling can disrupt the ecological balance in the Bay, [which] is a complex biological system in which microorganisms, plants, fish, waterfowl, and shorebirds live in a delicate balance created by nature, and in which seemingly minor changes . . . may have . . . highly destructive effects." The commissioners also noted the importance of maintaining the surface area and water volume of the bay to "maintain adequate levels of oxygen in its waters . . . the strength of tides necessary to flush [away] wastes" and sufficient air-cooling capacity to minimize "the frequency and intensity of temperature-inversions, which trap air pollutants."[54]

The attention given to these sorts of systemic environmental concerns was a far cry from the narrowly economic utilitarianism of the preceding decades. In fact, despite the quarrels that one might have with subsequent uses or misuses of San Francisco Bay, it is difficult to overestimate the significance of the Save the Bay movement and its political successes. The movement awakened tens of thousands of ordinary people to their love of an aspect of their environment that had become second nature to them, and it mobilized them in its defense. The movement permanently placed environmental policy on California's legislative agenda. Its ability to tap deeply into public yearnings for a "livable" urbanism helped win many subsequent regulatory battles, the first of which was the bid to transform the BCDC into a permanent agency in 1969. The movement also ensured that, for the first time, one of the greatest estuarine systems in the world would be forever understood as such. Rather than infrequent, piecemeal, and often crisis-driven evaluation of the bay environment, as occurred in response to old hydraulic mining debris in the 1910s or drought in the 1920s, the bay would now be subjected to ongoing scrutiny as a complex and integrated natural system of which human beings were a part.[55] Finally, much as the Reber Plan had characterized the centrality of the doctrine of economic growth from the 1930s through the 1950s, the BCDC's Bay Plan offered a qualified challenge to the "common assumption that the supreme goal of every community is to grow, to compete in the population sweepstakes . . . to expand in every direction, across the land and into the water."[56] The Save the Bay movement legitimized debate over the thorny question of how best to balance multiple human and environmental needs—the need for work, housing, recreation, breathable air, clean water, and natural beauty; the need sometimes to live, even in a city, among other species; and the need to maintain and uphold, in urban habitats, some broadly accepted definition of "quality of life." On this last score, Save the Bay was not alone.

The environmental saga of the bay from the Reber Plan of the 1930s through the conservationist struggle of the 1960s paralleled a similar story that linked bridge construction in the 1930s to San Francisco's freeway revolt two and three decades later. Though the movement to prevent further freeway construction within San Francisco sought to protect the built environment of the city's neighborhoods rather than to preserve a piece of pre-urban nature, the freeway revolt and Save the Bay shared important generational attributes. In both cases, the development of urban infrastructure that had been cast in the positive light of growth and progress in the 1930s and 1940s brought substantial public resistance by the late 1950s and 1960s. In both cases as well, an expanded base of middle- and upper-middle-class citizens proved to be most effective at agitating on behalf of a pleasing and aesthetic urban environment. Finally, both movements boosted the political stature of environmental concerns.

Conceived during the prosperous 1920s and brought to fruition during the Great Depression, San Francisco's bridges broke down the limits imposed by the city's peninsular geography, with both expected and unexpected results. One surprising impact of the completion of the San Francisco–Oakland Bay Bridge in 1936 was a sudden interest in water pollution control on the part of the East Bay municipalities. Until the bridge's completion, the principal transit link between the East Bay cities and San Francisco had been the electric interurban Key System railway, which carried passengers out though the Oakland/Emeryville mudflats by way of a long mole that ended in a ferry terminal not far from Yerba Buena Island. Many civic leaders, including Oakland's mayor W. J. McCracken, correctly anticipated the substantial increase in transbay private automobile traffic that eventually contributed to the collapse of the mass transit system. While neither prescient of, nor particularly concerned for, the fate of the rail system, McCracken and others did imagine that the ease of automobile travel would vastly augment the number of suburbanites who would choose to take up residence in the East Bay cities and maintain their jobs in San Francisco. Oakland alone forecast population growth of ninety thousand by the end of the decade, and San Francisco echoed this, fearfully anticipating a loss of thirty-four thousand people unless improvements were made to its own internal transit links to the city's western neighborhoods.[57]

East Bay officials, while hopeful of growth, were anxious and appalled at the thought of tens of thousands of middle-class people returning home in the evening every weekday over a bridge that landed them alongside the foul-smelling, industrially polluted tidal mudflats that lined the bay from Richmond to San Leandro. Faced with this prospect, in 1937 the city officials of Alameda,

Albany, El Cerrito, Emeryville, Piedmont, Richmond, and San Leandro joined with those of Oakland in forming the East Bay Municipal Executives Association, which in turn appointed a committee of engineers to conduct a sewage disposal study. As progress toward collective action was slow, San Leandro moved ahead alone with the construction of trunk sewers and treatment facilities. In 1940, the remaining seven cities resumed their investigation of a solution with an appropriation of funds for the East Bay Cities Sewage Disposal Survey. Since Oakland had initiated this entire line of inquiry, it was ironic that its city auditor, Harry G. Williams, had to be compelled by court order to authorize the city's contribution to the survey allocation. The judgment on behalf of the city in *The City of Oakland v. Williams* declared the existence of a "grave condition . . . threatening both health and property."[58] In their final report, consulting engineers Charles Gilman Hyde, Harold Farnsworth Gray, and A. M. Rawn concluded that the East Bay Municipal Utilities District was best equipped to take charge of sewage treatment and disposal and should be entrusted with that responsibility. In their assessment of the gravity of the problem, the engineers declared that "foul conditions . . . have rendered the shores and shore waters hardly utilizable for recreational uses . . . ; completely unsuitable for bathing; and a handicap to industrial development and shipping." And while the court affidavit cited the "illness of persons required to work in the vicinity," as well as "a pollution of shellfish," the engineers concluded more cautiously that the problem was essentially "one of aesthetics . . . rather than one . . . concerned with the public health."[59]

A few months after Hyde, Gray, and Rawn completed their report, Japanese armed forces attacked Pearl Harbor, and the United States entered the World War, deflecting public attention from bay pollution for some time to come. Nonetheless, the concern over waterfront health, function, and especially aesthetics that municipal leaders and local chambers of commerce had expressed for several years was significant in the promise it held for the postwar era. East Bay waterfront and industrial workers had already suffered decades of exposure to noxious gases and effluent without drawing much attention from civic leaders. In fact, in environmental terms, these sorts of laborers had enjoyed little beneficial change since the 1860s and 1870s, when working-class children in San Francisco swam in the industrially fouled waters of Mission Bay. But the growth of an urban and suburban middle class in the 1920s, stalled by the depression but accelerated in the aftermath of World War II, provided the basis for a more determined political will to defend environmental quality, at the very least in ways that suited the middle-class aesthetic.

While the depression-era discussion over the east-shore bay front had not been initiated by or principally on behalf of industrial workers, its social base was also quite unlike that of Nob and Rincon hills' battle against the south of Market slaughterhouses in the nineteenth century or Hillsborough's defeat of South San Francisco copper smelting in 1908. Instead, the debates of the 1930s took the Bay Area a small step in the direction of transforming the drive for environmental quality from an elitist to a broad popular movement. Though fueled by city governments that understood the connections between aesthetics and economic growth, and as yet lacking an ecological consciousness, this movement embodied a middle-class quest for cleanliness, wholesomeness, and order and a yearning for environmental amenities like space, quiet, and some element of natural beauty—all themes that would reassert themselves in a more significant way as more Americans achieved middle-class standards of living in the decades that followed the Second World War.

While East Bay civic leaders of the mid-1930s focused on water pollution, San Francisco leaders had different concerns stemming from the opening of the two bridges—population outflow to the suburbs and traffic. Local economy was again at the core of these concerns, and the proffered solutions were delivered top-down through technocratic channels. In 1931, City Engineer Michael O'Shaughnessy had already warned of the city's need to compete with expected reduced travel times from the East Bay by building rapid transit links to its own western neighborhoods. In 1934, the San Francisco Public Utilities Commission (SFPUC) echoed this warning and concluded that "the western part of San Francisco would be placed at a great disadvantage as it will require less time to cross the Bay via the Bridge than it will to reach a number of the desirable residence sections of the City by the present street car system."[60] Later in the year, the board of supervisors appropriated twenty-five thousand dollars to hire Robert Ridgway and Alfred Brahdy of the New York City Board of Transportation to recommend a plan for a San Francisco rapid transit system. In July 1935, Ridgway and Brahdy suggested that San Francisco was too small to warrant a New York–style system but that the city could benefit from something more modest and less expensive, the principal feature of which would be a subway under Market Street with east/west surface connections to and from Van Ness Avenue. The $53 million plan stalled in the face of resistance from supervisors who were alarmed at its cost; opposition from the owners and employees of the private Market Street Railway, which would have been barred from using the new subway tunnels; and protests from advocates of municipalization, who wished to consolidate existing services under municipal ownership before moving forward on any new plan.

At the same time, the nationally renowned traffic consultant Miller McClintock conducted a citywide survey to address the impact of the bridges on traffic flow on the city's streets. San Francisco did not suffer the predicted net outflow of population that leaders like O'Shaughnessy had feared, but the city did gain only 142 residents during the 1930s, while neighboring counties gained thousands. The bridges had made small towns and cities on the urban periphery viable as satellites of the big city. These satellites attracted the bulk of population influx into the Bay Area during that decade, promising a substantial increase in automobile traffic into and out of San Francisco on a daily basis. This new reality, coupled with the fact that motor vehicle registration in the city proper had risen from twelve thousand in 1914 to one hundred sixty thousand by 1937, led to substantial traffic congestion, especially downtown. McClintock's proposed remedy was a "Limited Way Plan" that consisted of sixty-five miles of elevated, depressed, and semi-depressed roadways similar to New York's Westside Highway, designed to move traffic at an average speed of forty miles per hour. These expressways were laid out with one continuous thoroughfare close to or along the bay on Third Street, the Embarcadero, and Marina Boulevard; two east/west connectors, one along California Street and the other through Golden Gate Park; and two north/south roadways along Van Ness and Potrero avenues, with two diagonal transverse roads from Market and Harrison streets out to points in the southwestern corner of the city. McClintock estimated the cost of the plan at $26 million, half the expense of the SFPUC's subway plan, and proposed it for the same reason—to help San Francisco compete for residents with areas made more accessible by the bridges.[61]

Despite their actual or potential environmental impact, the Bay Area's bridge and roadway plans were principally about economics and focused on the geographic distribution of the costs and benefits of growth. Consequently, the reason that East Bay cities felt compelled to deal with their malodorous wetlands was not fundamentally different than the motive of San Francisco engineers in promoting new transportation systems. Both groups were striving to enhance their regional competitive advantages in an increasingly integrated metropolitan system. Civic leaders at that time had no appreciation of regional ecology—nor did voters have any basis for judging the merits of a development plan other than its cost or perceived feasibility. After voters rejected expenditure on the subway plan by a three-to-two margin in November 1937, the McClintock proposal was shelved as well. No one could have imagined that state highway planners would propose a similar but grander plan fifteen years later that would arouse far greater controversy and grassroots resistance.

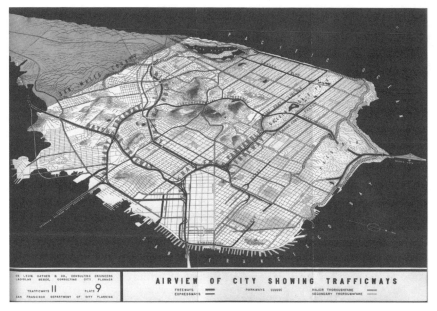

De Leuw, Cather and Company's 1948 San Francisco freeway proposal. Courtesy of the San Francisco History Center, San Francisco Public Library.

In 1947, California's Collier-Burns Act earmarked higher fuel taxes and auto license fees for urban freeway construction. The following year, the transportation engineering firm of De Leuw, Cather and Company presented San Francisco's Planning Commission with an expansive new roadway plan. In 1952, the State of California and the San Francisco Board of Supervisors approved a modified version of this as the San Francisco Trafficways Plan, which proposed an extensive network of freeways transecting the city. The plan was typical for a period in the nation's history during which highway development was seen as integral to economic growth, as further evidenced by President Eisenhower's signing of the National Interstate Defense and Highways Act in 1956. From the mid-1940s to the mid-1950s, business and labor leaders in San Francisco were united in the view that the city's competitive position in relation to regional rivals depended on enhancing road traffic to and through the city. The San Francisco Labor Council–AFL, the San Francisco Chamber of Commerce, and the Down Town Association all concurred with the plans proposed by state highway engineers. However, by early 1959 a group of neighborhood associations and environmental activists had convinced the board of supervisors to reverse the city's prior approval of seven out of the nine crosstown freeways slated for construction by the state highway department. Like its contemporary movement to save San Francisco Bay, the "freeway revolt" was driven in large part by its participants' powerful desire to protect the city's "treasured appearance."[62]

On one level, factions in the freeway battle supported different mechanisms of economic growth that harkened back to the debates surrounding the Burnham Plan. The earthquake of 1906 had buried the Burnham Plan and temporarily resolved the contest between commercial pragmatism and urban beauty in favor of the former, but, since a vital urban economy is not entirely inconsistent with aesthetic satisfaction and livability, the issue was not destined to rest forever. Although the resistance to intraurban freeways differed from the City Beautiful movement in that it sought to preserve rather than to transform the existing urban landscape, the city's business leaders and others were divided as to whether San Francisco's post–World War II economy would best be served by enhancing commercial traffic flow or by protecting the city's—now "old-fashioned"— aesthetic qualities. Decades of deindustrialization, accompanied by the growing importance of recreational tourism, eventually strengthened the hand of those who favored protecting the city's aesthetics. Though not always successful at first, many of the city's aesthetic defenders were politically well-connected. In 1956, when the planned Embarcadero Freeway threatened to sever the historic Ferry Building from the city, Charles Blyth, of the independent planning group known as the Blyth-Zellerbach Committee, appealed directly to his friend, Mayor George Christopher. Blyth secured the mayor's support for replacing the elevated freeway plan with an underground boulevard that would allow for a visually appealing Ferry Building Park at the foot of Market Street, but unfortunately no funds were available for the alternate design.

Scott Newhall, the executive editor of the *San Francisco Chronicle*, was another influential opponent of the Trafficways Plan. Although the *Chronicle* had initially endorsed the freeways, by the end of 1955 the paper was unequivocal in expressing its opposition. The shift can be explained in large part by Newhall's personal conversion. When his friend Karl Kortum, director of the Maritime Museum, showed him photographs of Seattle's newly completed and unsightly waterfront freeway, Newhall was aghast. The *Chronicle* soon began turning over its editorial pages to anti-freeway voices, including those of urban planner Francis Violich, columnist Herb Caen, and environmental writer Harold Gilliam, soon to be associated with the Save the Bay movement as well. Kortum soon discovered that his paper's environmentalist position was an asset in its circulation wars with its rival, the *Examiner*, and in fact the freeway debate played an important role in the *Chronicle*'s ultimate ascendancy.

The *Chronicle*'s assumption of an anti-freeway advocacy role paralleled the rise of grassroots resistance on the part of neighborhood associations in the Glen Park, Sunset, Telegraph Hill,and Marina districts, which was facilitated by revision of the California Streets and Highways Code to mandate public input on new freeway plans. Between 1955 and 1959, neighborhood associations and business owners from prosperous neighborhoods where hundreds faced displacement took on the state's Division of Highways. Reflecting once again the importance of a vastly expanded postwar middle class to the emergence of contemporary environmental values and politics, tens of thousands of Sunset District residents mobilized to prevent the construction of the Western Freeway that would have bisected their neighborhood. Operating under the banner slogan of "Protect YOUR home—YOUR neighborhood—YOUR community," they were led by the property developer and Sunset resident Christopher McKeon and millionaire politician William Blake.[63] The two men founded the anti-freeway Property Owners' Association of San Francisco, while Blake used his position as chairman of the board of supervisor's Committee on Streets to push the views of the various neighborhood associations before the city government. In January 1959, the movement succeeded. In a unanimous vote, the San Francisco Board of Supervisors rejected seven of the nine freeways proposed in the Trafficways Plan, including the Western Freeway.

The freeway revolt made the need to satisfy a restive public quite evident to Mayor Christopher, who empanelled a Citizens Freeway Committee to make recommendations on future freeway policy. When the committee issued a report ten months later and was subsequently dissolved, the grassroots movement to which it owed its existence did not dissipate. The Forest Hill Garden Club and the Potrero Hill Boosters and Merchants Association both opposed revised freeway plans in 1961, while plans to "cut and cover" the Golden Gate Park Panhandle for freeway development started down the road to defeat in 1964. In the latter case, local resident Sue Bierman helped launch the Haight Ashbury Neighborhood Council, which mobilized public opposition to the Panhandle Freeway and put pressure on the board of supervisors to reject the project. The board, despite Governor Edmund "Pat" Brown and Mayor John Shelley's aggressive support for freeways in Golden Gate Park, voted against pursuing any such projects in October 1964. The swing vote for the majority came from the city's only African American supervisor, Terry Francois, who later commented that freeway construction would harm the "unique and enviable character" of the Haight-Ashbury neighborhood as "one of the few pleasant well-integrated neighborhoods" in San Francisco.[64]

By the mid-1960s, it was evident that the citizens of San Francisco would not accept any further freeway development. The freeway revolt's success protected San Francisco's "treasured appearance" from what city planner Paul Oppermann had warned in 1955 would be "an expensive, unsightly, and very durable civic blunder for future generations to mourn over." Four decades later, after the Loma Prieta earthquake of 1989, San Francisco demolished the weakened Embarcadero Freeway—one of the two to have escaped the freeway rebels' axe. The city's decision to finally end the jarring isolation of the Ferry Building from Market Street and to reunite the people of the city with their beautiful waterfront was a reminder of the lasting legacy of the urban environmental aesthetic that took root during the freeway revolt of the 1950s and 1960s.[65]

By the mid-1960s, the San Francisco Bay region had established itself as a pioneer of urban environmentalism, owing principally to grassroots movements that rescued the bay from destruction by landfill and the city from girding in concrete viaducts. The common feature of these movements was the political engagement of a substantial number of prosperous middle-class citizens, intent upon defending or creating an aesthetically gratifying and livable urban environment. The new environmentalism did not impress itself on a blank historical slate. Like the proponents of the Burnham Plan, the new urban environmentalists believed that a cityscape's design mattered and that it should incorporate elements of visual beauty. Like the founders of Golden Gate Park, they understood that nature had a place in the city. On the same score, many of the freeway opponents, like the earlier park advocates, saw a connection between quality of life and property values and readily defended them both. The intergenerational persistence of material self-interest in urban design was accompanied as well by the resurgence of a sense of social mission. Harold Gilliam, for example, echoed the social environmentalism of the past in his expression of hope that by the recreational development of San Francisco Bay, which was flanked in many places by slums, "the horizons of children as well as adults would no longer be bound by the walls of the ghetto but would extend to the Bay and its far shores, [and bring] beauty . . . to the blighted areas."[66]

Yet the new movements also manifested novel traits. Thanks to the growth of the post–World War II middle class, the Save San Francisco Bay and anti-freeway movements enjoyed a much broader base of public support than was possible to achieve in the late nineteenth or early twentieth centuries. In California, this politically active and environmentally engaged public repeatedly displayed its concerns and expectations—not only in the Bay region proper, but elsewhere as well. In Sonoma County, residents launched a contemporaneous campaign against the Pacific Gas and Electric Corporation's plans to build a nuclear reactor on Bodega Bay.[67] Like their activist counterparts a few miles to the south, they too were successful. Perhaps most importantly, the mass movements of the 1950s and 1960s took the definition of urban livability out of the hands of experts or narrow elites. The urban park and City Beautiful advocates of an earlier time, however attractive their plans might have been, were inclined by profession, disposition, and social stature to satisfy perceived human needs with top-down efforts at urban design. The engineers in whom trust was vested in the 1930s and 1940s, however astute they were in weighing the consequences of human activity, measured need along only one axis—functionality. By comparison, the new middle-class environmentalists expressed and defended their own broadly experienced need for beauty, health, and comfort. They promoted an aesthetic of urban life that warranted no complex intellectual justification They sought, as is essential in an urban setting, a viable compromise between the city as a place to work and the city as a place to live.[68] They were fortunate that the setting for the San Francisco Bay metropolis offered so much inspiration for the yearning to achieve some sort of balance between urbanism and nature and stoked the drive for what we have come to think of as "human-scale" city life. Finally, they left us both a legacy of success and a reservoir of challenges—how will we shape our urban civilization to make "livability" tangible in the twenty-first century?

BEYOND BEAUTY AND COMFORT

The Save the Bay movement and the San Francisco freeway revolt of the 1960s were emblematic of a new wave of urban environmental activism that persists to this day. Their success derived from the increasing prevalence by midcentury of environmental values that fueled concerns about the role of nature in urbanized environments, the impact of urban industrial conditions on public health, and the impact of rising levels of population and production on the quality of life. In their efforts to address the qualitative problems of urban growth, San Franciscans and other Bay Area inhabitants have been part of a broader national trend. Urbanites in general, occupying spaces that are the direct result of human beings' most dramatic engagements with nature—and most profound transformation of the external world—have raised the loudest voices in defense of environmental quality. In fact, the centrality of the urban experience and of the urbanization of society as a whole to the emergence of contemporary environmental culture—including organizational life and politics—casts human capabilities in a very positive light. It demonstrates our ability to respond creatively to the consequences of our actions, despite our limited ability to weigh outcomes in the first instance. On the negative side, there are manifold and inevitable drawbacks with a perspective on nature that is rooted in an urban world. Like all people in all places at all times, contemporary American urbanites develop perspectives on life that are shaped by what is tangible and proximate to them. The material conditions of urban life, the received physical and social environment of the city, and the fact that the city becomes one's world all exert deep influence on instinctive patterns of thought. It is not easy for modern San Franciscans—any more than it would have been for the Yelamu, the missionaries of St. Francis, the Mexican rancheros, or the argonauts of 1849, and so on—to imagine a role for themselves in nature that is fundamentally outside of the parameters that their participation in a particular social and economic system appears to dictate.

It is one thing, for example, as the bay and freeway movements illustrated, to achieve some agreement on what constitutes an aesthetic of environmental beauty, however indefinable and unquantifiable. It is yet another to fully grasp the social implications as well as the environmental impacts, internal and external to the city, of the decisions one makes under the broad umbrella of "quality of life." To do this well, one needs to think beyond the bounds of one's immediate experience. While entirely possible, the challenge this presents has been shown time and again since the mid-1960s. The many examples include the contradictions manifest in ongoing struggles for green space and for the elimination of urban blight, and in the contention over urban growth limits and suburban sprawl.

The struggle to create the beautiful and extensive Golden Gate National Recreation Area (GGNRA) has been the most notable green space battle to be fought in the Bay Area in recent times, and it exemplifies the difficulty of achieving consensus on defining nature and its uses. San Francisco visitors and natives alike who have enjoyed the area's substantial coastal park can be grateful that President Nixon signed this pleasure ground into existence in 1972, but few are aware of why it is here. The brainchild of onetime Sierra Club president Edgar Wayburn, the project was avidly promoted by a grassroots organization called People for a Golden Gate National Recreation Area (PFGGNRA), while Congressman Philip Burton led the political charge in Washington, D.C. The drive to create the GGNRA was similar in many respects to the motive that had fueled the parks movement since the nineteenth century, which was largely to offer urbanites a natural refuge from the depths of the city. Yet the effort to create the GGNRA was fraught with much more conflict than the creation of Golden Gate Park and Yosemite Park in an earlier day. Unlike the formation of Golden Gate Park, where the only resistance came from nonhuman nature, or of Yosemite, where the Ahwahneechee Indians were too weak to resist the imposition of a park on their homes, the fate of the GGNRA was shaped by numerous powerful players. If further distinctions are to be made from the principal nineteenth-century examples described in this book, one can point to the facts that GGNRA was built in large part around the concept of preservation, while Golden Gate Park involved an almost total rearrangement of the landscape, and that GGNRA was to partly constitute a "wilderness area" in immediate proximity to the city, while Yosemite Park was at a sufficient distance to satisfy the then-prevalent definition of wilderness.

Much as the Sierra Club had come around to seeing the value of the Berkeley tea ladies' efforts at preserving the bay as an object of natural beauty within the metropolis, Wayburn had often taken the position that "wilderness begins in your own backyard."[1] Especially concerned with the small size of Marin

County's land reserves, Wayburn had labored to expand these as early as the 1940s. As exceptionally well told by historian Hal Rothman, the fulfillment of Wayburn's hopes and the GGNRA's fortunes were contingent on historical timing. In the wake of the urban riots of the 1960s, Secretary of the Interior Warren Hickel argued that "we have got to bring the natural world back to the people, rather than have them live in an environment where everything is paved over with concrete and loaded with frustration and violence."[2] Hickel's position was reminiscent of the social betterment arguments made by nineteenth-century and Progressive Era park advocates and was directly correlative to Harold Gilliam's vision of a recreational bay shore that would break down the "walls of the ghetto." Yet in none of these cases did the frustrated and the violent shape the contours or enjoy the principal benefits of the parks that were supposed to relieve their burdens.

Though the PFGGNRA was a very broad-based coalition, its success was influenced in part by the phenomenon we now call NIMBY, or "not in my backyard." As Rothman has adeptly put it: "In the battles of the 1960s in the Bay Area, local residents cloaked themselves in the quality-of-life environmentalism that rose to the fore as Americans came to believe that they could have it all without risk. . . . They regarded themselves as entitled to freedom from the consequences of the progress that gave them leisure, offering an environmentalism that depended on the affluence of their society for its claim to moral right."[3] Public responses to the proposed park in Marin County on the one hand and San Mateo County on the other illustrated the inseparability of environmental attitudes from collective and often narrowly conceived self-interest. In Marin, a coalition of ranchers, dairy farmers, other longtime rural residents, and more recent upper-middle-class and wealthy "escapees" from San Francisco supported park development as the most effective buffer against large-scale real estate development and continued suburban growth. For wealthy homeowners, the park promised to preserve or enhance the value of adjacent properties that served as second homes or suburban retreats. It also would close the door on future "quality of life" migrants whose presence in large numbers might destroy the very attributes that made Marin a refuge from the city in the first place.[4]

In San Mateo, the response to the park was markedly different. When a GGNRA southward-expansion proposal was floated subsequent to the Association of Bay Area Governments (ABAG) recommendation that the San Mateo coast be protected from development, locals from Pacifica, Pescadero, and elsewhere raised vehement objections. Ranchers feared that their lands might be confiscated under eminent domain, working-class residents wondered if they were about to be deprived of the mechanisms of growth and prosperity that their northerly neighbors had already enjoyed, and coastal communities as a whole worried about the prospect that their taxable land base would disappear. San Mateo residents confronted the PFGGNRA with their own PAGGNRA—People Against the Golden Gate National Recreation Area.[5] The contrasting responses and heterogeneous opposing alliances on both sides of the park issue demonstrate the extraordinary difficulty of forging a coherent vision and strategy of environmental engagement. While human beings have always been capable of contention over the proper uses and allocation of nature, the contest over best use in a modern urban industrial society such as ours is always heavily imbued with perspectives shaped by class, occupation, residence, and relative privilege. It is simply very difficult—to our own detriment and to that of our external world—for us to feel a part of the same nature, with all of the compromises and responsibilities that entails.

The debates that surround the proper uses of nature in the immediate hinterlands of the city have a correlate in the urban redevelopment arguments that have been characteristic of the late twentieth century. While the hinterland issue of preserving rural economic uses of land—agriculture and animal husbandry—obviously plays no part in the inner city planning process, that process has an ultimate and usually unexamined impact on land-use patterns external to the city. Further, both questions involve differing class-based visions of what constitutes an appropriate human environment as well. In the aftermath of World War II, the federal government committed itself to a sort of domestic Marshall Plan designed to revitalize American cities, which had suffered from declining investment during the depression years and inattention during the war. Though an objective phenomenon, the blight that urban redevelopment was designed to correct also happened to be a web in which the lives of many of the urban poor were deeply enmeshed. Consequently, what the more prosperous urbanites could comfortably refer to as "slum removal" came with certain social costs.

In San Francisco, redevelopment of the Western Addition neighborhood in the 1950s and 1960s displaced four thousand people. It produced an alienating physical landscape of apartment towers and institutional buildings that all seem oddly disjointed and disconnected from one another and that have done little to serve or enhance the public life of the street. It produced the Geary Expressway, which acts as a moat separating the largely African American Fillmore district from a reinvented—and arguably surreal—Japantown, as well as from wealthy Pacific Heights. It restored a small percentage of the area's blighted Victorian homes, once occupied by poor tenants, and made them accessible to a new and more affluent clientele.[6] Many of the displaced poor relocated to the Bayview-Hunters Point neighborhood never to return, while redevelopment did nothing to prevent the social problems associated with poverty from following them there. It is no wonder that today, as the San Francisco Redevelopment Agency proposes to bring half of Bayview—1,300 acres—under its jurisdiction, local residents are mistrustful and resistant. Despite the promise that redevelopment will cure the area's crime, poverty, and crumbling infrastructure, many residents, some of them aging Western Addition transplants, maintain justifiable fears that urban renewal means urban removal.

While the dialogue of urban renewal includes the voices of target communities to a far greater extent than it did half a century ago, it is still difficult for more prosperous urbanites to fully grasp the concerns of the poor or how to address them. This is especially so since gentrification produces an apparent enhancement of overall urban quality of life when the indices of this include safety, cleanliness, and the private capital investment that produces amenities of entertainment and leisure. Yet it is important to understand gentrification as another form of NIMBYism that displaces the essential problem it seeks to address and results in inequitable access to resources. San Francisco has not been much more successful than other cities in navigating the thorny contradictions endemic to urban redevelopment policies. In the words of Bayview community worker Patricia Wright, "Five dollar coffees and $20 mugs, that's all good . . . . But when you come in and build these things, where are we going to go?"[7]

Suburbanization is another comparable process, typically explained in terms of a space-to-land cost ratio, the supposedly immutable American urge to own a single-family home, and the desire to leave the troubles of urban life behind. The first of these factors may be quantifiable, but the second presumes—ahistorically—fixity of human need, and the third reflects an important strain of anti-urbanism that does in fact impinge on the environmentally rational use of space. It is not easy, for example, to fully disentangle the yearning for suburban living from the notion of a threatening "urban wilderness." As the established wealthy neighborhoods and newly gentrified areas of the city fall beyond the reach of middle-class people raising families, the affordable spaces occupied by the poor offer unacceptable alternatives that are laden with nightmarish visions of depravity and degradation. While wilderness as conceived in nonhuman nature—GGNRA, for example—carries with it the powerful appeal of a retreat from urban routines, a different sort of wilderness as imagined in an inner city context is colored by fears of human savagery. The two images operate in tandem to fuel a very prevalent anti-urban mentality that is partly responsible for and often reinforced by suburbanization. The consequence of this is spatial segregation by class and race on the one hand, with its attendant human costs, and an extraordinarily inefficient and insensible allocation of land and resources—the misuse of the wealth of nature—on the other, with all its attendant environmental costs.[8]

San Franciscans, proud of their city's urbanity, often take pleasure in mocking Los Angeles as a place with "no there there." Their offhand critique of L.A. as a fragmented metropolis of agglomerated bedroom communities sprawling pointlessly and destructively across the landscape has some validity, but the trouble is that neither San Franciscans nor other Americans should feel exempted from responsibility for the social and environmental costs of mismanaged growth and sprawl. Assuming such responsibility, however, requires a clear vision of how to accommodate the multiple and ultimately interdependent needs of human and nonhuman nature in an urban world—economic justice and environmental quality, production for use and ecological balance, the life of the city and the life of the Earth. Some critics of contemporary urban environmentalism, like Mike Davis, have derided the social base and limited vision of movements like Save the Bay as being a sort of patrician environmentalism with a Los Angeles analogue in the slow-growth movement of Southern California from the 1970s onward.[9] Though intentionally harsh in his assessment, Davis has correctly pointed out the false dichotomy of pro-growth versus slow growth that pits large developers against affluent homeowners and that was one of the elements at work in the GGNRA contest in Marin County as well. A debate that has been framed along these lines and reserved for these privileged constituencies ignores most people and most of nature. It is not, however, unchallenged in activist circles.

The history of environmentalism in the San Francisco Bay area has shown how the so-called patrician movement of the 1960s could and did evolve to grapple with the relationship between the social and the natural. In 1958, Dorothy Erskine and Jack Kent founded Citizens for Regional Recreation and Parks (CRRP), which became part of the coalition to save San Francisco Bay during the 1960s. In 1969, CRRP moved beyond its concern for urban recreational needs and became People for Open Space (POS) in recognition of the need to defend a proximate urban hinterland of ranches, farms, and wildlife preserves. In 1987, POS transformed itself once again, and became the Greenbelt Alliance, dedicated to grassroots activism and policy research. Over the subsequent decade, the organization focused on the relationships between suburban sprawl, farming, housing needs, and open space, and soon began to advocate urban infill development, higher density and affordable housing, and improved access to public transportation. It was essentially a program of planned urbanization that would deliver the best qualities of pedestrian-friendly urban liveliness to a broad section of the public while at the same time preserving local agricultural lands, recreational sites, and nonhuman habitats. In a progressive move, the alliance fostered the notion of urbanism as an environmental asset rather than as an environmental liability. It brought the idea of density minimums, rather than density maximums, into the political realm, opening the door ever so slightly to a post-suburban, post-automotive America. Though only a first step in the direction of environmental balance, the alliance has succeeded in securing twenty-one urban growth boundaries in the Bay Area since 1996. These are pointedly not designed to prevent the urbanization of the suburbs, but to achieve a sensible land-use balance in which multiple functions of the landscape are integrated at the regional level. Though it is far too early to visualize what the impact of this will be in another century, or to predict the outcome of the environmental political battles of future generations, it does indicate at least the prospect of imagining an urban world integrated into, rather than alienated from, the rest of nature.[10]

This integration, both physical and conceptual, stands as the main challenge of the future. Hundreds of years ago, the Yelamu occupants of San Francisco's pre-urban site had already built an integral world for themselves. They knew nature through their activities as hunters and gatherers, and they gave it meaning through animistic lenses that imbued all of creation with sentience and spiritual power. The Yelamu's ecological prescience was imperfect, but technological limits constrained their physical impact on the landscape. The Spanish missionaries and Mexican rancheros who supplanted the Yelamu knew nature as well—the former as horticulturists endowed with a divine right to cultivate and transform the wilderness, and the latter as masters of domesticated livestock. As different as they were from the Yelamu, they nonetheless understood their lives and livelihoods as inextricably bound to the fruits of the land, the passage of the seasons, and the cycles of deluge and drought. In contrast to all of these early inhabitants of the city's site, San Franciscans in the decades that followed the gold rush constructed an edifice of production, distribution, and habitation that divorced their daily routines and their experience of the world from its natural moorings. This was not unique, malevolent, or even foolish, but was part and parcel of a conventional entry into modern urban life. The passage of time, as we have seen, awakened in some a yearning to marry the benefits of urbanism to the lost world of external nature. From the urban parks movement to early efforts to protect distant wild hinterlands, from the aesthetic defense of home and neighborhood to a broadly targeted contemporary environmentalism, San

Franciscans have forged a path toward an urban future very unlike the city's formative boomtown past. It is a future of uncertain shape, but it will be entered consciously. Having repeatedly "improved upon" nature to serve the short-term interests of the city, like other urbanites, San Franciscans will face the question of how to build another "better nature" to serve their long-term needs—a nature built on environmental equity.

Over half a century ago, the pioneering ecologist Aldo Leopold formulated an ethical ideal for human relations with the rest of nature. Describing ethics as a limitation on freedom of action in the struggle for existence, Leopold posited the evolution of human ethical systems to include a broader and broader universe of relationships:

> The first ethics dealt with the relation between individuals, [as in] the Mosaic Decalogue. Later accretions dealt with the relation between the individual and society. The Golden Rule tries to integrate the individual to society; democracy to integrate social organization to the individual. . . . There is as yet no ethic dealing with man's relationship to land and to the animals and plants which grow upon it. . . . The extension of ethics to this third element in human environment is . . . an evolutionary possibility and an ecological necessity. . . . A land ethic changes the role of Homo sapiens from conqueror of the land-community to plain member and citizen of it.[11]

Let us excuse Leopold's culturally conditioned examples and consider the merits of his hopes. Arguably, ethical systems are as self-serving as they are noble. The capacity to perceive the "other" as "self"—to abide by the adage "there but for the grace of God go I"—is an accomplishment that draws on and feeds the virtue of compassion, and it is also an eminently practical strength. From an ecological perspective, it stands to reason that our species interest as conscious beings rests in effective management of the web of natural relations in which we are embedded and from which we are inseparable. To achieve this, we need scientific knowledge, social wisdom, collective action, and, yes— ethics. But how might Leopold's ethical evolution come to fruition? If there is an answer to be found in the twenty-first century, it will lie in an alteration of the relationship between urbanites and the rest of nature.

In the last two decades, ecologists and planners have developed provocative proposals for building sustainable urban futures. Some have advocated bioregionalism, which would break down the massive production and distribution apparatuses to which we have become accustomed—Central Valley industrial agriculture, for example—and restore the bonds between human activity and thought and the specific ecological qualities of their regional habitat. Others have argued for ecologically designed urban landscapes—wetlands that act as wastewater treatment sites, stormwater infiltration gardens planted with native vegetation, buildings aligned to make use of solar energy—that would remind urbanites on a daily basis of their presence within nature. These proposals, feasible or not, take aim at both practice and thought with the understanding that urban life demands of us an extra leap of consciousness, that we may imagine our continued links to the "external" world—in order to bridge the urban self and natural other.[12]

Maintaining ecological consciousness in an urban world in a way that becomes second nature is no small task that will require a new institutional framework for environmental decision making. But at the individual level, it may be that our attraction to certain indefinable qualities of natural beauty is our most potent tool. After all, it played a major role in all of the environmental reform efforts described in this book. If our aesthetic sensibilities are in fact pathways to grasping ecological processes, as some environmental philosophers and psychologists believe, then San Francisco is blessed indeed.[13] The beauty and drama of the city's setting, which few if any have been heard to challenge, present tremendous opportunities for reinventing nature here once again—this time further deepening the bonds between the human and nonhuman worlds that were reinvigorated by the emergence of the modern environmental movement.

The incontrovertible, sometimes enchanting, and often breathtaking beauty of San Francisco and its environs presents opportunities for environmental leadership that may not be so readily apparent in all urban settings. To as yet an insufficient extent, the area's inhabitants have accepted the responsibility that nature has thrust upon them. If San Franciscans assume the full mantle of this responsibility, the aesthetic sensibilities that have heretofore driven so much valuable civic engagement over the quality of life in a beautiful corner of the world will be substantially broadened. An aesthetic that admires a sustainable city in balance with the health of its hinterlands; that produces an ecologically sound distribution of population in which suburbs do not swallow farms, ranches, and wilderness; that leaves room for other species to share the Bay region with their human neighbors; and that achieves environmental justice by ceasing to foist the greatest burdens of environmental degradation on the poor and the powerless is an aesthetic that would most certainly reveal and achieve our better nature.

NOTES

PREFACE

1. Cronon, *Nature's Metropolis;* Hurley, *Common Fields;* Miller, *On the Border;* Colten, *Transforming New Orleans and its Environs;* Tarr, *Devastation and Renewal;* Deverell and Hise, *Land of Sunshine;* Melosi and Pratt, *Energy Metropolis;* Davis, *City of Quartz;* and *Ecology of Fear;* Brechin, *Imperial San Francisco;* Hays, *Beauty, Health, and Permanence;* and *Explorations in Environmental History;* Braudel, *Civilization and Capitalism.*

INTRODUCTION. NATURE AND THE CITY

1. The Chicago School is represented preeminently by Park, Burgess, and McKenzie, *The City.* See also Park, *The Collected Papers of Robert Ezra Park,* vol. 2, *Human Communities.* Contemporary writer Mike Davis adapted some of the Chicago School theories to his work on troubled Los Angeles in *The Ecology of Fear.*

2. See, for example, Starr, *Material Dreams.*

3. Gen. 1:28.

4. Cronon, "The Trouble with Wilderness," 89. Cronon credits others as well for similar interpretations: Jackson, "Beyond Wilderness," 71–91; and Pollan, *Second Nature.*

CHAPTER 1. COYOTE'S CHILDREN

1. Geiger and Meighan, *As the Padres Saw Them,* 1.

2. Ibid., 137.

3. Milliken, *A Time of Little Choice,* 260.

4. Ibid., 61–62.

5. Heizer and Elsasser, *The Natural World,* chaps. 3–4.

6. Nelson, "San Francisco Bay Shellmounds," 144.

7. http://www.muwekma.org/history/tribe.html

8. Cook, "Antiquity of San Francisco Bay Shellmounds," 202–205.

9. Davis, "Trade Routes," 23.

10. Davis, "Trade Routes," 12–13; Alfred L. Kroeber, "General Surveys," in Heizer and Whipple, *California Indians,* 41; Heizer, "Village Shifts," 482.

11. Gilliam, *The Natural World of San Francisco,* 33–34.

12. Beals and Hester, *Indian Occupancy,* 43–50; including Generalized Soil Map of California, UC College of Agriculture, Agricultural Experiment Station, Berkeley.

13. Milliken, *A Time of Little Choice,* 62.

14. Heizer and Elsasser, *The Natural World,* 95–98.

15. Nelson, "San Francisco Bay Shellmounds," 154–55.

16. Quoted in Browning, *San Francisco/Yerba Buena,* 99.

17. Lewis, "Patterns of Indian Burning," 55–116.

18. This is a condensation of an Ohlone creation story that appears online in a catalog of indigenous cultures at *http://members.tripod.com/~Sawols/ohlonestories.html*. A diverse collection of very similar tales appears in Bean, *The Ohlone Past and Present*.

19. Bean, "Power and its Applications," 408–20.

20. Geiger and Meighan, *As the Padres Saw Them*, 47–51.

21. Jackson and Castillo, *Indians, Franciscans, and Spanish Colonization*. The numbers derive from *Annual Reports*, Santa Barbara Mission Archive-Library; "Mission Statistics," Bancroft Library, UC Berkeley; and *Hartnell Mission Reports*, Bancroft Library, UC Berkeley.

22. Milliken, *A Time of Little Choice*, 63–64.

23. Ibid., 132.

24. Milliken, *A Time of Little Choice*, 68–69, 90–92, 137–38, 178–79, 200–201, derived from Mission San Francisco *Libro de Bautismos, 1776–1870*, Archives of the Archdiocese of San Francisco.

25. Jackson and Castillo, *Indians, Franciscans, and Spanish Colonization*, chap. 3.

26. Gen. 1:28.

CHAPTER 2. URBAN GENESIS

1. The political economy of the missions is well described in Jackson and Castillo, *Indians, Franciscans, and Spanish Colonization,* chap. 1. Brief commentary on the unique aspects of towns in Iberian America can be found in Braudel, *Civilization and Capitalism,* vol. 1, *The Structures of Everyday Life*, chap. 8.

2. Discussion of foreign mercantile role in urban development appears in Braudel, *Civilization and Capitalism*, vol. 3, *The Perspective of the World*, chap. 1.

3. William Antonio Richardson, "The Founding of Yerba Buena," in Browning, *San Francisco/Yerba Buena*; Lotchin, *San Francisco*, chap. 1.

4. McGloin, *San Francisco,* chaps. 2–3; Soulé, Gihon, and Nisbet, *The Annals of San Francisco*, pt. 2, chap. 2.

5. Eldredge, *The Beginnings of San Francisco*, chap. 14.

6. Lotchin, *San Francisco,* chap. 2.

7. Braudel, *Civilization and Capitalism,* vol. 1, *The Structures of Everyday Life*, 498–500.

8. *Random House Dictionary of the English Language,* unabridged ed.

9. Hittell, *A History of San Francisco,* cited in McIlroy and Praetzellis, *Vanished Community*, 70–71.

10. Ibid.

11. Todd, *The Sunset Land*, 263–64.

12. Ibid., 67–69.

13. Gray Brechin's *Imperial San Francisco* offers astute observations on the city's global role. Import statistics are from Soulé, Gihon, and Nisbet, *The Annals of San Francisco*, pt. 2, chap. 32. Mel Scott coined the phrase "mother of cities."

14. Lotchin, *San Francisco*, 46–48 (on imports); McIlroy and Praetzellis, *Vanished Community*, 84 (on gardens).

15. McIlroy and Praetzellis, *Vanished Community*, 85.

16. Lehmann, *Economic Development of the City of Santa Cruz*, 8–10.

17. Ibid., 14.

18. Lotchin, *San Francisco*, 174–180.

19. Schafer, *California Letters of Lucius Fairchild.*

20. Conzen, "A Saga of Families," chap. 9.

21. Shufelt, *A Letter from a Gold Miner.*

22. Soulé, Gihon, and Nisbet, *The Annals of San Francisco*, pt. 2, chap. 2.

23. Woods, *Sixteen Months at the Gold Diggings*, vii.

24. Boswell, "A Split Labor Market Analysis," 360.

25. Hill, *Gold,* 18–19, 94–97.

26. Todd, *The Sunset Land*, 53.

27. Brechin, *Imperial San Francisco*, chap. 1; Rohe, "Man as Geomorphic Agent," 5–16; Kelley, "The Mining Debris Controversy," 331–46.

28. Bailey, *Sam Brannan and the California Mormons.*

29. Lotchin, *San Francisco*, chap. 4.

30. Lotchin, *San Francisco*, chap. 7.

31. Brechin, *Imperial San Francisco*, chap. 1 (on silver).

32. Issel and Cherny, *San Francisco*, 53–57.

33. White, *"It's Your Misfortune and None of My Own,"* 337–40.

CHAPTER 3. GREENING THE CITY

1. On the parks movement, see Schuyler, *The New Urban Landscape*; and Spirn, "Constructing Nature," 91–113. For San Francisco specifically, see Young, *Building San Francisco's Parks*, chap. 1.

2. Rozenzweig and Blackmar, *The Park and the People.*

3. U.S. Bureau of the Census, "Population of the 100 Largest Cities . . . 1790–1990," Washington, D.C.: Bureau of the Census, June 1998; Demographia, "New York (Manhattan) Sectors Population & Density, 1800–1910," http://www.demographia.com/db-nyc-sector1800.htm.

4. Robert Woods, *The City Wilderness* (1898), excerpted in Merchant, *Major Problems* (1993 edition), 415–16.

5. Issel and Cherny, *San Francisco,* chap. 2.

6. Bancroft, *History of California*, vol. 7, 5:75–101n7 ("Manufactures").

7. McIlroy and Praetzellis, *Vanished Community*, 94.

8. *Daily Evening Bulletin*, quoted in Clary, *The Making of Golden Gate Park*, 3.

9. Hurley, "Busby's Stinkboat," 145–62.

10. Peter Stuck, "Butchertown—A Fragrant Memory," *San Francisco Chronicle*, October 9, 1971.

11. Hays, *Explorations in Environmental History*, 72.

12. Larsen, *The Far West,* 38.

13. Trollope, "Nothing to See in San Francisco," 318–19.

14. San Francisco Board of Supervisors, *San Francisco Municipal Reports* (1865–66), 395, quoted in Young, *Building San Francisco's Parks,* 47.

15. Todd, *The Sunset Land*, 263.

16. Soulé, Gihon, and Nisbet, *The Annals of San Francisco*, pt. 2, chap. 1.

17. *Daily Evening Bulletin*, July 25, 1865, 2.

18. Olmsted was quoted in San Francisco Board of Supervisors, *San Francisco Municipal Reports* (1865–66), 397, excerpted in Clary, *The Making of Golden Gate Park*, 2.

19. Olmsted, "Parks, Parkways and Pleasure Grounds," 253–54.

20. The whole Olmsted plan is presented in detail in Olmsted, "Preliminary Report in Regard to a Plan of Public Pleasure Grounds," 518–46. The main features of the plan are well summarized in Young, *Building San Francisco's Parks*, 52–56. Olmsted's visual observations

regarding the specific topographic contours and elevations of the proposed park site are given specificity by modern-day USGS aerial mapping.

21. Young, *Building San Francisco's Parks*, 58–60.

22. Young, *Building San Francisco's Parks*, 61–66; Clary, *The Making of Golden Gate Park*, 3–5.

23. Clary, *The Making of Golden Gate Park*, 26.

24. Excerpt from Hall's unpublished manuscript "Romance of a Woodland Park" (ca.1926), quoted in Young, *Building San Francisco's Parks*, 82–83. While Hall occasionally espoused the public virtues of urban parks in the 1870s, it should be noted that the manuscripts in which he elaborated most profusely on his thinking were written late in life. After a half century, it is likely that his recollections were embellished and his interpretation deepened by his later experiences.

25. Young, *Building San Francisco's Parks*, 84–86.

26. Clary, *The Making of Golden Gate Park*, 22–26; Young, *Building San Francisco's Parks*, 87–97. Much of this material is drawn from Hall's unpublished manuscript "The Story of a City Park" (ca.1919); and Giffen and Giffen, *The Story of Golden Gate Park*.

27. *Daily Morning Call,* December 12, 1875.

28. Rosenzweig and Blackmar, *The Park and the People*, 63–64. Quoted from the *Evening Post*, May 13, 1856; and Egbert Viele, "Topography of New York and Its Park System," in Wilson, *The Memorial History of the City of New York*.

29. Excerpt from Hall, "Our Park Sites as Nature Made Them," 6–7, in "The Making of a City Park" (unpublished manuscript; ca. 1915), quoted in Young, *Building San Francisco's Parks*, 60, 68–69, 102.

30. All material on the Bois de Boulogne is drawn from an excellent book by French environmental historian Jean Michel Derex, who specializes in forest and hydrological history. His *Histoire Du Bois De Boulogne* is not available in English. Consequently, the translations are my own.

31. Ray, "Modoc Childhood," 424–30; Blackburn, "Ceremonial Integration," 225–43; Park, "San Franciscans at Work and at Play," 44–51.

32. The problem of water pollution caused by slaughterhouse and tannery wastes was addressed repeatedly by the San Francisco Board of Supervisors in successive editions of the *Health Officers Report,* Fiscal Year 1865–1866 through at least Fiscal Year 1874–1875.

33. Spirn, "Constructing Nature," 93.

34. *Paterson Intelligencer,* July 9, 1828, quoted in Johnson, "'Art' and the Language of Progress," 434.

35. Johnson, "'Art' and the Language of Progress," 433–49.

36. Ibid., 437.

37. Hall's expectations are in Clary, *The Making of Golden Gate Park*, 22. Downing is quoted in Schuyler, *The New Urban Landscape*, 65–66.

38. Rosenzweig and Blackmar, *The Park and the People*, 104–105, 233–36.

39. Park, "San Franciscans at Work and at Play," 48.

40. Charles Warren Stoddard, *In the Footprints of the Padres*, quoted in McIlroy and Praetzellis, *Vanished Community*, 83.

41. Young, *Buiding San Francisco's Parks*, 37–38; McIlroy and Praetzellis, *Vanished Community*, 77–82; *San Francisco Chronicle*, November 9, 1913, 25.

42. *San Francisco Chronicle*, November 9, 1913, 25; from Ethel Malone Brown, "Woodward's Gardens," in Palmer, *Vignettes of Early San Francisco Homes and Gardens*, 15–19, found in Young, *Building San Francisco's Parks*, 39–43.

43. Leslie, *California,* chap. 19.

44. Runte, *Yosemite,* chap. 2.

45. Ibid., chap. 3.

46. Hall, *To Preserve from Defacement,* 21–25.

47. Warren Baer, "A Trip to Yosemite Falls," *Mariposa Democrat*, August 5, 1856.

48. Spence, *Dispossessing the Wilderness,* 105–19; Godfrey, "Yosemite Indians"; Bunnell, *Discovery of the Yosemite,* chap. 15.

49. Olmsted, *The Yosemite Valley.*

50. William Cronon's "The Trouble with Wilderness" offers a compelling philosophical discussion of wilderness as a state of mind (69–90).

51. *San Francisco Chronicle*, November 9, 1913, 25.

52. San Francisco Board of Park Commissioners, *Third Biennial Report,* 16.

CHAPTER 4. WATER

1. Roth, "Cholera," 527–51. The quote from Derbec appears in Nasatir, *A French Journalist,* 163–64.

2. Lotchin, *San Francisco*, 182; Delgado, "The Humblest Cottage," 26–27.

3. *Evening Picayune*, August 23, 1851, and December 8, 1851. Reproduced in Johnson, *San Francisco As It Is,* 194–95, 235–36.

4. Delgado, "The Humblest Cottage," 27–29.

5. Braudel, *Civilization and Capitalism*, vol. 1, *The Structures of Everyday Life,* 229–31.

6. Lotchin, *San Francisco*, 182; Delgado, "The Humblest Cottage," 29–31; Braudel, *Civilization and Capitalism*, vol. 1, *The Structures of Everyday Life,* 228.

7. Lotchin, *San Francisco*, 182.

8. *Alta California*, April 12, 1851.

9. Merguerian, "A History of the NYC Water Supply System"; *Alta California*, April 12, 1851.

10. Delgado, "The Humblest Cottage," 32–33; Lotchin, *San Francisco*, 183.

11. Delgado, "The Humblest Cottage," 35–37.

12. Brechin, *Imperial San Francisco*, 77–80.

13. Pisani, "'Why Shouldn't California,'" 347–60.

14. *Daily Territorial Enterprise* (Virginia City, Nev.), February 23, 1870, quoted in Pisani, "'Why Shouldn't California.'"

15. *The Daily Bee* (Sacramento), March 19, 1870; *Marysville Union* editorial reprinted in Sacramento *Union*, October 30, 1871; and *Alta*, March 12, 1870, all quoted in Pisani, "'Why Shouldn't California,'" 341.

16. U.S. Congressional Documents and Debates.

17. *Pacific Railway Act*, July 2, 1864, http://www.cprr.org/Museum/Pacific_Railroad_Acts.html\#1864.

18. Pisani, "'Why Shouldn't California,'" 354–60.

19. River Law Project, *River Law: Who Owns the Rivers?*

20. Igler, *Industrial* Cowboys, chap. 4.

21. *Debates and Proceedings of the Constitutional Convention of the State of California, convened at the City of Sacramento, Saturday, September 28, 1878,* ed. E. B. Willis and P. K. Stockton, 1880, sup. n. 7, quoted in Hartley, "Spring Valley Water Works," 299.

22. Kahrl, "Water for California Cities," 17–18.

23. Clements, "Engineers and Conservationists," 283–86.

24. Clements, "Engineers and Conservationists," 283–86; San Francisco Public Utilities Commission, *SFPUC History.*

25. Pourade, *The Glory Years*, chap. 2 (on rail access); Hennessey, "George White Marston," 230–53 (on harbor development); Fogelson, *The Fragmented Metropolis*, 46 (on Crocker).

26. Fogelson, *The Fragmented Metropolis*, 55.

27. Lieutenant Ord is quoted in Gumprecht, *The Los Angeles* River, chap. 2, p. 55; originally from E. O. C. Ord, *The City of Angels and the City of Saints: or, a Trip to Los Angeles and San Bernardino in 1856* (San Marino: Huntington Library, 1978).

28. Gumprecht, *The Los Angeles* River, 104–105. See also Hundley, *The Great Thirst*, chap. 4.

29. Issel and Cherny, *San Francisco*, 85–88, 154–61, 174–75; Long, "Pipe Dreams," 22–23.

30. Pinchot, *Breaking New Ground*, 326.

31. Turner, *The Frontier in American History*, 37.

32. Marsh, *Man and Nature*, 29.

33. Pinchot, *Breaking New Ground*, 326.

34. For a fine biography of John Wesley Powell, see Wallace Stegner's *Beyond the Hundredth Meridian*.

35. Knapp, "The Other Side of Conservation," 465–81.

36. Clements, "Engineers and Conservationists," 289; and "Politics and the Park," 189.

37. An excellent brief account of Muir's life, as well as the Hetch Hetchy controversy, appears in Nash's *Wilderness and the American Mind*, chaps. 8–10.

38. *Sierra Club History*, "Origins and Early Outings," http://www.sierraclub.org/history/origins.

39. Italicized emphasis added. Full text of the pamphlet is available online: http://www.sfmuseum.org/john/muir.html.

40. Wolfe, *John of the Mountains,* 317.

41. Olwig, "Reinventing Common Nature." 397.

42. Vilas, "How the Raker Act Affects Hetch Hetchy."

43. Foster, "Honeymoon in Hetch Hetchy," 10–15.

44. Long, "Pipe Dreams," 24–25.

45. Kent and Roosevelt are quoted in Nash, *Wilderness and the American Mind*, pages 153 and 151 respectively; originally from William Kent, "Out Doors," Kent Family Papers, Historical Manuscripts Room, Yale University; and Theodore Roosevelt, "Wilderness Reserves: The Yellowstone Park," in *The Works of Theodore Roosevelt,* ed. Hermann Hagedorn (New York: Scribner, 1923–26), 3:311–12.

46. Kent's role is described in Nash, *Wilderness and the American Mind*, chap. 10, based largely on material from the Kent Family Papers.

47. Freeman, *On the Proposed Use,* 17–51.

48. Muir, *The Yosemite*, 196–97.

49. Ibid., 4.

50. Sanborn, *Yosemite,* 238.

51. Runte, *Yosemite*, 61–62.

52. For a discussion of the uniquely American concern with natural versus cultural landscapes, see Olwig, "Reinventing Common Nature," 379–408.

53. Excerpt from *Congressional Record*, 63rd Congress, 2nd session, (December 19, 1913), 1189, quoted in Nash, *Wilderness and the American Mind*, 179–80.

54. John R. Freeman, *On the Proposed Use*, 77–79.

CHAPTER 5. THE QUEST FOR LIVABILITY

1. Hays, *Explorations in Environmental History*, 86–87.

2. *San Francisco Bulletin*, December 5, 1899, quoted Blackford, *The Lost Dream*.

3. *San Francisco Examiner*, December 12, 1899, quoted in Blackford, *The Lost Dream*.

4. *San Francisco Bulletin*, January 7, 1904, quoted in Blackford, *The Lost Dream*.

5. Daniel Hudson Burnham and Edward H. Bennett, *Report on a Plan for San Francisco* (San Francisco: City of San Francisco, 1905), 41, quoted in Blackford, *The Lost Dream*.

6. Charles Lathrop to Phelan, April 30, 1906, Carton 20, AIASF File, Phelan Papers, quoted in Blackford, *The Lost Dream*.

7. *San Francisco Chronicle*, May 9, 1906, quoted in Blackford, *The Lost Dream*.

8. *Merchants' Association Review*, June 1909, quoted in Blackford, *The Lost Dream*.

9. *San Francisco Examiner*, May 2, 1912, quoted in Blackford, *The Lost Dream*.

10. Walker, "Industry Builds Out the City," 9.

11. Ibid., 11.

12. San Francisco Chamber of Commerce *Journal*, 1, no. 9 (July 1912): 1, quoted in Scott, *The San Francisco Bay Area*, 137.

13. Scott, *The San Francisco Bay Area*, 203.

14. Allen, "The Salt Water Barrier," 24–25.

15. San Francisco Board of Supervisors, Resolution No. 2241, November 18, 1941, San Francisco Bay Saline Water Barrier Collection (SFBSWBC), Water Resources Center Archives (WRCA), University of California, Berkeley (UCB), Box 1, Folder 4.

16. State of California, Senate Resolution No. 5, December 20, 1941, SFBSWBC, WRCA, UCB, Box 1, Folder 4.

17. Rear Admiral U.S. Navy John Greenslade to Mr. David A. Barry, Clerk, San Francisco Board of Supervisors, April 30, 1942, SFBSWBC, WRCA, UCB, Box 1, Folder 4.

18. "Disadvantages of the Reber Plan," Drysdale and Schedler, Industrial Engineers, presented before Joint Army-Navy Board on Second Bay Crossing, San Francisco, August 1945, SFBSWBC, WRCA, UCB, Box 2, Folder 18.

19. "Analysis of the Reber Plan," B. C. Allin, Consulting Engineer, presented before Joint Army-Navy Board on Second Bay Crossing, August 12, 1945, SFBSWBC, WRCA, UCB, Box 2, Folder 19.

20. "Report of the Joint Army-Navy Board on an Additional Crossing of San Francisco Bay," January 25, 1947, quoted in C. W. Schedler, "The Reber Plan," February 21, 1948, SFBSWBC, WRCA, UCB. Box 1, Folder 8.

21. "An Address on the Reber Plan," Brigadier General Philip G. Bruton (Ret.), to the Irrigation Districts Association of California, 1948, SFBSWBC, WRCA, UCB, Box 1, Folder 5.

22. "Comments on the Reber Plan," C. W. Schedler, Consulting Engineer, prepared for Senator Downey at the Hearing of the Public Works Committee, San Francisco, California, December 1949, SFBSWBC, WRCA, UCB, Box 2, Folder 20.

23. "Statement by the Bureau of Reclamation Relative to the Water Problems of the San Francisco Bay Area," prepared for the U.S. Senate Hearing of the Public Works Committee, San Francisco, December 1949, SFBSWBC, WRCA, UCB, Box 1, Folder 11.

24. "Recreational Aspects of the Reber Plan," remarks by Josephine D. Randall, Superintendent of Recreation, City and County of San Francisco, Senate Hearing on the Reber Plan, San Francisco, December 5, 1949, SFBSWBC, WRCA, UCB, Box 1, Folder 11.

25. "Report on the Development of the San Francisco Bay Region," John L. Savage, Consulting Engineer, Denver, Colorado, and International Engineering Company, Inc., San

Francisco, California, prepared for the Fact-Finding Committee of the California Assembly on Tidelands Reclamation and Development, Related Traffic Problems and Relief of Congestion on Transbay Crossings, January 1951, SFBSWBC, WRCA, UCBB, Box 2, Folder 21.

26. Frank J. Taylor, "They Want to Rebuild San Francisco Bay," *Saturday Evening Post*, November 18, 1950.

27. "Resolution of the Santa Clara County Farm Bureau Board of Directors," R. Ken Wilhelm, Secretary, July 7, 1952; W. R. Reaves, Norman Dill, Elmer Verrue, Chet Ridgeway, Prosper Bergon, and John O'Neal, officers, Madera County National Farm Loan Association, Madera, California, to The Honorable Earl Warren, Governor of California, March 12, 1953, both in SFBSWBC, WRCA, UCB, Box 1, Folder 4.

28. Paterson, "The Great Salt Water Panacea," 319.

29. "Barriers in the San Francisco Bay System. A Statement Presented to the Assembly, California Legislature," Walter G. Schulz, Principal Hydraulic Engineer, Division of Water Resources, California Department of Public Works, April 29, 1955, SFBSWBC, WRCA, UCB, Box 1, Folder 11.

30. San Francisco Labor Council, *Official Bulletin*.

31. Ibid.

32. U.S. Army Corps of Engineers, San Francisco District, *Technical Report on Barriers*, 184.

33. Hays, *Beauty, Health, and Permanence*, 87.

34. Odell, *The Saving of San Francisco Bay*, 13.

35. Gilliam, *Between the Devil and the Deep Blue Bay*, 5.

36. Chall, *Save San Francisco Bay Association*.

37. Ibid., 2.

38. Ibid., 15.

39. Odell, *The Saving of San Francisco Bay*, 13.

40. Gilliam, *Between the Devil and the Deep Blue Bay*, 97.

41. Chall, *Save San Francisco Bay Association*, 6.

42. Scott, *The Future of San Francisco Bay*, i—ii, 1.

43. Ibid., chap. 1 and app. A.

44. Ibid., chap. 3.

45. Ibid., 48.

46. Ibid., 60.

47. Ibid., 65–66.

48. Ibid., 107–108.

49. Senator Eugene McAteer to Professor Mel Scott, reproduced in afterword to Chall's *Save San Francisco Bay Association*.

50. Chall, *Save San Francisco Bay Association*, 25.

51. The entire background story to the passage of the McAteer-Petris Act is well recounted in Odell, *The Saving of San Francisco Bay*, 17–33.

52. San Francisco Bay Conservation and Development Commission (SFBCDC), *The San Francisco Bay Plan*, introduction.

53. Scott, *The San Francisco Bay Area*, 317.

54. SFBCDC, *The San Francisco Bay Plan*, sec. 5.

55. For a good historical account of the prolonged lack of interest in San Francisco Bay as an estuarine environment, see Hedgpeth, "San Francisco Bay."

56. Gilliam, *Between the Devil and the Deep Blue Bay*, 115.

57. Scott, *The San Francisco Bay Area*, 232–33; originally from Tomaschke-Eliott, Inc., *The Effect of Bridge Construction on Population Movement: A Study of Eastern Cities,* prepared for the Residential Development Committee of the Oakland Chamber of Commerce (Oakland, 1934).

58. *The City of Oakland v. Williams*.

59. Scott, *The San Francisco Bay Area*, 242; originally from *Report upon the Collection, Treatment and Disposal of Sewage and Industrial Wastes of the East Bay Cities to the Mayor and Council Representing the City of Berkeley as the Sponsoring Agent for the Seven Cooperating Cities by the Board of Consulting Engineers* (Berkeley, 1941), 8–9.

60. San Francisco Public Utilities Commission, *Report,* 143.

61. Scott, *The San Francisco Bay Area*, 237–39.

62. Issel, "'Land Values,'" 611–46. The phrase "treasured appearance" appeared in a San Francisco Board of Supervisors' resolution of 1963.

63. Issel, "'Land Values,'" 629–30, 630n31.

64. *San Francisco Chronicle*, October 14, 1965, 1.

65. The narrative of the freeway revolt presented here is based almost entirely on Issel's recounting of the same.

66. Gilliam, *Between the Devil and the Deep Blue Bay*, 144.

67. See Wellock, *Critical Masses*.

68. This binary formulation belongs to Samuel Hays. See his *Explorations in Environmental History*, 72.

CONCLUSION. BEYOND BEAUTY AND COMFORT

1. Quoted in Rothman, *The New Urban Park,* 24.

2. Ibid., 34.

3. Ibid., 18.

4. Ibid., chaps. 1–2.

5. Ibid., chaps. 3–4.

6. A good summary of this history can be found in Habert, "50 Years of Redevelopment."

7. Cecilia Vega, "Some in Bayview Fear the 'R' Word," *San Francisco Chronicle*, February 28, 2006.

8. Two thoughtful articles on the problem of ghettoization and urban renewal are Light, "Boyz in the Woods"; and Bennett, "Manufacturing the Ghetto."

9. See Davis, *City of Quartz*.

10. A document of particular contemporary interest is the Greenbelt Alliance's "Bay Area Smart Growth Scorecard, 2006," available online as a PDF file at

http://www.greenbelt.org/downloads/resources/smartgrowthscorecard/smartgrowthscorecard.pdf.

11. Leopold, "The Land Ethic," 201–204.

12. On bioregionalism, see Dasmann and Berg, "Reinhabiting California," 399–410. On sustainable urban design, see Eisenstein, "Ecological Design."

13. See, for example, the work of environmental psychologists Rachel and Stephen Kaplan at the University of Michigan, and philosopher Marcia Mulder Eaton.

BIBLIOGRAPHY

Allen, Ben. "The Salt Water Barrier." Address before Purchasing Agents Association, March 7, 1930, reprinted in *Pacific Purchasor* 12, no. 4 (April 1930): 24–25.

Bailey, Paul. *San Brannan and the California Mormons*. Los Angeles: Westernlore Press, 1953.

Bakken, Gordon Morris, and Brenda Farrington, eds. *The Urban West*. New York: Garland Publishing, 2000.

Bancroft, Hubert Howe. *The Works of Hubert Howe Bancroft*. Vol. 23–24, *History of California*, Vol. 6–7. San Francisco: History Company, 1888.

Barth, Gunther. *Instant Cities: Urbanization and the Rise of San Francisco and Denver.* New York: Oxford University Press, 1975.

Beals, Ralph L., and Joseph A. Hester. *Indian Occupancy, Subsistence, and Land Use Patterns in California*. New York: Garland Publishing, 1974.

Bean, Lowell John, ed. *The Ohlone Past and Present: Native Americans of the San Francisco Bay Region*. Menlo Park, Calif.: Ballena Press, 1994.

———. "Power and its Applications in Native California." In Bean and Blackburn, *Native Californians,* 408–20.

Bean, Lowell John, and Thomas C. Blackburn. *Native Californians: A Theoretical Perspective.* Ramona, Calif.: Ballena Press, 1976.

Bennett, Michael. "Manufacturing the Ghetto: Anti-urbanism and the Spatialization of Race." In Bennett and Teague, *The Nature of Cities,* 169–88.

Bennett, Michael, and David Teague, eds. *The Nature of Cities: Ecocriticism and Urban Environments*. Tucson: University of Arizona Press, 1999.

Blackburn, Thomas. "Ceremonial Integration and Social Interaction in Aboriginal California." In Bean and Blackburn, *Native Californians*, 225–43.

Blackburn, Thomas, and Kat Anderson, eds. *Before the Wilderness: Environmental Management by Native Californians*. Menlo Park, Calif.: Ballena Press, 1993.

Blackford, Mansel G. *The Lost Dream: Businessmen and City Planning on the Pacific Coast, 1890–1920*. Columbus: Ohio State University Press, 1993.

Boswell, Terry E. "A Split Labor Market Analysis of Discrimination Against Chinese Immigrants, 1850–1882." *American Sociological Review* 51, no. 3 (June 1986): 352–71.

Braudel, Fernand. *Civilization and Capitalism, 15th—18th Centuries*. Vol. 1, *The Structures of Everyday Life*. Vol. 3, *The Perspective of the World*. New York: Harper and Row, 1979.

Brechin, Gray. *Imperial San Francisco: Urban Power, Earthly Ruin*. Berkeley: University of California Press, 1999.

Browning, Peter, ed. *San Francisco/Yerba Buena: From the Beginning to the Gold Rush, 1769–1849*. Lafayette, Calif.: Great West Books, 1998.

Bunnell, Lafayette Houghton. *Discovery of the Yosemite, and the Indian war of 1851, which Led to That Event*. New York: F. H. Revell, 1892.

Chall, Malca. *Save San Francisco Bay Association, 1961–1986*. Berkeley: Regional Oral History Office, Bancroft Library, University of California, 1987.

Chandler, Arthur, comp. *Old Tales of San Francisco*. Dubuque, Iowa: Kendall/Hunt, 1987.

Cherny, Robert, and William Issel. *San Francisco: Presidio, Port, and Pacific Metropolis*. San Francisco: Boyd and Fraser, 1981.

The City of Oakland v. Williams, 15 Cal. 2d 542 (1940).

Clary, Raymond. H. *The Making of Golden Gate Park: The Early Years, 1865–1906*. San Francisco: California Living Books, 1980.

Clements, Kendrick A. "Engineers and Conservationists." *California History* 58, no. 4 (1979–80): 282–303.

———. "Politics and the Park: San Francisco's Fight for Hetch Hetchy, 1908–1913." *Pacific Historical Review* 48, no. 2 (1979): 185–215.

Colten, Craig, ed. *Transforming New Orleans and its Environs: Centuries of Change*. Pittsburgh: University of Pittsburgh Press, 2001.

Conzen, Kathleen Neils. "A Saga of Families." In Milner, O'Connor, and Sandweiss, *The Oxford History of the American West*, 315–58.

Cook, Sherburne F. "Antiquity of San Francisco Bay Shellmounds." In Heizer and Whipple, *The California Indians*, 202–205.

Cranz, Galen. "Women in Urban Parks." *Signs* 5 (1980): S79—S95.

Cronon, William. *Nature's Metropolis: Chicago and the Great West*. New York: W. W. Norton, 1991.

———. "The Trouble with Wilderness." In Cronon, *Uncommon Ground*, 69–90.

———, ed. *Uncommon Ground: Rethinking the Human Place in Nature*. New York: W. W. Norton, 1996.

Dasmann, Raymond, and Peter Berg. "Reinhabiting California." *The Ecologist* 7, no. 10 (1980): 399–410.

Davis, James T. "Trade Routes and Economic Exchange Among the Indians of California." In Heizer, *Aboriginal California*, 1–79.

Davis, Mike. *City of Quartz: Excavating the Future in Los Angeles*. London: Verso, 1990.

———. *Ecology of Fear: Los Angeles and the Imagination of Disaster*. New York: Metropolitan Books, 1998.

Delgado, James P. "The Humblest Cottage Can In A Short Time Afford . . . Pure and Sparkling Water: Early Efforts to Solve Gold Rush San Francisco's Water Shortage." *The Pacific Historian* 26, no. 3 (1982): 26–39.

Derex, Jean Michel. *Histoire Du Bois De Boulogne*. Paris: Éditions l'Harmattan, 1997.

Deverell, William, and Greg Hise, eds. *Land of Sunshine: An Environmental History of Metropolitan Los Angeles*. Pittsburgh: University of Pittsburgh Press, 2005.

Eisenstein, William. "Ecological Design, Urban Places, and the Culture of Sustainability." San Francisco Planning and Urban Research Association, *SPUR Newsletter*, September 1, 2001.

Eldredge, Zoeth Skinner. *The Beginnings of San Francisco*. San Francisco: Z. S. Eldredge, 1912.

Fogelson, Robert M. *The Fragmented Metropolis: Los Angeles, 1850–1930*. Berkeley: University of California Press, 1967.

Foster, Laura. "Honeymoon in Hetch Hetchy." *The American West* 8, no. 3 (1971): 10–15.

Freeman, John R. *On the Proposed Use of a Portion of the Hetch Hetchy, Eleanor and Cherry Valleys Within and Near to the Boundaries of the Stanislaus U.S. National Forest Reserve and the Yosemite National Park as Reservoirs for Impounding Tuolumne River Flood Waters and Appurtenant Works for the Water Supply of San Francisco, California, and Neighboring Cities: A Report to James Rolph, Mayor of San Francisco, and Percy V. Long, City Attorney*. San Francisco: Rincon, 1912.

Geiger, Maynard, and Clement Meighan. *As The Padres Saw Them, California Indian Life and Customs as Reported by the Franciscan Missionaries 1813–1815.* Santa Barbara: Santa Barbara Mission Archive Library, 1976.

Giffen, Guy, and Helen Giffen. *The Story of Golden Gate Park* (San Francisco: Phillips and Van Orden, 1949).

Gilliam, Harold. *Between the Devil and the Deep Blue Bay: The Struggle to Save San Francisco Bay.* San Francisco: Chronicle Books, 1969.

———. *The Natural World of San Francisco.* Garden City, NY: Doubleday, 1967.

Godfrey, Elizabeth. "Yosemite Indians: Yesterday and Today." *Yosemite Nature Notes* 20, no. 7 (1941): 49–72.

Greenbelt Alliance. *Bay Area Smart Growth Scorecard, 2006.* http://www.greenbelt.org/downloads/resources/smartgrowthscorecard/smartgrowthscorecard.pdf

Gumprecht, Blake. *The Los Angeles River: Its Life, Death, and Possible Rebirth.* Baltimore: Johns Hopkins University Press, 1999.

Habert, David. "50 Years of Redevelopment." San Francisco Planning and Urban Research Association, *SPUR Newsletter*, March 1999.

Hall, William Hammond. *To Preserve from Defacement and Promote the Use of Yosemite Valley.* Sacramento: California State Printing Office, 1882.

Hartley, Katha G. "Spring Valley Water Works v. San Francisco: Defining Economic Rights in San Francisco." *Western Legal History* 3, no. 2 (1990): 287–308.

Hays, Samuel P. *Beauty, Health, and Permanence: Environmental Politics in the United States, 1955–1985.* Cambridge: Cambridge University Press, 1987.

———. *Explorations in Environmental History.* Pittsburgh: University of Pittsburgh Press, 1998.

Hedgpeth, Joseph. "San Francisco Bay: The Unsuspected Estuary." Paper delivered at the Fifty-Eighth Annual Meeting of the Pacific Division of the American Association for the Advancement of Science, SFSU, San Francisco, California, June 12–16, 1977. In *San Francisco Bay: The Urbanized Estuary,* edited by T. John Conomos. http://www.estuaryarchive.org/archive/conomos_1979

Heizer, Robert F., ed. *Aboriginal California, Three Studies in Culture History.* Berkeley: published for the University of California Archaeological Research Facility by the University of California, 1963.

———. "Village Shifts and Tribal Spreads in California Prehistory." In Heizer and Whipple, *The California Indians,* 480–84.

Heizer, Robert F., and Albert Elsasser. *The Natural World of the California Indians.* Berkeley: University of California Press, 1980.

Heizer, Robert F., and M. A. Whipple, eds. *The California Indians; A Source Book.* Berkeley: University of California Press, 1971.

Hennessey, Gregg R. "George White Marston and Conservative Reform in San Diego." *The Journal of San Diego History* 32, no. 4 (1986): 230–53.

Hill, Mary. *Gold: The California Story.* Berkeley: University of California Press, 1999.

Hittell, John S. *A History of San Francisco and Incidentally of the State of California.* San Francisco: A. L. Bancroft, 1878.

Hundley, Norris. *The Great Thirst: Californians and Water—A History.* Berkeley: University of California Press, 2001.

Hurley, Andrew. "Busby's Stinkboat and the Regulation of Nuisance Trades, 1865–1918." In Hurley, *Common Fields,* 145–62.

————, ed. *Common Fields: An Environmental History of St. Louis*. St. Louis: Missouri Historical Society Press, 1997.

Igler, David. *Industrial Cowboys: Miller and Lux and the Transformation of the Far West, 1850–1920*. Berkeley: University of California Press, 2001.

Issel, William. "'Land Values, Human Values, and the Preservation of the City's Treasured Appearance': Environmentalism, Politics, and the San Francisco Freeway Revolt." *Pacific Historical Review* 68, no. 4 (1999): 611–46.

Issel, William, and Robert W. Cherny. *San Francisco 1865–1932: Politics, Power, and Urban Development*. Berkeley: University of California Press, 1986.

Jackson, John Brinckerhoff. "Beyond Wilderness." In *A Sense of Place, A Sense of Time*. New Haven: Yale University Press, 1994. 71–91.

Jackson, Joseph Henry, ed. *The Western Gate: A San Francisco Reader*. New York: Farrar, Straus and Young, 1952.

Jackson, Robert H., and Edward Castillo. *Indians, Franciscans, and Spanish Colonization: The Impact of the Mission System on California Indians*. Albuquerque: University of New Mexico Press, 1995.

Johnson, Kenneth M., ed. *San Francisco As It Is: Gleanings From the Picayune*. Georgetown, Calif.: Talisman Press, 1964.

Johnson, Paul. "'Art' and the Language of Progress in Early-Industrial Paterson: Sam Patch at Clinton Bridge." *American Quarterly* 40 (1988): 433–49.

Kahrl, William. "Water for California Cities: Origins of the Major Systems." *The Pacific Historian* 27, no. 1 (1983): 17–23.

Kelley, Robert. "The Mining Debris Controversy in the Sacramento Valley." *Pacific Historical Review* 25 (1956): 331–46.

Kelman, Ari. *A River and Its City: The Nature of Landscape in New Orleans*. Berkeley: University of California Press, 2003.

Knapp, George L. "The Other Side of Conservation." *North American Review* 191 (1910:) 465–81. Reprinted in Merchant, *Major Problems*. 2nd ed. 321–23.

Kroeber, Alfred L. "Elements of Culture in Native California." In Heizer and Whipple, *The California Indians*, 3–65.

Larsen, Lawrence Harold. *The Urban West at the End of the Frontier*. Lawrence: Regents Press of Kansas, 1978.

Lehmann, Susan. *Economic Development of the City of Santa Cruz, 1850–1950: Fully Developed Context Statement for the City of Santa Cruz*. Santa Cruz, Calif.: City of Santa Cruz Planning and Development Department, 2000.

Leopold, Aldo. "The Land Ethic." In *A Sand County Almanac and Sketches Here and There*. New York: Oxford University Press, 1987.

Leslie, Mrs. Frank. *California: A Pleasure Trip from Gotham to the Golden Gate, April, May, June, 1877*. 1877. Reprint, Nieuwkoop, Netherlands: B. De Graaf, 1972.

Lewis, Henry T. "Patterns of Indian Burning in California." In Blackburn and Anderson, *Before the Wilderness*, 55–116.

Light, Andrew. "Boyz in the Woods: Urban Wilderness in American Cinema." In Bennett and Teague, *The Nature of Cities*, 3–14.

Long, David R. "Pipe Dreams: Hetch Hetchy, the Urban West, and the Hydraulic Society Revisited." *Journal of the West* 34, no. 3 (1995): 19–31.

Lotchin, Roger. *San Francisco, 1846–1856, From Hamlet to City*. Urbana: University of Illinois Press, 1997.

Marsh, George Perkins. *Man and Nature*. Edited by David Lowenthal. 1864. Reprint, Cambridge: Belknap Press of Harvard University Press, 1965.

McCarthy, Elizabeth. *Layperson's Guide to Water Rights Law*. Sacramento: Water Education Foundation, 2000.

McGloin, John Bernard. *San Francisco, The Story of a City*. San Rafael: Presidio Press, 1978.

McIlroy, Jack, and Mary Praetzellis, eds. *Vanished Community: 19th-Century San Francisco Neighborhoods: From Fourth Street to Mission Creek and Beyond*. Prepared for the California Department of Transportation, with contributions by Nancy Olmsted and Roger W. Olmsted. Rohnert Park, Calif.: Anthropological Studies Center, Sonoma State University, 1997.

Melosi, Martin V., and Joseph A. Pratt, eds. *Energy Metropolis: An Environmental History of Houston and the Gulf Coast*. Pittsburgh: University of Pittsburgh Press, 2007.

Merchant, Carolyn, ed. *Major Problems in American Environmental History*. Lexington, Mass.: D.C. Heath, 1993; and 2nd ed. Boston: Houghton Mifflin, 2005.

Merguerian, Charles. "A History of the NYC Water Supply System." Lecture at Long Island Geologists Meeting, October 4, 2000. http://people.hofstra.edu/charles_merguerian/Abstracts%20and%20Papers/CM2000c.htm

Miller, Char, ed. *On the Border: An Environmental History of San Antonio*. Pittsburgh: University of Pittsburgh Press, 2001.

Milliken, Randall. *A Time of Little Choice: The Disintegration of Tribal Culture in the San Francisco Bay Area, 1769–1810*. Menlo Park, Calif.: Ballena Press, 1995.

Milner, Clyde A., Carol A. O'Connor, and Martha A. Sandweiss, eds. *The Oxford History of the American West*. New York: Oxford University Press, 1994.

Muir, John. *The Yosemite*. 1912. Reprint, San Francisco: Sierra Club Books, 1988.

Muscatine, Doris. *Old San Francisco: The Biography of a City from Early Days to the Earthquake*. New York: Putnam, 1975.

Muwekma Ohlone. "History." http://www.muwekma.org/history/tribe.html

Nasatir, Abraham P., ed. *A French Journalist in the California Gold Rush: The Letters of Étienne Derbec*. Georgetown, Calif.: Talisman Press, 1964.

Nash, Roderick. *Wilderness and the American Mind*. New Haven: Yale University Press, 1967.

Nelson, Nels C. "San Francisco Bay Shellmounds." In Heizer and Whipple, *The California Indians*, 144–57.

Odell, Rice. *The Saving of San Francisco Bay: A Report on Citizen Action and Regional Planning*. Washington, D.C.: Conservation Foundation, 1972.

Olmsted, Frederick Law. "Parks, Parkways and Pleasure Grounds." *Engineering Magazine* 9 (1895): 253–54.

———. "Preliminary Report in Regard to a Plan of Public Pleasure Grounds for the City of San Francisco." In *The Papers of Frederick Law Olmsted*. Vol. 5, *California Frontier, 1863–1865*. Edited by Victoria Post Ranney. Baltimore: Johns Hopkins University Press, 1990.

———. *The Yosemite Valley and the Mariposa Big Tree Grove: A Preliminary Report, 1865*. Introduction by Laura Wood Roper. Yosemite, Calif.: Yosemite Association, 1995.

Olwig, Kenneth R. "Reinventing Common Nature: Yosemite and Mount Rushmore—A Meandering Tale of a Double Nature." In Cronon, *Uncommon Ground*, 379–408.

Park, Robert Ezra. *The Collected Papers of Robert Ezra Park*. Vol. 2, *Human Communities: The City and Human Ecology*. Glencoe, Ill.: Free Press, 1952.

Park, Robert Ezra, Ernest W. Burgess, and Roderick Duncan McKenzie. *The City*. Chicago: University of Chicago Press, 1925.

Park, Roberta. "San Franciscans at Work and at Play, 1846–1869." *Journal of the West* 22 (1983): 44–51.

Paterson, Alan M. "The Great Fresh Water Panacea: Salt Water Barrier Proposals for San Francisco Bay." *Arizona and the West* 22, no. 4 (1980): 307–22.

Pinchot, Gifford. *Breaking New Ground.* Washington, D.C.: Island Press, 1947.

Pisani, Donald J. "'Why Shouldn't California Have the Grandest Aqueduct in the World?' Alexis Von Schmidt's Lake Tahoe Scheme." *California Historical Quarterly* 53, no. 4 (1974): 347–60.

Pollan, Michael. *Second Nature: A Gardener's Education.* New York: Atlantic Monthly Press, 1991.

Pourade, Richard F. *The Glory Years.* San Diego: Union-Tribune, 1964.

Ray, Verne. "Modoc Childhood." In Heizer and Whipple, *California Indians,* 424–30.

Reps, John W. *Cities of the American West: A History of Frontier Urban Planning.* Princeton, N.J.: Princeton University Press, 1979.

River Law Project. *River Law: Who Owns the Rivers?* Colorado Springs, Colo.: National Organization for Rivers, 2004.

Rohe, Randall. "Man as Geomorphic Agent: Hydraulic Mining in the American West." *The Pacific Historian* 27 (1983): 5–16.

Rosenzweig, Roy, and Elizabeth Blackmar. *The Park and the People: A History of Central Park.* Ithaca, N.Y.: Cornell University Press, 1992.

Roth, Mitchel. "Cholera, Community, and Public Health in Gold Rush Sacramento and San Francisco." *Pacific Historical Review* 66, no. 4 (1997): 527–51.

Rothman, Hal K. *The New Urban Park: Golden Gate National Recreation Area and Civic Environmentalism.* Lawrence: University Press of Kansas, 2004.

Runte, Alfred. *Yosemite: Embattled Wilderness.* Lincoln: University of Nebraska Press, 1990.

Sanborn, Margaret. *Yosemite: Its Discovery, Its Wonders and Its People.* Yosemite, Calif.: Yosemite Association, 1989.

San Francisco Bay Conservation and Development Commission. *The San Francisco Bay Plan.* Sacramento: San Francisco Bay Conservation and Development Commission, 1969.

San Francisco Bay Saline Water Barrier Collection, multiple documents. Water Resources Center Archives, University of California at Berkeley, two boxes.

San Francisco Board of Park Commissioners. *Third Biennial Report of the San Francisco Park Commissioners, 1874–75.* San Francisco: San Francisco Board of Parks Commission, 1875.

San Francisco Board of Supervisors. *Health Officers Report.* In *San Francisco Municipal Reports,* various years. San Francisco: Towne and Bacon, 1866; Joseph Winterburn, 1867; and Cosmopolitan Printing, 1868–1875.

San Francisco Labor Council, *Official Bulletin* 8, no. 1 (January 9, 1957).

San Francisco Public Utilities Commission. *Report of the San Francisco Public Utilities Commission, Fiscal Year 1935–1936.* San Francisco: San Francisco Public Utilities Commission, 1936.

———. *SFPUC History: The Sierra Nevada.* San Francisco: SFPUC Communications and Public Outreach, 2002. http://sfwater.org/detail.cfm/MC_ID/18/MSC_ID/114/MTO_ID/520/C_ID/808

Schafer, Joseph, ed. *California Letters of Lucius Fairchild.* Madison: State Historical Society of Wisconsin, 1931.

Schuyler, David. *The New Urban Landscape: The Redefinition of City Form in Nineteenth-Century America.* Baltimore: Johns Hopkins University Press, 1986.

Scott, Mel. *The Future of San Francisco Bay*. Berkeley: Institute of Governmental Studies, 1963.

———. *The San Francisco Bay Area: A Metropolis in Perspective*. Berkeley: University of California Press, 1959.

Shufelt, S. *A Letter from a Gold Miner, Placerville, California, October 1850*. San Marino, Calif.: Friends of Huntington Library, 1941.

Soulé, Frank, John H. Gihon, and James Nisbet. *The Annals of San Francisco*. San Francisco: D. Appleton, 1855.

Spence, Mark David. *Dispossessing the Wilderness: Indian Removal and the Making of the National Parks*. New York: Oxford University Press, 1999.

Spirn, Anne Whiston. "Constructing Nature: The Legacy of Frederick Law Olmsted." In Cronon, *Uncommon Ground*, 91–113.

Starr, Kevin. *Material Dreams: Southern California Through the 1920s*. New York: Oxford University Press, 1990.

Stegner, Wallace. *Beyond the Hundredth Meridian: John Wesley Powell and the Second Opening of the West*. 1954. Reprint, New York: Penguin Books, 1992.

Tarr, Joel A., ed. *Devastation and Renewal: An Environmental History of Pittsburgh and Its Region*. Pittsburgh: University of Pittsburgh Press, 2003.

Todd, John. *The Sunset Land*. Boston: Lee and Shepard, 1870.

Trollope, Anthony. "Nothing to See in San Francisco." In Jackson, *The Western Gate*, 318–19.

Turner, Frederick Jackson. *The Frontier in American History*. 1920. Reprint, New York: Dover, 1996.

U.S. Army Corps of Engineers, San Francisco District. *Technical Report on Barriers*. Washington, D.C.: U.S. Army Corps of Engineers, 1963.

U.S. Congressional Documents and Debates, 1774–1875, "Bills and Resolutions, Senate, 41st Congress," Library of Congress, American Memory Collection. http://memory.loc.gov/ammem/amlaw/browse/llsb_041_comm.html

Vilas, Martin S. "How the Raker Act Affects Hetch Hetchy, San Francisco, and the Rest of California." *The American City,* February 1914, 175–81.

Walker, Richard. "Industry Builds Out the City: The Suburbanizaton of Manufacturing in the San Francisco Bay Area, 1850–1940." In *The Manufactured Metropolis*, edited by Robert Lewis. Philadelphia: Temple University Press, 2004.

Webb, Edith Buckland. *Indian Life at the Old Missions*. Lincoln: University of Nebraska Press, 1952.

Wellock, Thomas Raymond. *Critical Masses: Opposition to Nuclear Power in California, 1958–1978*. Madison: University of Wisconsin Press, 1998.

White, Richard. *"It's Your Misfortune and None of My Own": A History of the American West*. Norman: University of Oklahoma Press, 1991.

Wilson, James Grant, ed. The Memorial History of the City of New York. New York: New York History Company, 1893.

Wolfe, Linnie Marsh, ed. *John of the Mountains: The Unpublished Journals of John Muir*. 1938. Reprint, Madison: University of Wisconsin Press 1979.

Woods, Daniel B. *Sixteen Months at the Gold Diggings*. New York: Harper and Brothers, 1851.

Young, Terence. *Building San Francisco's Parks, 1850–1930*. Baltimore: Johns Hopkins University Press, 2004.

INDEX

References to illustrations are in italic type.

Abella, Fray Ramón, 11, 12
Abshire-Kelly Salinity Control Barrier
  Act, 161
Acorns, 15, 16–17, 18, 27
Acquaroli, 104
AFL (American Federation of Labor),
  180
Agriculture: gold rush and, 38, 45, 52,
  53, 55, 57; Hewes and, 46; Los
  Angeles, Calif., 122; market
  gardening and, 47; Native Americans
  and, 19, 25; real estate
  speculation/development (1860s) and,
  45; Reber Plan and, 155, 156, 158;
  Spanish colonialism/missions and, 25,
  26, 27, 31, 32, 57; subsistence
  farming vs. commercial, 58;
  urbanization and, 188, 191, 193;
  water and, 111, 127, 154; Yerba
  Buena and, 36, 45
Aguirre, Juan Miguel, 103
Ahwahneechee Indians, 98–99, 139
Alameda, Calif., 150, 158, 176
Alameda County (Calif.), 124, 141, 149
Alexander, Barton, 83
Allen, Ben, 154
Allin, B. C., 157, 160
Alta California, 50, 105
American Alpine Club, 131
American River, 66, 110, 120, 124
Amuctac village, 12, 13
Animal husbandry, 19, 25, 26, 27, 47–48,
  52, 188
Anti-freeway Property Owners'
  Association of San Francisco, 182

Antiquities Act, 136
Appalachian Mountain Club, 126, 132
Appropriative rights, 115, 116
Aqueducts, 105, 107, 124, 129, 141, 158
Arancel, 33
Arnold v. Mundy, 114
Association for the Improvement and
  Adornment of San Francisco
  (AIASF), 145–47
Association of Bay Area Governments
  (ABAG), 187
Association of Industrial Water Users of
  Contra Costa/Solano counties, 154
Atchison, Topeka & Santa Fe Railroad,
  43

Baer, Warren, 98
Balanophagy, 16–17
Balderston, Fred, 168
Ballinger, Richard, 130
Bank of California, 63
Barbary Coast, 71, 89, 93
Barton, A. M., 157, 160
Bay Area Transportation Study
  Commission, 174
Bay Cities Water Company, 124, 125
Bay Conservation and Development
  Commission, 171
Bay Miwok language, 12, 19–20
Bayview-Hunters Point neighborhood,
  189
Benicia, 27, 39
Bennett, Tony, 6
Bensley Company, 106, *107*, 107–108,
  116

213